Social Aggregations and Distributional Ethics

This coursebook looks at four distinct areas of social choice theory and welfare economics: nonstrategic choice, Harsanyi's aggregation theorems, distributional ethics, and strategic choice. It analyzes Arrow's social welfare ordering and addresses issues relating to social choice functions. It studies practical applications of social welfare functions and looks at welfare-theoretic approaches to the measurement of both single and multidimensional inequality. Harsanyi's social aggregation theorems are studied to explain how individual utility functions can be aggregated into a social utility function under the assumption that individual and social preferences satisfy expected utility hypotheses.

The methodology employed in the book is analytical and geometric. Each chapter is supplemented with bibliographical notes, and technical terms and operations employed to discuss the results are explained in a comprehensive and accessible way.

The book has developed out of two different courses on social choice theory regularly taught at the level Master of Science in Quantitative Economics. It will be useful material for students and researchers interested in this frontline area of study, both in India and globally.

Key features include:

- Review questions
- Numerical examples and non-technical explanations
- Graphical representations of concepts and results

Satya R. Chakravarty is a non-resident honorary distinguished fellow at the Indira Gandhi Institute of Development Research, Mumbai, and an honorary visiting professor of economics at the Indian Statistical Institute, Kolkata. He is a renowned name in the fields of studies of voting game theory and measurement of inequality, poverty, and polarization, and has published widely, both books and in reputed journals. He authored *A Course on Cooperative Game Theory* with Manipushpak Mitra and Palash Sarkar, which was published by the Press in 2015.

Manipushpak Mitra is professor of economics at the Indian Statistical Institute, Kolkata. His research interests are game theory, individual and collective choice, industrial organization, and mechanism design.

Suresh Mutuswami is professor of economics at the School of Business, University of Leicester. His research interests are social choice and microeconomic theory.

Social Aggregations and Distributional Ethics

Satya R. Chakravarty
Manipushpak Mitra
Suresh Mutuswami

CAMBRIDGE
UNIVERSITY PRESS

CAMBRIDGE
UNIVERSITY PRESS

University Printing House, Cambridge CB2 8BS, United Kingdom

One Liberty Plaza, 20th Floor, New York, NY 10006, USA

477 Williamstown Road, Port Melbourne, vic 3207, Australia

314 to 321, 3rd Floor, Plot No.3, Splendor Forum, Jasola District Centre, New Delhi 110025, India

103 Penang Road, #05-06/07, Visioncrest Commercial, Singapore 238467

Cambridge University Press is part of the University of Cambridge.

It furthers the University's mission by disseminating knowledge in the pursuit of education, learning and research at the highest international levels of excellence.

www.cambridge.org
Information on this title: www.cambridge.org/9781108832045

First published 2022

Printed in India by Avantika Printers Pvt. Ltd.

A catalogue record for this publication is available from the British Library

ISBN 978-1-108-83204-5 Hardback

ISBN 978-1-108-92763-5 Paperback

Cambridge University Press has no responsibility for the persistence or accuracy of URLs for external or third-party internet websites referred to in this publication, and does not guarantee that any content on such websites is, or will remain, accurate or appropriate.

CONTENTS

PREFACE

Social aggregation theory deals with the problem of amalgamation of the values assigned by different individuals to alternative social or economic states in a society into values for the entire society. A social state provides a description of materials that are related to the well-being of a population in different ways. One fundamental question that arises at the outset is how an individual can rank two alternative states in a well-defined manner. The problem of social aggregation theory can then be regarded as one of clubbing individual rankings into a social ranking in a meaningful way.

Chapter 1 presents an introductory outline of the materials analyzed in the remaining chapters. Chapter 2 of the monograph formally defines individual and social rankings of alternative states of affairs. Chapter 3 provides a rigorous discussion on May's remarkable theorem on "social choice functions," which represents group or collective decision rules, limited to two alternatives. In Chapter 4 we analyze Arrow's social welfare function, a mapping from the set of all possible profiles of individual orderings of social states to the set of all possible orderings. We discuss this with some elaboration in view of the fact that Arrow's model forms the basis of almost the entire social choice theory. Chapter 5 investigates to what extent the "dictatorship" result can be avoided when some of Arrow's axioms are relaxed. In Arrow's framework, when individual preferences are represented by utility functions, utilities are of the ordinal and non-comparable types. Arrow's theorem with utility functions constitutes a part of Chapter 6 of the book. We use geometric technique to prove this fundamental result. In the recent past, the non-comparability assumption has been relaxed to partial and full comparability assumptions. A discussion on alternative notions of measurability and comparability of utility functions is also presented in Chapter 6. Simple numerical examples have been provided to illustrate the ideas. Possibilities of social welfare functions are expanded as a consequence of interpersonal comparability. Proofs of most theorems in the literature are sophisticated mathematically, which may not be easygoing for non-specialist readers. In view of this, we use simple graphical proofs for many such results.

Harsanyi's social aggregation theorems indicate how individual utility functions can be aggregated into a social utility function under the assumption that individual and social preferences satisfy the expected utility hypotheses. There is a clear line of demarcation between the Arrowian approach and the Harsanyi approach. This is because in the former and its variants, decision-making by different individuals takes place in an environment characterized by certainty. On the contrary, uncertainty has an impact on the behavior of different individuals in the latter. We include a discussion on Harsanyi's theorems in Chapter 7.

Chapters 8 and 9 present real life applications of social welfare functions by analyzing welfare-theoretic approaches to the measurement of both single and multidimensional inequalities. An inequality index determines the size of welfare loss resulting from the existence of inequality. There will be extensive discussions on policy implications of the underlying indices.

Social choice functions are addressed with greater detail in Chapters 10–11. While Chapter 10 mainly concentrates on the well-known Gibbard–Satterthwaite theorem, Chapter 11 deals with "strategyproof" decision rules.

Chakravarty and Mitra have used different chapters of the book to offer a course on social choice and welfare economics at the level of Master of Science in Quantitative Economics, a graduate program offered at the Indian Statistical Institute, Kolkata. Mitra has also used different chapters of the book as part of the Game Theory Course at the level of Master of Science in Economics, a graduate program offered at the University of Calcutta. Some parts of Chapters 2, 4, 5, 10, and 11 have been taken from the online notes of Debasis Mishra and Arunava Sen.[1] We thank Debasis Mishra and Arunava Sen for allowing us to use their notes. We also thank Sreoshi Banerjee, Parikshit De, and Arindam Paul for their suggestions and constructive feedback.

---

[1] For Debasis Mishra's notes, see https://www.isid.ac.in/~dmishra/game.html (accessed on August 17, 2022) and for Arunava Sen's notes, see https://www.isid.ac.in/~asen/teach.html (accessed on August 17, 2020).

A major advantage of this book is that it covers four distinct but not unrelated areas of social choice theory and welfare economics, namely, nonstrategic choice, Harsanyi's aggregation theorems, distributional ethics, and strategic choice. The book will therefore serve as a useful resource for students or researchers interested in this area of research. Since the materials presented in the book are distinct but not unrelated, for a researcher interested in one or more of the topics covered, it will work as a device used to connect his research areas to some other closely associated issues. A concrete example is the analysis of fairness in network resource allocation. This may be regarded as an added advantage of our monograph.

There are several innovative features of the book that are worth noting. The methodology of the book is analytical and geometric. The technical terms and mathematical operations employed to discuss the results are explained in a non-technical language and intuitive explanations of the mathematical results are given. Wide coverage of the topics and their analytical, articulate, and authoritative presentation make the book theoretically and methodologically quite contemporary and inclusive. Often analytical examples are used to illustrate the results. Integration of theory and practice helps students understand the theoretical issues first and then see their practical relevance.

We express our sincere gratitude to the students who encouraged us to teach this course. We are grateful to them for the joys and immense benefit we have derived through interactive teaching.

INTRODUCTION

1

Social aggregation theory is concerned with investigating methods of clustering values that individuals in a society attach to different social or economic states into values for the society as a whole. Loosely speaking, a social state, a state of affairs, represents a sketch of the amount of commodities possessed by different individuals, quantities of productive resources invested in different productive activities and different types of collective activities (Arrow 1950). The values that individuals attach to different social states are reflections of respective preferences. Consequently, the problem of social aggregation is to combine individual preferences into a social preference in an unambiguous way. In this monograph, we will use the terms "social aggregation" and "social choice" interchangeably.

Modern social aggregation theory started with the publication of Kenneth J. Arrow's pioneering contribution *Social Choice and Individual Values*, his PhD dissertation, in 1951. It can be regarded as the foundation to laying the groundwork of social aggregation theory in view of its innovative facture and revolutionary influence. The idea of aggregating individual preferences into a collective choice rule predates Arrow (1950) by more than 150 years. In 1785, the French mathematician and philosopher Marie-Jean de Condorcet considered the problem of collective decision-making with regard to majority voting. According to majority voting,

1

in a choice between two alternatives x and y, x is declared as the winner if it gets more votes than y. He established that the method of pair-wise majority voting may give rise to cyclicality in social preference. This paradoxical result, popularly known as the *Condorcet voting paradox*, appears to draw inspiration, to a certain extent, from an earlier contribution by the French mathematician Jean-Charles de Borda (de Borda 1781). In this alternative voting system, known as the Borda count method, voters rank candidates in order of preference.[1]

One of the major goals of this monograph is the analysis of the Arrovian approach to the theory of collective aggregation and later developments on it. We, therefore, focus now on Arrow's impossibility theorem, which is generally acknowledged as the formative basis of modern social aggregation rules. Arrow's seminal work examines the possibility of the aggregation of individual preferences into a social preference in order to obtain a social ranking of alternative states of affairs. Each individual preference relation (or ordering) designed with the objective of ranking alternative social states is assumed to satisfy *completeness, reflexivity*, and *transitivity*. Each of these assumptions may be regarded as a value judgment, a subjective statement that cannot be verified by factual evidence. Completeness means that the individual can compare and rank any two social states. That is, between any two state of affairs x and y, the person regards either x as at least as good as, y, y as at least as good as x or both. Reflexivity demands that each social state should be always as good as itself. According to the transitivity of three social states x, y, and z, if a person regards x as at least as good as y, y as at least as good as z, then he must regard x as at least as good as z. If a continuity assumption is made, the preference relation can be represented by a utility function. Continuity means that of the three social states x, y, and z, if x is treated as better than y and y is treated as better than z, then any curve connecting x and z must cross the indifference curve

---

[1] Contributions along this line also came from Pierre-Simon Laplace (1812), Charles Lutwidge Dodgson (better known as Lewis Carroll) Dodgson (1873, 1874, 1876), Isaac Todhunter (1865), Edward J. Nanson (1882), and Francis Galton (1907). Two important references for detailed discussions in this context, which are beyond the scope of this monograph, are Black (1958) and Suzumura (2002).

containing y. For a continuous preference ordering, there can be no sudden jump from being better than an alternative to being worse than the alternative. Continuity ensures that if the person prefers all states that are close to x' to y', then x' should be preferred to y'. Thus, utility expresses the intensity of individual preferences.

Arrow's fundamental result on preference aggregation shows that there is no way to aggregate person-by-person preferences for arriving at a social preference relation or social welfare ordering (social ordering, for short), satisfying five highly plausible value judgments such that all social states can be ranked unambiguously by the ordering. The five value judgments that are required to be fulfilled by an Arrovian social ordering are: (a) completeness, reflexivity, and transitivity, (b) universality or unrestricted domain, (c) weak Pareto principle, (d) non-dictatorship, and (e) independence of irrelevant alternatives. According to universality, an Arrovian social preference ordering should work irrespective of what individual preferences happen to be. In other words, there is a lack of restriction on the domain. The weak Pareto principle demands that of two alternatives x and y, if everybody strictly prefers x to y then x must be regarded as socially better than y. That is, a gain by each individual must be acknowledged as a social enrichment. A social ordering is called a dictatorship if there is someone whose strict preferences depict social preferences. Non-dictatorship requires that a social ordering must make nobody a dictator. Independence of irrelevant alternatives demands that a social ranking between any two states of affairs should be independent of the individual orderings over other states of affairs. Thus, Arrow's theorem looks for a complete, reflexive, and transitive social ordering that can be represented as a social welfare function under continuity. While individual and social orderings are presented analytically in Chapter 2, Chapters 4 and 6 analyze Arrow's theorem with preferences and utilities respectively.

Arrow's theorem casts doubts on all concepts that implicitly or explicitly incorporate a societal preference. Examples that can be included within this purview are "a social contract," "a social benefit," "a public good," and so on. Evidently, any notion that casts so much perplexity will invite a lot of feedback. Consequently the investigations advanced along the lines of looking for aggregations of individual preferences so that alternative states of affairs can be evaluated in a satisfactory way. Some prior value judgment is required to be made for pooling of individual preferences into an aggregated preference. One such value judgment in the current context is the assumption about measurability and comparability of individual preferences.

For expositional ease, the remaining discussions on these lines, will be in terms of individual and social utility functions.[2] In the Arrovian framework when individual preferences are portrayed in terms of utility functions, it is said that utility functions are ordinally measurable and interpersonally non-comparable. The measurability of a utility function refers to the meaningfulness of the real numbers attached to a given person's utility levels. It is formalized by considering the type of transformations that can be applied to the utility function such that the information conveyed by the original utility function is retained by its transformed counterpart. Since such a transformation maintains the original information, it is referred to as an information invariance assumption. Sen (1970a) and many others have relaxed the non-comparability assumption and demonstrated the possibilities of existence of social aggregation rules.

To understand the measurability and comparability notions more explicitly, let the real valued function U_i denote person i's utility function defined on the set of alternatives. Thus, between two states of affairs x and y, if the person regards x as at least as good as y, then in terms of utility we express this as $U_i(x) \geq U_i(y)$. Consider the least restrictive measurability assumption that U_i is measurable on an ordinal scale. Under the ordinal measurability assumption, we can say that for any increasing transformation f_i defined on the set of real numbers, $U_i(x) \geq U_i(y)$ if and only if $f_i(U_i(x)) \geq f_i(U_i(y))$. In words, ordinal scale measurability allows the utility function of an individual to be rescaled using any ordinal or increasing transformation of it. For instance, $f_i(t)$ can be t^r, where $r > 0$ is any positive real number. (The real number t is any element in the range of U_i.) A second example can be $\log(t)$ given that $t > 0$ and so on. A stricter type of

---

[2]   A social utility function, expressed as a function of individual utilities, is referred to as a social welfare or evaluation functional.

measurability assumption is cardinal scale measurability. Under this notion of measurability, the only allowable transformation is an affine transformation, that is, $f_i(t) = a_i + b_i t$, where $b_i > 0$ and a_i are arbitrary real numbers. The relationship between centigrade and Fahrenheit temperature scales is a standard example of cardinal equivalence. Thus, if C and F stand for temperatures on the centigrade and Fahrenheit scales respectively, then the relationship between the two scales is given by $C = -160/9 + 5F/9$. Another strict notion of measurability is ratio scale measurability, which claims that the only admissible transformation under which the utility and its transformed counterpart convey to us the same information is $f_i(t) = b_i t$, where $b_i > 0$ is any arbitrary real number. An example can be the measurement of weight of a person. It does not matter whether we measure the weight of a person in grams or in kilograms, since we can convert the latter into the former by multiplying with 1,000.

The problem of interpersonal comparisons of utility is simply the problem of comparing different person's utilities. It means how the real numbers attached to different individuals' utility levels can be compared in a meaningful way. A simple example can be as follows. Suppose a person C is given the option of being person A or person B in a situation. He claims that he prefers to be person B rather than be person A in the situation. Implicit under this comparability by person C is an interpersonal comparison.

However, the idea of interpersonal comparison has been criticized on the grounds that exact numerical scales of utility cannot be contrived or there may be difficulties involved in the process of such comparisons.[3] Nevertheless, if we cannot compare different individuals' utilities, it may be difficult to evaluate situations where a change in the social state increases the utility of one or more individuals at the cost of reduction of the utility of at least one other individual. This means that we may not be able

---

[3] See, for example, Robbins (1932, 139–142), and Arrow (1963, 9). Harsanyi (1955, 317n20) offered the logical basis of such comparisons. The possibility of interpersonal comparisons was also discussed by Little (1957). Waldner (1972) analyzed the problem of interpersonal comparisons using the notion of empirical meaningfulness. For generalization and justifications of Waldner's approach, see List (2003).

to settle distributive justice. Nonetheless, it has been noted in the literature that in many situations social evaluation involves only limited comparability.

Alternative notions of interpersonal comparisons can be formalized by making assumptions about the information invariance transformations applied to individual utility functions. For instance, under ordinal scale measurability, if the increasing transformations f_is are not necessarily identical across persons, then we have ordinally measurable, non-comparable utilities. If the increasing transformations f_is are assumed to be same for every person, then the situation is the one of ordinal scale measurability combined with full comparability of utilities. While under full comparability the utility levels are comparable across persons, under non-comparability this is not so. More precisely, under full comparability, for any two individuals i and j, it is possible to make claims such as $U_i(x) \geq U_j(x)$ if and only if $f(U_i(x)) \geq f(U_j(x))$, where the transformation f is increasing. Likewise, with cardinally measurable utilities, if the scalars a_is and b_is are non-identical across persons, then we have full non-comparability under cardinal scale measurement. In this case, intrapersonal, but not interpersonal, comparability of utility differences is allowed. That is, for any person i one can compare utility gains or losses of the form $U_i(x) - U_i(y)$ for i only, not across persons. If, however, the multiplicative scalar $b_i > 0$ is the same for all persons but a_is are distinct, then the setting comes to be the one of cardinally measurable unit-comparable utilities. In this case of interpersonal comparison, comparability of utility differences across persons is allowed, but comparison of utility levels is not permitted. More precisely, for any two individuals i and j, differences of the type $U_i(x) - U_i(y)$ and $U_j(x) - U_j(y)$ can be compared but not utility levels such as $U_i(x)$ and $U_j(x)$. The utilitarian social evaluation functional, the sum of individual utilities, has been characterized using this notion of information invariance (d'Aspremont and Gevers 1977). Following Bentham's (1789) usage, the classical economists John Stuart Mill, Alfred Marshall, Francis Y. Edgeworth, Henry Sidgwick, and Arthur Pigou employed the sum of cardinal utilities to evaluate public policies from the viewpoint of increase or decrease in the sum of satisfaction.

A scheme of classification of different measurability and comparability assumptions was provided by Sen (1974, 1977, 1986).[4] Chapter 6 of this monograph deals with a detailed taxonomy of alternative notions of measurability and comparability. Aggregation theorems, along with the Arrow theorem, under alternative notions of measurability and comparability are presented in Chapter 6.

In the Arrovian framework, the objective was to find whether a profile of individual preference relations can be aggregated into a social preference relation. This goal turned out as an impossibility. An alternative natural line of inquiry can be investigating whether a profile of relations can be converted into a single winner or a single best alternative. The single-winner problem arises in many practical situations. For instance, in a single-winner election the election process has to declare exactly one of the contestants as the winner. A rule that transforms preference profiles into a single winner is called a social choice function. The question now boils down to this: Is there a trustworthy social choice function which can claim that this alternative is on top?

To understand this in greater detail, we need to figure out what we mean by trustworthy. For illustrative purposes, let us consider the problem of (private) provision of a public good using the Lindahl tax scheme. A vector of tax shares and an output level g for the public good is said to constitute a Lindahl equilibrium if g maximizes individual utility functions subject to respective budget constraints. At a Lindahl equilibrium, the marginal utility of a person, evaluated at g, is equated with his tax share, establishing that what the person receives is the same as what he pays. The public good output quantity g is the optimal level of the public good as well and the tax shares are optimal. The determination of Lindahl equilibrium, thus, needs information on the utility maximizing tax shares. Now, if a person truthfully reveals his preference about public good production quantity, then he will have to pay what the public good is worth to him. Consequently, if he is asked by the public good authority to communicate his preference for the public good, he may behave strategically and underreport his preference with the anticipation that others will pay for it and he can take

---

[4] See also Blackorby, Donaldson, and Weymark (1984); and d'Aspremont and Gevers (2002).

a free ride. Therefore, the Lindahl tax scheme is not trustworthy. Equivalently, we can say that it is not foolproof or cheat proof.[5]

If a social choice function does not come up with any inducement for strategic behaviour in the sense of falsification of preference by anybody irrespective of what others are doing, then it can be regarded as strategyproof or non-manipulable. Therefore, in our public good example, strategyproofness or non-manipulability requires everybody to reveal their preferences truthfully irrespective of what others are doing.

Apart from non-manipulability, the two other value judgments we impose on a social choice function are non-degeneracy and universality. According to non-degeneracy, any state of affairs must be included in the range of the social choice function. Universality is the same as in the Arrovian case. A social choice function is called dictatorial if the social choice is always the favourite alternative of a person. A social choice function is non-dictatorial if it is not dictatorial.

Gibbard (1973) and Satterthwaite (1975) demonstrated that there is no non-dictatorial social choice function that satisfies universality, non-degeneracy, and non-manipulability. Equivalently, the Gibbard–Satterthwaite theorem says that any social choice function satisfying universality, non-degeneracy, and non-manipulability must be dictatorial. The theorem definitely does not claim that there can be no useful social choice functions. The theorem does not even claim that no social decision can be taken in a given situation. There can be some choice functions that are superior to dictatorship. We provide extensive discussion along this line in Chapter 10 of the monograph. Moreover, in Chapter 10, we also impose a domain restriction called single-peakedness and provide two non-dictatorship results due to Moulin (1980). Another kind of domain restriction is achieved by allowing for side-payments and assuming that the agents have quasi-linear preferences. In Chapter 11, we assume quasi-linear preferences and discuss the Vickrey–Clarke–Groves mechanisms (see Vickrey 1961; Clarke 1971; Groves 1973). In Chaper 11, we also discuss Roberts'

---

[5]   See Feldman and Serrano (2006).

mechanisms that generalize the Vickrey–Clarke–Groves mechanisms (see Roberts 1980).

A possibility result on the existence of a social choice function in the two-alternative case was demonstrated by May (1952). May's theorem says that a two-candidate group decision function is the simple majority rule if and only if it satisfies *decisiveness, anonymity, neutrality,* and *strong monotonicity.* Decisiveness requires a group decision function to be well defined for all profiles of individual voters' preferences and single valued. Anonymity means that the individuals should be treated symmetrically; a reordering of voters should not change the outcome. Neutrality demands symmetric treatment of alternatives. A monotonicity condition stipulates that increased support for a candidate may help it to win. According to May's theorem, in a preference between two alternatives, if the number of individuals liking the former over the latter is more than the number of individuals liking the latter over the former, then the group recommends the choice of the former. Thus, May's theorem identifies a winner on a majority rule basis. A rigorous discussion on May's theorem is presented in Chapter 3 of this text.

Harsanyi (1955, 1977) investigated the social aggregation problem from a different standpoint. In the Harsanyi framework, social evaluation judgments are made behind a veil of ignorance. Both individual ex-ante and social utilities, defined over a set of lotteries, are assumed to fulfill the von Neumann–Morgenstern expected utility axioms. Harsanyi assumed ex-ante Pareto indifference for a social preference over lotteries, which claims that if two lotteries are judged as equally valuable by all individuals then it should be treated as equally valuable by society as well. It then turns out that the social evaluation functional can be expressed as a weighted sum of individual utilities. The literature refers to this as *Harsanyi's social aggregation theorem.* According to Harsanyi, this social evaluation functional is of the utilitarian type. As expected, Harsanyi's contributions have invited a lot of responses from different angles. We provide extensive discussions on Harsanyi's aggregation theorem and related issues in Chapter 7 of this monograph.

The social aggregation theorems do not tell us anything about the welfare implications of inequality resulting from unequal distribution implicit in the states of affairs. Often from the policy point of view it becomes worthwhile to look at distributional implications of states of affairs in terms of equity. This issue is addressed from single and multidimensional perspectives in Chapters 8 and 9, respectively. In this context, by a state of affairs we mean a description of individuals' achievements in a single dimension, say income, or in multiple dimensions, depending on whether our concern is a unidimensional or a multidimensional analysis. More precisely, while in the single dimensional structure a state of affairs describes a distribution of income, in the multidimensional structure it represents the achievements of different individuals in different dimensions of well-being, say income, wealth, health, literacy, and so on. A state of affairs here gives information on individual achievements but not on tastes and preferences.

The two different approaches to welfare evaluations adopted here are direct and inclusive measures of well-being. In the former, welfare is defined directly on dimensional achievements while the latter parallels an idea implicit under a social evaluation functional rule. Thus, the latter methodology assigns each person a well-being number, as indicated by his utility, by aggregating all the welfare-relevant dimensions in his life while taking account of his achievement in each dimension. For the sake of convenience, we use the common term social evaluation function for welfare metric in the current context. Three value judgments that are assumed for a social evaluation function are efficiency (size), equity (distribution), and anonymity. Efficiency is taken care of by the strong Pareto principle, which requires welfare to increase if the achievement of a person, under *ceteris paribus* assumption, increases. Well-defined notions of equity that ensure welfare increase under equitable redistributions are assumed. Anonymity means that any feature other than achievements is irrelevant to welfare assessment. Intrinsic to the notion of multidimensional welfare evaluation is inter-dimensional correlation of achievements that enables us to distinguish among dimensions in terms of substitutability, complementarity, and independence.

While welfare evaluation is concerned with both size and distribution, the only concern of inequality is distribution. Size independence property of inequality analysis can be taken care of by considering inequality metrics of both relative and absolute categories. For a relative metric, the unvarying criterion is ratio scale invariance, invariance of inequality under rescaling of dimension-wise achievements. In the absolute case the corresponding invariability postulate is translation scale invariance, which demands inequality to remain unaltered with respect to equal absolute changes in dimension-wise achievements. Each of these two postulates enables us to convert different-sized achievement distributions into equal-sized distributions without altering inequality.

Since our concern with ethical approaches to inequality stems from the idea that a reduction in inequality should raise welfare under *ceteris paribus* assumptions, it seems worthwhile to design inequality evaluation standards from social evaluation functions, which can be direct or inclusive-measure based, and vice versa. This is the methodology underlying the single-dimensional relative indices of Gini (1936), Atkinson (1970), Kolm (1969), and Sen (1973); the single-dimensional absolute indices of Blackorby and Donaldson (1980) and Kolm (1976); and their multidimensional counterparts proposed respectively by Kolm (1977) and Tsui (1995). Each of these inequality evaluation standards has interesting policy implications. The general metrics are illustrated using several inequality indices, including the well-known Atkinson (1970) and Kolm (1976), indices and their multidimensional twins.

Dimensional achievements may often be characterized with risk or uncertainty. For instance, individual incomes may take the form of returns on risky prospects. Measurement of inequality needs a separate treatment in a set-up marked by uncertainty since we do not have information on achievements with certainty. We make use of the Harsanyi (1953, 1955) and the Ben-Porath et al. (1997) frameworks to address this problem in Chapters 8 and 9, respectively. If the set of opportunities available to a person enlarges, the quality of his life is expected to increase. Individual opportunity sets are likely to differ across persons. Therefore, the study of opportunity equality becomes a worthwhile exercise. This issue is analyzed rigorously in a section of Chapter 8. Fairness is a highly important scrutiny in a distribution system, where a given amount of resource is to be shared by a set of users. There is a newly emerging network analysis literature on fairness in discrete division models. A brief discussion on fair allocation of resources considered in network analysis is taken up in Chapter 8. Additional issues we address in this chapter are evaluation of inequality in a dimension in which both achievement and shortfall inequalities are of interest, inequality for an ordinally significant dimension of human well-being, and inequality as an ordinal notion.

REFERENCES

Arrow, K. J. 1950. "A Difficulty in the Concept of Social Welfare." *Journal of Political Economy* 58 (4): 328–346.

———. 1963. "Uncertainty and the Welfare Economics of Medical Care." *American Economic Review* 53 (5): 941–973.

Atkinson, A. B. 1970. "On the Measurement of Inequality." *Journal of Economic Theory* 2 (3): 244–263.

Ben-Porath, E., I. Gilboa, and D. Schmeidler. 1997. "On the Measurement of Inequality under Uncertainty." *Journal of Economic Theory* 75 (1): 194–204.

Bentham, Jeremy. 1789. "An Introduction to the Principles of Morals and Legislation." McMaster University archive for the History of Economic Thought, London.

Black, D. 1958. *The Theory of Committees and Elections.* Cambridge: Cambridge University Press.

Blackorby, C., and D. Donaldson. 1980. "A Theoretical Treatment of Indices of Absolute Inequality." *International Economic Review* 21 (1): 107–136.

Blackorby, C., D. Donaldson, and J. A. Weymark. 1984. "Social Choice with Interpersonal Utility Comparisons: A Diagrammatic Introduction." *International Economic Review* 25 (2): 327–356.

Clarke, E. H. 1971. "Multi-Part Pricing of Public Goods." *Public Choice* 11 (September): 17–33.

d'Aspremont, C., and L. Gevers. 1977. "Equity and the Informational Basis of Collective Choice." *Review of Economic Studies* 44 (2): 199–209.

———. 2002. "Social Welfare Functionals and Interpersonal Comparability." In *Handbook of Social Choice and Welfare,* edited by K. Arrow, A. K. Sen and K. Suzumura, 1:459–541. Amsterdam, The Netherlands: North-Holland.

de Borda, Jean-Charles. (1781) 1995. "Surles élections au scrutin." In *Mémoires de l'Académie royale des sciences année*, 657–665. Reprinted as "On Elections by Ballot," in *Classics of Social Choice*, edited by I. McLean and A. Urken, 83–89. Ann Arbor: University of Michigan Press.

Dodgson, C. L. (1873) 1958. "A Discussion of the Various Methods of Procedure in Conducting Elections." Reprinted in D. Black, *The Theory of Committees and Elections*, 214–222. London: Cambridge University Press

———. (1874) 1958. "Suggestions as to the Best Method of Taking Votes, When More than Two Issues Are to be Voted On." Reprinted in D. Black, *The Theory of Committees and Elections*, 222–224. London: Cambridge University Press.

———. (1876) 1958. "A Method of Taking Votes on More than Two Issues." Reprinted in D. Black, *The Theory of Committees and Elections*, 224–234. London: Cambridge University Press.

Feldman, A. M., and R. Serrano. 2006. *Welfare Economics and Social Choice Theory*. 2nd ed. Boston, MA: Springer.

Galton, F. 1907. "Vox Populi." *Nature* 75 (March): 450–451.

Gibbard, A. 1973. "Manipulation of Voting Schemes: A General Result." *Econometrica* 41 (4): 587–601.

Gini, C. 1936. "On the Measure of Concentration with Special Reference to Income and Statistics." General Series no. 208, Colorado College Publication, 73–79.

Groves, T. 1973. "Incentives in Teams." *Econometrica* 41 (4): 617–631.

Harsanyi, J. C. 1953. "Cardinal Utility in Welfare Economics and in the Theory of Risk-Bearing." *Journal of Political Economy* 61 (5): 434–435.

———. 1955. "Cardinal Welfare, Individualistic Ethics, and Interpersonal Comparisons of Utility." *Journal of Political Economy* 63 (4): 309–321.

———. 1977. "Rule Utilitarianism and Decision Theory." *Erkenntnis* 11 (1): 25–53.

Kolm, S-C. 1969. "The Optimal Production of Social Justice." In *Public Economics*, edited by J. Margolis and H. Guitton, 145–200. London: Macmillan.

——. 1976. "Unequal Inequalities I." *Journal of Economic Theory* 12 (3): 416–442.

——. 1977. "Multidimensional Egalitarianisms." *Quarterly Journal of Economics* 91 (1): 1–13.

Laplace, Pierre-Simon. 1812. *Théorie analytique des probabilités*. Paris: Courcier.

List, C. 2003. "Are Interpersonal Comparisons of Utility Indeterminate?" *Erkenntnis* 58 (March): 229–260.

Little, I. M. D. 1957. *A Critique of Welfare Economics*. 2nd ed. Oxford: Oxford University Press.

May, K. 1952. "A Set of Independent, Necessary and Sufficient Conditions for Simple Majority Decision." *Econometrica* 20 (4): 680–684.

Moulin, H. 1980. "On Strategyproofness and Single Peakedness." *Public Choice* 35 (4): 437–455.

Nanson, E. J. (1882) 1995. "Methods of Elections." *Transactions and Proceedings of the Royal Society of Victoria* 18 (954): 197–240. Reprinted in *Classics of Social Choice*, edited by I. McLean and A. Urken, 321–359. Ann Arbor: University of Michigan Press.

Robbins, L. 1932. *An Essay on the Nature and Significance of Economic Science*. 2nd ed. London: Macmillan.

Roberts, K. W. S. 1980. "Price Independent Welfare Prescriptions." *Journal of Public Economics* 13 (3): 277–297.

Satterthwaite, M. 1975. "Strategyproofness and Arrow's Conditions: Existence and Correspondence Theorems for Voting Procedures and Social Welfare Functions." *Journal of Economic Theory* 10 (2): 187–217.

Sen, A. K. 1970. *Collective Choice and Social Welfare*. Amsterdam, The Netherlands: Elsevier.

——. 1973. *On Economic Inequality*. Oxford: Clarendon.

——. 1974. "Informational Bases of Alternative Welfare Approaches." *Journal of Public Economics* 3 (4): 387–403.

——. 1977. "On Weights and Measures: Informational Constraints in Social Welfare Analysis." *Econometrica* 45 (7): 1539–1572.

——. 1986. "Social Choice Theory." In *Handbook of Mathematical Economics III*, edited by K. J. Arrow and M. D. Intriligator, 1073–1181. Amsterdam: North-Holland.

Suzumura, K. 2002. "Introduction." In *Handbook of Social Choice and Welfare*, edited by K. J. Arrow, A. K. Sen, and K. Suzumura, 1:1–32. Amsterdam, The Netherlands: North-Holland.

Todhunter, I. 1865. *A History of the Mathematical Theory of Probability from the Time of Pascal to That of Laplace*. Cambridge; London: Macmillan.

Tsui, K. Y. 1995. "Multidimensional Generalizations of the Relative and Absolute Indices: The Atkinson–Kolm–Sen Approach." *Journal of Economic Theory* 67 (1): 251–265.

Vickrey, W. S. 1961. "Counterspeculation, Auctions and Competitive Sealed Tenders." *Journal of Finance* 16 (1): 8–37.

Waldner, I. 1972. "The Empirical Meaningfulness of Interpersonal Utility Comparisons." *Journal of Philosophy* 69 (4): 87–103.

INDIVIDUAL AND SOCIAL ORDERINGS

2.1 INTRODUCTION

In this chapter, we introduce some basic concepts that will be used throughout this book. In Section 2.2, we start by defining the "at least as good as" relation $\succsim$ that describes the preferences of the individuals over the set of alternatives that they face. We specify certain properties associated with these preference relations. In Section 2.3, we introduce the notion of maximal sets (or choice sets) and link it with the properties of $\succsim$. Finally, in Section 2.4, we discuss social orderings, that is, given a set of agents in a society along with their preferences, how do we aggregate them into social preferences. Specifically, in Section 2.4, we discuss some well-known social aggregation rules like plurality rule, Borda count, anti-plurality rule, oligarchy, and pairwise majority rule.

2.2 RELATIONS

Let $A = \{x, y, z, w \ldots\}$ be the set of alternative states of affairs (alternatives, for short). A *relation* $\succsim$ on A is a subset of $A \times A$. We shall write $x \succsim y$ if $(x, y) \in \succsim$. We say that x and y are *unordered by* $\succsim$ if neither $x \succsim y$ nor $y \succsim x$. They are *ordered by* $\succsim$ if they are not unordered, that is, either $x \succsim y$ holds or $y \succsim x$ holds. We will call $\succsim$ as the "at least as good as" relation defined on the set of alternatives A. Given $\succsim$, let $\succ$ and $\sim$ be the asymmetric and the symmetric parts of $\succsim$. That is, $x \succ y$ if and only if $x \succsim y$ and $\neg(y \succsim x)$, where $\neg(y \succsim x)$ means that $y \succsim x$ is not true. Moreover, $x \sim y$ if and only if $x \succsim y$ and $y \succsim x$. We will also refer to $\succ$ as the strict preference part of $\succsim$ and we will also refer to $\sim$ as the indifference part of $\succsim$. In words, for any person (society) with the preference relation $\succsim$, between any two alternatives x and y, $x \succ y$ means that the person (society) strictly prefers x to y and $x \sim y$ means that the person (society) is indifferent between x and y.

The relation $\succsim$ is *reflexive* if $x \succsim x$ for all $x \in A$ and it is *irreflexive* if $\neg(x \succsim x)$ for all $x \in A$. The relation $\succsim$ is *symmetric* if for all $x, y \in A$, $x \succsim y$ if and only if $y \succsim x$ and it is *anti-symmetric* if for all $x, y \in A$ with $x \neq y$, $x \succsim y$ implies $\neg(y \succsim x)$. $\succsim$ is *transitive* if for all $x, y, z \in A$, $x \succsim y$ and $y \succsim z$ implies $x \succsim z$. A weaker form of transitivity is *quasi-transitivity*, which requires that transitivity only holds for the strict relation $\succ$. Finally, $\succsim$ is *complete* if for all $x, y \in A$, $x \succsim y$ or $y \succsim x$. Observe that if $\succsim$ is complete, then it is reflexive as well. Hence, whenever $\succsim$ is reflexive and complete, many authors simply specify that $\succsim$ is complete. However, to keep completeness and reflexivity separate, some authors define completeness by specifying that it holds only for all $x, y \in A$ such that $x \neq y$, that is, $\succsim$ is *complete* if for all $x, y \in A$ with $x \neq y$, we have $x \succsim y$ or $y \succsim x$. We will follow the latter definition of completeness to keep reflexivity different from completeness.

The following types of relations $\succsim$ on A are of importance:

- *Binary relation*: If $\succsim$ is reflexive and complete

- *Weak order (or simply an order)*: If $\succsim$ is reflexive, complete, and transitive

- *Partial order*: If $\succsim$ is reflexive, transitive, and anti-symmetric

- *Equivalence relation*: If $\succsim$ is reflexive, symmetric, and transitive

- *Linear order*: If $\succsim$ is reflexive, complete, transitive, and anti-symmetric

One may verify the following results:

(1) If a binary relation $\succsim$ on A is transitive, then by definition $\succsim$ on A is a weak order.

(2) If $\succsim$ on A is a weak order, then its asymmetric part $\succ$ on A is a partial order. This is formally proved in Proposition 4.1 (a) of Chapter 4.

(3) If $\succsim$ on A is a weak order, then its symmetric part $\sim$ on A is an equivalence relation. This is established in Proposition 4.1 (b) of Chapter 4.

(4) If $\succsim$ on A is a binary relation and its asymmetric part $\succ$ and its symmetric part $\sim$ are both transitive, then $\succsim$ on A is a weak order. In an exercise of Chapter 4, you are asked to prove this result.

(5) If $\succsim$ on A is a weak order and there does not exist $x, y \in A$ such that $x \neq y$ and $x \sim y$, then $\succsim$ on A is a linear order. This follows from the definition of a linear order.

2.3 PREFERENCE RELATIONS AND CHOICE SETS

We consider the problem of a decision maker (also called an agent or a player or an individual) who faces a set of finite alternatives A. Let $\mathcal{A}$ be the collection of all possible non-empty subsets of A, that is, $\mathcal{A} = \{S \subseteq A : S \neq \emptyset\}$. Given the relation $\succsim$ on A and any set S in $\mathcal{A}$, we define the *maximal set* associated with the set S and the preference relation $\succsim$ on A as: $M(S; \succsim) = \{x \in S \mid \nexists y \in S$ such that $y \succ x\}$. Observe that $M(S; \succsim)$ is the best or top-ranked alternative in S according to the relation $\succsim$ defined on A. Usually, $M(S; \succsim)$ is called the *choice set* corresponding to $\succsim$ and S because it is natural to assume that, given S and $\succsim$ on A, the chosen alternatives are those included in $M(S; \succsim)$. That is, the decision maker selects from the feasible alternatives that he faces the best alternative(s) from his point of view. This assumption is called the *rationality principle*. The behavioral pattern that it implies is called *rational behavior*.

(1) The relation $\succsim$ on A is a binary relation if it is reflexive and complete. If the relation $\succsim$ on A is also a binary relation, then $M(S; \succsim) = \{x \in S \mid x \succsim y \,\forall\, y \in S\}$.

(2) Reflexivity of the relation $\succsim$ on A is a necessary condition for ensuring the existence of a non-empty choice set $M(S; \succsim)$ in those cases where S consists of a single alternative. Completeness is a necessary condition for ensuring the existence of a non-empty choice set $M(S; \succsim)$ in those cases where S includes two alternatives.

What are the properties of the relation $\succsim$ on A that ensures that, for any given subset of alternatives S, the choice set $M(S; \succsim)$ is non-empty? To answer this question we first define two more important properties of the relation $\succsim$ on A which are used for both individual and social orderings.

- *Quasi-transitive*: If for all $x, y, z \in A$ such that $x \succ y$ and $y \succ z$, we have $x \succ z$.

- *Acyclic*: If for any positive integer $k \geq 3$ and any k-alternatives $x_1, \ldots, x_k \in A$ such that $x_1 \succ x_2, x_2 \succ x_3 \succ \ldots \succ x_{k-1} \succ x_k$, then $\neg(x_k \succ x_1)$.

If $\succsim$ on A is a binary relation, then acyclicity requires that for any positive integer k and any $x_1, \ldots, x_k \in A$ such that $x_1 \succ x_2$, $x_2 \succ x_3, \ldots, x_{k-1} \succ x_k$, we have $x_1 \succsim x_k$ (since completeness means that if $\neg(x_k \succ x_1)$, then $x_1 \succsim x_k$). Let $\mathcal{Q}$ be the set of all possible weak orders on A, $\mathcal{Q}^q$ be the set of all possible binary relations on A that are quasi-transitive, and $\mathcal{Q}^a$ be the set of all possible binary relations on A that are acyclic.

(1) The binary relation $\succsim$ on A is a quasi-order if it satisfies quasi-transitivity. In Lemma 5.4 of Chapter 5, it is proved that a binary relation $\succsim$ on A (with three or more alternatives in the set A, that is, with $|A| \geq 3$) is a quasi-ordering if and only if for every triple $x, y, z \in A$, $x \succ y$ and $y \succsim z$ implies $x \succsim z$.[1]

---

[1] For any set X, the notation $|X|$ denotes the cardinality, the number of elements, of the set X.

(2) The binary relation $\succsim$ on A is a weak quasi-order if it is acyclic. In Proposition 5.2 of Chapter 5, it is established that the set $M(S;\succsim)$ is non-empty for every non-empty set of alternatives $S \in \mathcal{A}$ if and only if $\succsim \in \mathcal{Q}^a$, that is, the set $M(S;\succsim)$ is non-empty for every $S \in \mathcal{A}$ if and only if $\succsim$ is acyclic. In other words, reflexivity, completeness, and acyclicity taken together are both necessary and sufficient for the existence of a non-empty choice set under all circumstances (that is, for all sets in $\mathcal{A}$).

(3) In Proposition 5.1 of Chapter 5, it is established that if the set of alternatives A has three or more elements, then $\mathcal{Q} \subset \mathcal{Q}^q \subset \mathcal{Q}^a$. Here we provide an intuitive argument for this result by taking four alternatives. Therefore, assume that $A = \{x,y,z,w\}$ and consider the following possibilities:

(a) If $\succsim$ on A is such that $x \succ y$, $y \sim z$, $x \succ z$, $x \succ w$, $y \sim w$, and $z \sim w$, then one can verify that $\succsim \in \mathcal{Q} \subset \mathcal{Q}^q \subset \mathcal{Q}^a$.

(b) If $\succsim$ on A is such that $x \succ y$, $z \sim y$, $x \sim z$, $x \succ w$, $y \succ w$, and $z \succ w$, then one can verify that $\succsim \in \mathcal{Q}^q \subset \mathcal{Q}^a$. However, $\succsim \notin \mathcal{Q}$ since $x \sim z$, $z \sim y$ and yet we do not have $x \sim y$ (since $x \succ y$). Transitivity of the symmetric part $\sim$ of $\succsim$ on A is violated.

(c) If $\succsim$ on A is such that $x \succ y$, $y \succ z$, $x \sim z$, $x \succ w$, $y \succ w$, and $z \succ w$, then it follows that $\succsim \in \mathcal{Q}^a$ since maximal set of all non-empty subsets of A are non-empty. Specifically, $M(A;\succsim) = \{x\}$, $M(\{x,y,z\};\succsim) = \{x\}$, $M(\{x,y,w\};\succsim) = \{x\}$, $M(\{x,z,w\};\succsim) = \{x,z\}$ and $M(\{y,z,w\};\succsim) = \{y\}$. However, $\succsim \notin \mathcal{Q}$ and $\succsim \notin \mathcal{Q}^q$ since $x \succ y$, $y \succ z$ and yet we do not have $x \succ z$ (since $x \sim z$). Transitivity of the asymmetric part $\succ$ of the relation $\succsim$ on A is violated.

(4) The binary relation $\succsim$ on A with A having at least three alternatives is a quasi-order if it satisfies quasi-transitivity, that is, transitivity of strict preferences (that is, $\succsim \in \mathcal{Q}^q$). If a binary relation $\succsim$ on A is a quasi-order, then $M(S;\succsim)$ is non-empty for any set of alternatives $S \in \mathcal{A}$ since $\mathcal{Q}^q \subset \mathcal{Q}^a$. Therefore, reflexivity, completeness, and quasi-transitivity are also sufficient conditions for the existence of a non-empty choice set under all circumstances.

(5) The binary relation $\succsim$ on A having three or more alternatives in A is an order if it satisfies transitivity (that is, $\succsim \in \mathcal{Q}$). If a binary relation $\succsim$ on A is an order, then $M(S; \succsim)$ is non-empty for any set of alternatives $S \in \mathcal{A}$ since $\mathcal{Q} \subset \mathcal{Q}^q \subset \mathcal{Q}^a$. In other words, reflexivity, completeness, and transitivity are also sufficient conditions for the existence of a non-empty choice set under all circumstances.

2.4 SOCIAL ORDERINGS, QUASI-ORDERINGS, AND WEAK QUASI-ORDERINGS

We have the following definition of an Arrovian social welfare function. Suppose that there is a set $N = \{1, \ldots, n\}$ of n-agents in a society (with $n \geq 2$) such that each agent $i \in N$ has a preference ordering (or simply an ordering) $\succsim_i \in \mathcal{Q}$. A profile of preferences or a state of the world is given by $(\succsim_1, \ldots, \succsim_n) \in \mathcal{Q}^n$. An *Arrovian social welfare function* or simply a social welfare function F is a mapping from the set of all possible profiles $\mathcal{Q}^n$ to the set of all possible orderings $\mathcal{Q}$, that is, $F : \mathcal{Q}^n \to \mathcal{Q}$. Thus, an Arrovian social welfare function requires that the set of all profiles drawn from the set $\mathcal{Q}^n$ must be mapped to an ordering $\mathcal{Q}$. As we will see later, often this is a strong requirement. As a relaxation one may often want to concentrate on requirements like social quasi-ordering or social weak quasi-ordering. Formally, F^q is a *social quasi-ordering* if $F^q : \mathcal{Q}^n \to \mathcal{Q}^q$, that is, a social quasi-ordering is a mapping from the set of all possible profiles $\mathcal{Q}^n$ to the set of all possible quasi-transitive binary relation $\mathcal{Q}^q$ on A. Similarly, F^a is a *social weak quasi-ordering* if $F^a : \mathcal{Q}^n \to \mathcal{Q}^a$, that is, a social weak quasi-ordering is a mapping from the set of all possible profiles $\mathcal{Q}^n$ to the set of all possible acyclic binary relation $\mathcal{Q}^a$ on A. We first provide examples of some well-known social welfare functions $F : \mathcal{Q}^n \to \mathcal{Q}$.

2.4.1 *Scoring rules*

Let $|A| = p$ and $s = (s_1, \ldots, s_p)$, where $s_1 \geq s_2 \geq \ldots \geq s_p \geq 0$ and $s_1 > s_p$. The vector s is called a scoring vector. For all $i \in N$, $\succsim_i \in \mathcal{Q}, x \in A$, define the rank of x in $\succsim_i$ as $r(x; \succsim_i) = |\{y \in A \setminus \{x\} \mid y \succ_i x\}| + 1$. That is, the rank of an element in a non-increasingly ordered set of elements is the number of elements that are strictly preferred to it in the reduced set, obtained by excluding the element itself from the original set, plus one. To understand this, consider the ordering $x \sim_i y \succ_i w \succ_i z$ for some agent $i \in N$. Suppose we wish to determine the rank of w for agent i. The number of elements that are preferred to w in the reduced set $\{x, y, z\}$ is two (x and y). Hence, the rank of w for agent i is $2 + 1 = 3$. Likewise, one can verify that for agent i the rank of both x and y is 1 and that of z is 4. The score of rank $r(x; \succsim_i)$ is $s_{r(x;\succsim_i)}$, that is, if the rank is $r(x; \succsim_i) = k$, then the score is $s_{r(x;\succsim_i)} = s_k$. For every profile $\succsim = (\succsim_1, \ldots, \succsim_n) \in \mathcal{Q}^n$, compute the score of alternative $x \in A$ as $s(x; \succsim) = \sum_{i \in N} s_{r(x;\succsim_i)}$.

Definition 2.1 The scoring rule $F^s : \mathcal{Q}^n \to \mathcal{Q}$ is defined as follows: For all $x, y \in A$, for all $\succsim = (\succsim_1, \ldots, \succsim_n) \in \mathcal{Q}^n$, we have $xF^s(\succsim)y$ if and only if $s(x; \succsim) \geq s(y; \succsim)$.

It is easy to see that $F^s : \mathcal{Q}^n \to \mathcal{Q}$ *defines an ordering*, that is, any scoring rule satisfies reflexivity, completeness, and transitivity. It is also obvious that we have strict preference for society, that is, we get $x\hat{F}^s(\succsim)y$ if and only if $s(x; \succsim) > s(y; \succsim)$. Similarly, we have indifference for society, that is, we have $x\overline{F}^s(\succsim)y$ if and only if $s(x; \succsim) = s(y; \succsim)$. Here are some special cases of the scoring rules.

- **Plurality rule (F^{sP}):** This is the scoring rule with $s = (1, 0, \ldots, 0)$. The decision associated with the plurality rule is what is followed under plurality voting. Plurality voting is an electoral system in which each voter is allowed to vote for only one candidate, and the candidate who polls the most among their counterparts (a plurality) is elected. The plurality voting system is often used to elect members of a legislative assembly or executive officers.[2]

- **The Borda rule (F^{sB}):** This is the scoring rule when $s = (p - 1, p - 2, \ldots, 1, 0)$. The decision associated with the Borda rule is what is followed under the Borda count single-winner

---

[2] Plurality rule is the most common form of the system, and is used in Canada, the lower house (Lok Sabha) in India, most elections in the United Kingdom (excluding some Scottish and Northern Irish elections), and most elections in the United States.

elections. The Borda count is a single-winner election method in which voters rank options or candidates in order of preference. The Borda count determines the outcome of a debate or the winner of an election by giving each candidate, for each ballot, a number of points corresponding to the number of candidates ranked lower.[3]

- **Anti-plurality rule (F^{sAP}):** This is the scoring rule when $s = (1, 1, \ldots, 1, 0)$. The decision associated with the anti-plurality rule is what is followed under anti-plurality voting. Anti-plurality voting describes an electoral system in which each voter votes against a single candidate, and the candidate with the fewest votes against him or her wins. The anti-plurality rule can be applied when a set of employees N in a firm wants to select a manager from a set of potential managerial candidates A. While selecting a manager it is often felt reasonable to select that person as the manager who is the least hated person in A and hence the anti-plurality rule is helpful in this context.

It is important to note that when there are exactly two alternatives, that is, if $|A| = 2$, then the plurality rule, the Borda count, and the anti-plurality rule are equivalent. However, it is easy to verify that each is different from the other two for $|A| \geq 3$.

2.4.2 *Oligarchies: a quasi-ordering for the society*

We provide an example of a well-known social quasi-ordering. Let $Q \in Q^n$ be a preference profile and consider a non-empty group of agents $G \subseteq N$. The oligarchic social quasi-ordering $F_G^{OL}(\succsim)$ (with a strict part $\hat{F}_G^{OL}(\succsim)$ and an indifference part $\overline{F}_G^{OL}(\succsim)$) is defined as follows: For all $x, y \in A$ we have $x F_G^{OL}(\succsim)y$ if and only if there exists $i \in G$ such that $x \succsim_i y$. In other words, $x \hat{F}_G^{OL}(\succsim)y$ if and only if for

---

[3] The Borda count is named for the 18th-century French mathematician and naval engineer Jean-Charles de Borda, who devised the system in 1770. It is currently used to elect members of the Parliament of Nauru and two ethnic minority members of the National Assembly of Slovenia, in modified forms to determine which candidates are elected to the party list seats in Icelandic parliamentary elections, and for selecting presidential election candidates in Kiribati.

all $i \in G$ we have $x \succ_i y$. Thus, given $F_G^{OL}(\succsim)$, for any pair $x, y \in A$ we have the following possibilities:

(OL1) $x F_G^{OL}(\succsim) y$ if and only if for all $i \in G$ we have $x \succ_i y$,

(OL2) $y \hat{F}_G^{OL}(\succsim) x$ if and only if for all $i \in G$ we have $y \succ_i x$, and

(OL3) $x \overline{F}_G^{OL}(\succsim) y$ if there exists $i \in G$ such that $x \succsim_i y$ and there also exists an agent $i' \in G \setminus \{i\}$ such that $y \succsim_i x$.

Let $\succsim \in \mathcal{Q}^n$ be a preference profile and consider a non-empty group of agents $G \subseteq N$. An oligarchic binary relation essentially means that the group G is all powerful in the sense that whenever all members of this group agree on strict preference over some pair of alternatives, society also follows that same strict ordering over that pair. Moreover, every member $i \in G$ has a veto power in the following sense. If for any member $i \in G$ we have $x \succsim_i y$, then, under the oligarchy, the society either says $x \succ y$ or $x \sim y$, that is, this member i has the veto power in the sense that society cannot select $y \succ x$ (given $x \succsim_i y$). In an exercise provided at the end of this chapter, you are asked to prove the following results: (a) for all profiles $\succsim \in \mathcal{Q}^n$, $F_G^{OL}(\succsim)$ is a quasi-ordering, (b) if $|G| = 1$, then $F_G^{OL}(\succsim)$ is an ordering, and (c) if $|G| \geq 2$, then quasi-ordering of $F_G^{OL}(\succsim)$ is not an ordering.

2.4.3 Pairwise majority rule

Given any $\succsim = (\succsim_1, \ldots, \succsim_n) \in \mathcal{Q}^n$, let $N(x, y; \succsim) = |\{i \in N \mid x \succ_i y\}|$. Alternative x defeats (is at least as good as) another alternative y in pairwise majority voting under any given preference ordering $\succsim = (\succsim_1, \ldots, \succsim_n) \in \mathcal{Q}^n$ if $N(x, y; \succsim) > (\geq) N(y, x; \succsim)$. Thus under the pairwise majority rule, between any pair of alternatives x and y, the former defeats the latter if the majority of the voters prefer the former.

Definition 2.2 For every $\succsim \in \mathcal{Q}^n$, define the pairwise majority relation $\succsim^{maj}(\succsim)$ as follows: for all $x, y \in A$ we have $x \succsim^{maj}(\succsim) y$ if and only if $N(x, y; \succsim) \geq N(y, x; \succsim)$.

We write $x \succ^{maj}(\succsim) y$ if and only if $N(x, y; \succsim) > N(y, x; \succsim)$. Therefore, it is obvious that $x \succ^{maj}(\succsim) y \Leftrightarrow [x \succsim^{maj}(\succsim$

$)y$ and $\neg(y \succsim^{maj} (\succsim)x)]$. Similarly, we write $x \sim^{maj} (\succsim)y$ if and only if $N(x, y; \succsim) = N(x, y; \succsim)$ and hence $x \sim^{maj} (\succsim)y \Leftrightarrow [x \succsim^{maj} (\succsim)y$ and $y \succsim^{maj} (\succsim)x]$. Thus, the social preference relation $\succsim^{maj} (\succsim)$ when operated over all pairs $x, y \in A$ for any given $\succsim \in \succsim^n$ generates a binary relation. However, if there are three or more alternative (that is, if $|A| \geq 3$), then $\succsim^{maj}$ need not be transitive. This point is explained in the following example due to Condorcet. The Condorcet paradox (also known as the voting paradox) is a situation noted by the Marquis de Condorcet in the late 18th century, in which collective preferences can be cyclic, even if the individual preferences are orderings.

Example 2.1   *The Condorcet paradox:* Consider $A = \{x, y, z\}$ and $N = \{1, 2, 3\}$. Let $\succsim_1$: $x \succ_1 y \succ_1 z$, $\succsim_2$: $z \succ_2 x \succ_2 y$ and $\succsim_3$: $y \succ_3 z \succ_3 x$. Given $N(x, y; \succsim) > N(y, x; \succsim)$ we have $x \succ^{maj} (\succsim)y$. Moreover, from $N(y, z; \succsim) > N(z, y; \succsim)$ we get $y \succ^{maj} (\succsim)z$ and from $N(z, x; \succsim) > N(x, z; \succsim)$ we get $z \succ^{maj} (\succsim)x$. Thus, for $\succsim = (\succsim_1, \succsim_2, \succsim_3) \in \mathcal{Q}^3$, $x \succ^{maj} (\succsim)y \succ^{maj} (\succsim)z \succ^{maj} (\succsim)x$. Therefore, if we consider pairwise majority voting then x is preferred to y, y is preferred to z, and z is preferred to x, and we have a violation of transitivity of social preference.

Thus, when there are three or more alternatives, then we need to define "appropriate" restrictions on preference profiles, that is, we need to define $D \subset \mathcal{Q}^n$ (with $D \neq \mathcal{Q}^n$) such that the pairwise majority relation is also transitive on the restricted domain D. As an example, suppose $N = \{1, 2, 3\}$, $A = \{x, y, z\}$, and let $\mathcal{Q}^* = \{\succsim^{(a)}, \succsim^{(b)}, \succsim^{(c)}, \succsim^{(d)}\}$ be a strict subset of orderings from $\mathcal{Q}$, where $\succsim^{(a)}$: $x \succ y \succ z$, $\succsim^{(b)}$: $y \succ x \succ z$, $\succsim^{(c)}$: $y \succ z \succ x$, and, $\succsim^{(d)}$: $z \succ y \succ x$. Observe that $\mathcal{Q}^*$ picks out only four possible orders from $\mathcal{Q}$.[4] $\mathcal{Q}^*$ allows for strict preferences only (that is, there does not exist any pair of alternatives that are indifferent). Moreover, $\mathcal{Q}^*$ also rules out two strict preferences where the alternative y is the least preferred alternative (that is, it rules out $x \succ z \succ y$ and $z \succ x \succ y$).

---

[4] With three alternatives given by $A = \{x, y, z\}$, the set of all possible orders is given by $\mathcal{Q} = \{x \succ y \succ z, x \succ z \succ y, y \succ x \succ z, y \succ z \succ x, z \succ x \succ y, z \succ y \succ x, x \succ y \sim z, y \succ x \sim z, z \succ x \sim y, x \sim y \succ z, x \sim z \succ y, y \sim z \succ x, x \sim y \sim z\}$. Note that $|\mathcal{Q}| = 13$.

One can show that if $N = \{1, 2, 3\}$, $A = \{x, y, z\}$, and the domain of preferences is $D^* = \{Q^*\}^3 \subset Q^3$, then the pairwise majority binary relation defined on the restricted domain D^* is also transitive. The domain restriction D^* is a particular kind of domain restriction called "single-peakedness." For more on this see Chapter 5.

From our discussion it follows that the pairwise majority rule with three or more alternatives neither generates a social ordering nor a social quasi-ordering nor a social weak quasi-ordering unless we restrict the domain appropriately. However, if there are only two alternatives (that is, if $A = \{x, y\}$ so that $|A| = 2$), then pairwise majority rule or simple *the majority rule* is a binary relation. In many electoral systems, there are only two contesting candidates and hence in that context majority rule can be used as it generates a binary relation. For this case of only two alternatives why the majority rule is a nice concept is the subject matter of the next chapter.

2.5 **EXERCISES**

For explanations or definitions of the notation, see the main text of Chapter 2.

(E-2.1) A relation $\succsim$ on A is *negative transitive* if for all $x, y, z \in A$ with $\neg(x \succsim y)$ and $\neg(y \succsim z)$, we have $\neg(x \succsim z)$. Show that if a relation $\succsim$ is anti-symmetric and negative transitive, then $\succsim$ is transitive.

(E-2.2) Show that a relation $\succsim$ on A is negative transitive if and only if $x \succsim z$ implies that for all $y \in A$, either $x \succsim y$ or $y \succsim z$.

(E-2.3) Show that any scoring rule $F^s : Q^n \to Q$ is an ordering, that is, show that any scoring rule F^s is reflexive, complete, and transitive.

(E-2.4) Let $\succsim \in Q^n$ be a preference profile and consider a non-empty group of agents $G \subseteq N$. Show that for all profiles $\succsim \in Q^n$, the oligarchic relation $F_G^{OL}(\succsim)$ is a quasi-ordering. Moreover, if $|G| = 1$, then show that $F_G^{OL}(\succsim)$ is an ordering. Finally, show that if $|G| \geq 2$, then quasi-ordering of the oligarchic binary relation $F_G^{OL}(\succsim)$ is not an ordering.

2.6 **BIBLIOGRAPHICAL NOTES**

- More on the results discussed in Section 2.2 can be found in Chambers and Echenique (2016).

- A very detailed discussion on preferences and choice sets (as discussed in Section 2.3 of this chapter) can be found in Nitzan (2010).

- The Borda count was characterized by Young (1974). A survey on characterizations of different scoring rules can be found in Chebotarey and Shamis (1998).

REFERENCES

Chambers, C. P., and F. Echenique. 2016. *Revealed Preference Theory.* Cambridge, United Kingdom: Cambridge University Press.

Chebotarey, P. Y., and E. Shamis. 1998. "Characterizations of Scoring Methods for Preference Aggregation." *Annals of Operations Research* 80 (January): 299–332.

Nitzan, S. 2010. *Collective Preference and Public Choice.* Cambridge, United Kingdom: Cambridge University Press.

Young, H. P. 1974. "An Axiomatization of Borda's Rule." *Journal of Economic Theory* 9 (1): 43–52.

MAY'S THEOREM

3.1 INTRODUCTION

In this chapter, we restrict our attention to the decisive voting rule with only two contesting candidates (or alternatives). A decisive voting rule maps for every possible vote (or preference) of the set of agents over the two contesting candidates (say, x and y) to either a winner or two non-losers. May's theorem, which is the main subject matter of this chapter, specifies the importance of majority voting rule by arguing that it is the unique rule that satisfies four important democratic principles. These four key democratic principles are decisiveness of the voting rule, anonymity, neutrality, and positive responsiveness. Decisiveness of the voting rule requires that the voting rule must specify a unique decision even if the decision is indifference for any set of individual preferences over the two contesting candidates. Anonymity (or symmetry across agents) requires that a voting rule must treat all voters alike, in the sense that if any two voters traded ballots, the outcome of the election would remain the same. Neutrality (or anonymity across alternatives) requires that a voting rule must treat all candidates alike, rather than favor one over the other. Finally, positive responsiveness (a type of monotonicity property) requires that if the group decision is indifference or favorable to some alternative x, and if individual preferences remain the same except that a single individual changes his or her vote in favor of x, then the group decision should be x. Formally, May's theorem states that among the class of all decisive voting rules, the majority voting rule is the only one that satisfies anonymity, neutrality, and positive responsiveness.

The chapter is organized as follows: Section 3.2 provides the framework. In Section 3.3 we state and prove May's theorem. In Section 3.4 we check the robustness of the axioms used in May's theorem.

3.2 THE FRAMEWORK

We consider preferences of a finite set of agents $N = \{1, \ldots, n\}$ of a society voting over two alternatives x and y. Thus, the set of alternatives is $A = \{x, y\}$. An agent i's preference is a binary relation on $A = \{x, y\}$ and given that we have only two alternatives it can be denoted by

$$
\alpha_i = \begin{cases} -1 & \text{if } y \succ_i x, \\ 0 & \text{if } x \sim_i y, \\ 1 & \text{if } x \succ_i y. \end{cases}
$$

Therefore, $\alpha_i = -1$ indicates that the agent prefers y over x, $\alpha_i = 0$ indicates that the agent is indifferent between x and y, and $\alpha_i = 1$ indicates that the agent prefers x over y. The family of agents' preferences between the two alternatives can be described by a profile $\alpha = (\alpha_1, \ldots, \alpha_n) \in \{-1, 0, 1\}^n$. We introduce some notations that will be used. For any $\alpha, \alpha' \in \{-1, 0, +1\}^n$, (i) $\alpha \geq \alpha'$ means $\alpha_i \geq \alpha_i$ for all $i \in N$, (ii) $\alpha \neq \alpha'$ means that there exists $i \in N$ such that $\alpha_i \neq \alpha_i'$, (iii) $\alpha \geq 0$ means $\alpha_i \geq 0$ for all $i \in N$, (iv) $\alpha \leq 0$ means $\alpha_i \leq 0$ for all $i \in N$, and (v) $\alpha \neq 0$ means that there exists $i \in N$ such that $\alpha_i \neq 0$.

Definition 3.1 A *decisive voting rule* is a rule F that assigns a social preference $F(\alpha) \in \{-1, 0, 1\}$ to every possible profile of the agents' preferences. Thus, we have $F : \{-1, 0, 1\}^n \to \{-1, 0, 1\}$ and

$$F(\alpha) = \begin{cases} -1 & \text{if } y \succ x, \\ 0 & \text{if } x \sim y, \\ 1 & \text{if } x \succ y. \end{cases}$$

Here $x \succsim y$ means that "x is at least as good as y" for the society given the decisive voting rule F. Therefore, $F(\alpha) \geq 0$ if and only if $x \succsim y$ and $F(\alpha) \leq 0$ if and only if $y \succsim x$. Hence, $x \succ y$ means that "x is strictly preferred to y" and then we have $F(\alpha) = 1$. Similarly, $y \succ x$ means that "y is strictly preferred to x" and then we have $F(\alpha) = -1$. Finally, $x \sim y$ means that "x is indifferent to y" for the society and then we have $F(\alpha) = 0$. Implicit in the definition of the decisive voting rule is the decisiveness of the voting rule that requires that it must specify a unique decision even if the decision is indifference for any set of individual preferences α over the two contesting candidates. Observe that the decisive voting rule F is an alternative way of representing the Arrovian social welfare function F defined in the previous chapter by following the numerical representation -1, 0, and $+1$ for the three possible individual preferences of y preferred to x, x indifferent to y, and x preferred to y, respectively. Before going into the properties of F, we introduce one more definition. Let $a \in (-\infty, \infty)$.

$$sign\, a = \begin{cases} -1 & \text{if } a < 0, \\ 0 & \text{if } a = 0, \\ 1 & \text{if } a > 0. \end{cases}$$

Definition 3.2 A decisive voting rule F satisfies *weak Pareto* if it respects the unanimity of strict preference on the part of the agents, that is, if $F(1, \dots, 1) = 1$ and $F(-1, \dots, -1) = -1$.

Weak Pareto requires that if all agents unanimously feel that x is preferred to y, that is, if $\alpha_i = 1$ for all $i \in N$, then the society must as well feel the same, that is, $F(1, \dots, 1) = 1$. Similarly, if all agents unanimously feel that y is preferred to x (that is, $\alpha_i = -1$ for all $i \in N$), then society must as well, that is, $F(-1, \dots, -1) = -1$.

Let $\beta = (\beta_1, \dots, \beta_n)$ be any vector of non-negative numbers (not all zero). Then $F_\beta(\alpha) = sign \sum_{i \in N} \beta_i \alpha_i$ is a decisive voting rule satisfying weak Pareto. Suppose T is any non-empty subset of N. We call a voting rule the *T-agent voting rule* if $\beta_i = 1$ for all $i \in T$ and $\beta_i = 0$ for all $i \in N \setminus T$ so that for every $\alpha \in \{-1, 0, +1\}^n$, $F_T(\alpha) = sign \sum_{i \in T} \alpha_i$.

(1) If $T = N$, then it follows that $F_N(\alpha) = sign \sum_{i \in N} \alpha_i$ for all profiles $\alpha \in \{-1, 0, +1\}^n$ and we have the well-known *majority voting rule*.

(2) If for any given $d \in N$, $T = \{d\}$ (so that $|T| = 1$), then we have $F_{\{d\}}(\alpha) = sign \, \alpha_d = \alpha_d$ for all profiles $\alpha \in \{-1, 0, +1\}^n$ and it is the well-known *dictatorial voting rule*.

Despite the fact that a dictatorial voting rule satisfies weak Pareto, a society never wants a dictatorial voting rule as the views of only one agent (that of the dictator) matters for the society. The majority voting rule not only satisfies weak Pareto, but it also has a democratic appeal in the sense that the views of every voter matters.

Before going to the next section, we provide an alternative representation of the majority voting rule $F_N(\alpha)$ which for each $\alpha \in \{-1, 0, +1\}^n$ is given by $F_N(\alpha) = sign \sum_{i \in N} \alpha_i$. For any profile $\alpha = (\alpha_1, \ldots, \alpha_n) \in \{-1, 0, 1\}^n$, define $n^+(\alpha) = |\{i \in N \mid \alpha_i = 1\}|$ and $n^-(\alpha) = |\{i \in N \mid \alpha_i = -1\}|$. Therefore, $n^+(\alpha)$ is the number of agents who strictly prefer x to y under the profile α and $n^-(\alpha)$ is the number of agents who strictly prefer y to x under the profile α.

Definition 3.3 A decisive voting rule F_N is the *majority voting rule* if

$$F_N(\alpha) = \begin{cases} -1 & \text{if } n^+(\alpha) < n^-(\alpha), \\ 0 & \text{if } n^+(\alpha) = n^-(\alpha), \\ 1 & \text{if } n^+(\alpha) > n^-(\alpha). \end{cases}$$

3.3 MAY'S THEOREM

We provide a characterization of the majority voting rule due to May (1952). May's characterization uses three properties defined below.

Definition 3.4 A decisive voting rule F is *symmetric among agents* (or anonymous) if the names of the agents do not matter, that is, if a permutation of preferences across agents do not alter the social preference.

Let $\pi : N \to N$ be an onto function (that is, for any $i \in N$, there exists an h such that $\pi(h) = i$).[1] If $F(\alpha)$ satisfies symmetry, then for any profile α we have $F(\alpha) = F(\alpha_\pi)$.

Definition 3.5 A decisive voting rule F is *neutral between alternatives* if for all $\alpha \in \{-1,0,1\}^n$, $F(\alpha) = -F(-\alpha)$, that is, the social preference is reversed when we reverse the preference of all agents.

Neutrality requires that a voting rule must treat all candidates alike.

Definition 3.6 A decisive voting rule F is *positive responsive* if for all $\alpha, \alpha' \in \{-1,0,1\}^n$ such that $\alpha \geq \alpha'$, $\alpha \neq \alpha'$ and $F(\alpha') \geq 0$, we have $F(\alpha) = 1$.

Positive responsiveness requires that if x is preferred or indifferent to y for the society and some agents raise their consideration of x, then x becomes socially preferred.

Theorem 3.1 A decisive voting rule F satisfies symmetry, neutrality, and positive responsiveness if and only if $F = F_N$, that is, F is the majority voting rule.

Proof. We first show that F_N satisfies symmetry, neutrality, and positive responsiveness. To check symmetry, consider any onto function $\pi : N \to N$. $F_N(\alpha_\pi) = sign \sum_{k=1}^{n} \alpha_{\pi(k)} = sign \sum_{i \in N} \alpha_i = F_N(\alpha)$. For neutrality, observe that $-F_N(-\alpha) = -sign \sum_{i \in N}(-\alpha_i) = sign \sum_{i \in N} \alpha_i = F^m(\alpha)$. To verify positive responsiveness, consider α' such that $F_N(\alpha') \geq 0$. Let $\alpha \geq \alpha'$ and $\alpha \neq \alpha'$. We can have two

---

[1] Since $|N| = n$ is a finite number, $\pi : N \to N$ is an onto function, which means that $\pi : N \to N$ is one-to-one as well. A function is one-to-one onto if every element of the range of the function corresponds to exactly one element of its domain.

possibilities: (*a*) $F_N(\alpha') = 0$, and (*b*) $F_N(\alpha') = 1$. If $F_N(\alpha') = 0$, then $n^+(\alpha') = n^-(\alpha')$. Since $\alpha \geq \alpha'$ and $\alpha \neq \alpha'$, there exists $j \in N$ such that $\alpha_j > \alpha'_j$ and it follows that $n^+(\alpha) > n^-(\alpha)$. Thus if (*a*) holds, then $F_N(\alpha) = 1$. If $F_N(\alpha') = 1$, then $n^+(\alpha') > n^-(\alpha')$. Since $\alpha \geq \alpha'$ and $\alpha \neq \alpha'$, it is obvious that $n^+(\alpha) > n^-(\alpha)$. Thus, if (*b*) holds, then also we have $F_N(\alpha) = 1$. Hence, F_N is positive responsive.

Using three steps we prove that if F satisfies symmetry, neutrality, and positive responsiveness, then $F = F_N$.

In the first step it is argued that if a decisive voting rule F satisfies symmetry and neutrality, and if we have a profile where the number of agents preferring x over y is the same as the number of agents preferring y over x, then the social preference must be indifferent between x and y.

Step 1: If F satisfies symmetry and neutrality and if $n^+(\alpha) = n^-(\alpha)$, then $F(\alpha) = 0$.

Proof of Step 1: If F satisfies symmetry, then the names of the players do not matter and hence for each $\alpha \in \{-1, 0, 1\}^n$, $F(\alpha) = G(n^+(\alpha), n^-(\alpha))$. Moreover, if for a profile α, $n^+(\alpha) = n^-(\alpha)$, then $n^+(\alpha) = n^-(-\alpha) = n^+(-\alpha) = n^-(\alpha)$. By applying neutrality we get $F(\alpha) = G(n^+(\alpha), n^-(\alpha)) = G(n^-(-\alpha), n^+(-\alpha)) = F(-\alpha) = -F(\alpha)$. Hence, whenever $n^+(\alpha) = n^-(\alpha)$, $F(\alpha) = -F(\alpha)$ implying that $2F(\alpha) = 0$ and, as a result, we have $F(\alpha) = 0$.   □

Using Step 1, symmetry and positive responsiveness, in Step 2 it is shown that if the number of agents preferring x over y is more than the number of agents preferring y over x, then the society must prefer x over y.

Step 2: From symmetry, positive responsiveness, and Step 1, it follows that if $n^+(\alpha) > n^-(\alpha)$, then $F(\alpha) = 1$.

Proof of Step 2: Consider a profile α such that $n^+(\alpha) > n^-(\alpha)$. Let $H = n^+(\alpha)$ and $J = n^-(\alpha)$ so that $H > J$. Using symmetry we can assume that α is such that $\alpha_i = 1$ for all integers $i \leq H$ and $\alpha_i \leq 0$ for all integers $i > H$. Construct α' in the following way: $\alpha'_i = 1$ for all positive integers $i \leq J$, $\alpha'_i = 0$ for all positive integers $J < i \leq H$, and $\alpha'_i = \alpha_i$ for all positive integers $i > H$. From the construction it follows that for α', $n^+(\alpha') = n^-(\alpha')$. Moreover, given α and α', it also follows that $\alpha \geq \alpha'$ and $\alpha \neq \alpha'$ since $\alpha_{J+1} = 1 > \alpha'_{J+1} = 0$. Therefore, from Step 1 we get $F(\alpha') = 0$ since $n^+(\alpha') = n^-(\alpha')$ and by applying positive responsiveness of F we also get $F(\alpha) = 1$ since $\alpha \geq \alpha'$ and $\alpha \neq \alpha'$. □

Finally, using Step 2 and neutrality, in Step 3 it is proved that if the number of agents preferring x over y is less than the number of agents preferring y over x, then the society must prescribe that y is preferred to x.

Step 3: From neutrality and Step 2 it follows that if $n^+(\alpha) < n^-(\alpha)$, then $F(\alpha) = -1$.

Proof of Step 3: Consider α such that $n^+(\alpha) < n^-(\alpha)$. Note that in this case $n^+(-\alpha) > n^-(-\alpha)$ and hence by Step 2, $F(-\alpha) = 1$. By applying neutrality we get $F(-\alpha) = 1 = -F(\alpha) \Rightarrow F(\alpha) = -1$. □

From Steps 1–3, the necessity of F_N follows. □

Note that for the characterization result we only require positive responsiveness with respect to only one alternative (x in the above definition). Positive responsiveness with respect to y requires the following: For all $\alpha, \alpha' \in \{-1, 0, 1\}^n$ such that $\alpha \leq \alpha'$, $\alpha \neq \alpha'$, and $F(\alpha') \leq 0$, we have $F(\alpha) = -1$. We *do not need* positive responsiveness *with respect to the other alternative y.*

3.4 ROBUSTNESS OF THE AXIOMS

One should verify the robustness of the axioms used in the characterization result, that is, one should verify that none of the axioms is redundant for the characterization of the majority voting rule. This means that we should find decisive voting rules that (*a*) satisfy symmetry, neutrality, but not positive responsiveness, (*b*) satisfy symmetry, positive responsiveness, but not neutrality, and (*c*) satisfy neutrality, positive responsiveness, but not symmetry. Before going into the robustness check we define another important axiom.

Definition 3.7 A decisive voting rule F is *non-trivial* if there exists $\alpha, \alpha' \in \{-1, 0, 1\}^n$ such that $F(\alpha) = 1$ and $F(\alpha') = -1$.

Non-triviality is a basic requirement specifying that we must find some profile where the decisive voting rule specifies that x is strictly preferred to y, and we must also find at least one profile where the decisive voting rule specifies that y is strictly preferred to x. Any decisive voting rule satisfying weak Pareto also satisfies non-triviality but the converse is not necessarily true. In an exercise you are asked to prove that if a decisive voting rule F satisfies non-triviality and positive responsiveness, then it must satisfy weak Pareto. We impose the restriction that for a robustness check all the examples we give must also satisfy non-triviality and weak Pareto.

We first give an example of a non-trivial decisive voting rule that satisfies symmetry and neutrality but not positive responsiveness.

$$F^*(\alpha) = \begin{cases} -1 & \text{if } n^-(\alpha) = n, \\ 1 & \text{if } n^+(\alpha) = n, \\ 0 & \text{otherwise.} \end{cases} \tag{3.1}$$

Verify that F^* given by (3.1) satisfies non-triviality, weak Pareto, symmetry, and neutrality but not positive responsiveness.

Next, we provide an example of a non-trivial decisive voting rule that satisfies symmetry and positive responsiveness but fails to satisfy neutrality. Let $\tilde{F}$ be a decisive voting rule such that

$$\tilde{F}(\alpha) = \begin{cases} -1 & \text{if } n^+(\alpha) \leq n^-(\alpha), \\ 0 & \text{if } n^+(\alpha) = n^-(\alpha) + 1, \\ 1 & \text{if } n^+(\alpha) > n^-(\alpha) + 1. \end{cases} \tag{3.2}$$

Verify that $\tilde{F}$ given by (3.2) satisfies non-triviality, symmetry and positive responsiveness but fails to satisfy neutrality.

Finally, we provide an example of a non-trivial decisive voting rule that satisfies neutrality and positive responsiveness but fails to satisfy symmetry. Let $\bar{F}$ be a decisive voting rule such that for all $\alpha \in \{-1, 0, 1\}^n$,

$$\bar{F}(\alpha) = sign \left[\gamma\alpha_1 + \sum_{i \in N \setminus \{1\}} \alpha_i \right],$$

where $\gamma \in (0, 1)$. An equivalent way of representing $\bar{F}$ is the following:

$$\bar{F}(\alpha) = \begin{cases} -1 & \text{if } n^+\left(\alpha_{N \setminus \{1\}}\right) < n^-\left(\alpha_{N \setminus \{1\}}\right), \\ 1 & \text{if } n^+\left(\alpha_{N \setminus \{1\}}\right) > n^-\left(\alpha_{N \setminus \{1\}}\right), \\ \alpha_1 & \text{if } n^+\left(\alpha_{N \setminus \{1\}}\right) = n^-\left(\alpha_{N \setminus \{1\}}\right). \end{cases} \tag{3.3}$$

Here $\alpha_{N\setminus\{1\}} \in \{-1,0,1\}^{n-1}$ represents the profile of all but agent 1. Verify that $\overline{F}$ given by (3.3) satisfies non-triviality, neutrality, and positive responsiveness but fails to satisfy symmetry. The decisive voting rule $\overline{F}$ given by (3.3) is a majority of all but agent 1 except for the case when the majority of all but agent 1 gives indifference. In the case when the majority of all but agent 1 gives indifference, the society follows the recommendation of agent 1. So it is only when the majority of all but agent 1 cannot reach an unambiguous strict ordering over the alternatives x and y that the role of agent 1 becomes important. If the majority of all but agent 1 can reach an unambiguous strict ordering over the alternatives x and y, then agent 1's vote does not matter.

3.5 EXERCISES

For explanations or definitions of the notation, see the main text of Chapter 3.

(E-3.1) Any decisive voting rule F that satisfies non-triviality and positive responsiveness must satisfy weak Pareto.

(E-3.2) Find a decisive voting rule F that satisfies non-triviality, weak Pareto, and neutrality but fails to satisfy both symmetry and positive responsiveness.

(E-3.3) We say that a decisive voting rule $F : \{-1,0,+1\}^n \to \{-1,0,+1\}$ satisfies Pareto if the following conditions hold: (a) $F(\alpha) = 1$ whenever $\alpha \geq 0$ and $\alpha \neq 0$ and (b) $F(\alpha) = -1$ whenever $\alpha \leq 0$ and $\alpha \neq 0$. Show that the majority voting rule satisfies Pareto and the dictatorial voting rule fails to satisfy it.

(E-3.4) Consider the decisive voting rule $F^{**} : \{-1,0,+1\}^n \to \{-1,0,+1\}$ given by the following condition:

$$F^{**}(\alpha) = \begin{cases} -1 & \text{if } \alpha \leq 0 \text{ and } \alpha \neq 0, \\ 1 & \text{if } \alpha \geq 0 \text{ and } \alpha \neq 0, \\ 0 & \text{otherwise.} \end{cases}$$

Is F^{**} identical to the majority voting rule for all $n \geq 2$? What happens if $n = 2$? Justify your answers.

3.6   BIBLIOGRAPHICAL NOTES

- A significant portion of this chapter is taken from Mas-Colell et al. (1995).

- Dasgupta and Maskin (2008) argue that the simple majority rule is the most robust voting rule and characterize it. Recently, Freixas and Pons (2021) provide an extension and an alternative characterization of May's theorem.

- Bartholdi et al. (2021), by assuming strict preferences across agents, show that a weakening of May's symmetry assumption allows for a far richer set of rules that still treat voters equally.

REFERENCES

Bartholdi, L., W. Hann-Caruthers, M. Josyula, O. Tamuz, and L. Yariv. 2021. "Equitable Voting Rules." *Econometrica* 89 (2): 563–589.

Dasgupta, P., and E. Maskin. 2008. "On the Robustness of Majority Rule." *Journal of the European Economic Association* 6 (5): 949–973.

Freixas, J., and M. Pons. 2021. "An Extension and an Alternative Characterization of May's Theorem." *Annals of Operations Research* (July): 137–150.

Mas-Colell, A., M. D. Whinston, and J. R. Green. 1995. *Microeconomic Theory*. New York: Oxford University Press.

May, K. 1952. "A Set of Independent, Necessary and Sufficient Conditions for Simple Majority Decision." *Econometrica* 20 (4): 680–684.

ARROW'S THEOREM WITH INDIVIDUAL PREFERENCES

4

4.1 INTRODUCTION

Kenneth J. Arrow (see Arrow 1950) provided a striking answer to a basic problem of democracy: how can the preferences of a set of individuals be aggregated into a social ordering? The answer, known as Arrow's impossibility theorem, was that every conceivable aggregation method has some flaw. That is, a handful of reasonable-looking axioms, which one thinks an aggregation procedure should satisfy, lead to an impossibility. This impossibility theorem created a large literature and the major field called social choice theory, which is one of the main subject matters of this book. Specifically, Arrow's impossibility theorem or the general possibility theorem or Arrow's paradox is an impossibility theorem stating that when agents face three or more distinct alternatives (options), every social welfare function that can convert the preference ordering of all the individuals into a social ordering while also meeting unrestricted domain, weak Pareto, and independence of irrelevant alternatives must be dictatorial. Unrestricted domain (also called universality) is a property in which all possible preferences of all individuals are allowed in the domain. Weak Pareto requires that the unanimous preferences of individuals must be respected, that is, if every agent strictly prefers one alternative over the other, then society must also strictly prefer the same alternative over the other. Social preference orderings satisfy the independence-of-irrelevant-alternatives criterion if the relative societal ranking of any two alternatives depends only on the relative ranking of those two alternatives of all the individuals and not on how the individuals rank other alternatives. A dictatorial social welfare function is one in which there is a single agent whose strict preferences are always adopted by the society. In this chapter, we present a detailed analysis of Arrow's impossibility theorem and then provide two proofs of the theorem.

4.2   THE FRAMEWORK

Consider a society with n agents and we denote this society by $N = \{1, \ldots, n\}$. Each agent $i \in N$ has an ordering $\succsim_i$ defined on A and assume that $|A| \geq 3$. The assumption that $\succsim_i$ is an order on A has implications for the strict preference relation $\succ_i$ and the indifference relation $\sim_i$. These implications are summarized in the next proposition.

Proposition 4.1   If $\succsim_i$ on A for agent $i \in N$ is an order, then we have the following:

(a) $\succ_i$ is both *irreflexive* ($x \succ_i x$ never holds) and *transitive* (if $x \succ_i y$ and $y \succ_i z$, then $x \succ_i z$).

(b) $\sim_i$ is *reflexive* ($x \sim_i x$ for all $x \in A$), *transitive* (if $x \sim_i y$ and $y \sim_i z$, then $x \sim_i z$), and *symmetric* (if $x \sim_i y$, then $y \sim_i x$).

(c) If $x \succ_i y \succsim_i z$, then $x \succ_i z$.

Proof.   (a) We first prove that the strict preference relation $\succ_i$ is *irreflexive*. Suppose it is not. Then there exists $x \in A$ such that $x \succ_i x$. But from the definition of strict preference $\succ_i$, it follows that $x \succ_i x$ if and only if $[x \succsim_i x$ and $\neg(x \succsim_i x)]$. Since $x \succsim_i x$ and $\neg(x \succsim_i x)$ cannot hold simultaneously, we have a contradiction. Hence, $\succ_i$ is irreflexive. Next, we prove that the strict preference relation $\succ_i$ is *transitive*. Suppose it is not. Then there exists $x, y, z \in A$ such that

$x \succ_i y$, $y \succ_i z$, and $\neg(x \succ_i z)$. Since $\succsim_i$ is complete, $\neg(x \succ_i z)$ is equivalent to (i) $z \succsim_i x$. From the definition of strict preference $\succ_i$, it follows that $x \succ_i y$ is equivalent to $[x \succsim_i y$ and $\neg(y \succsim_i x)]$, which implies that (ii) $x \succsim_i y$. From (i), (ii), and transitivity of $\succsim_i$, we get $z \succsim_i y$, which contradicts our assumption $y \succ_i z$ since $y \succ_i z$ implies that $\neg(z \succsim_i y)$.

(*b*) We first prove that the indifference relation $\sim_i$ is *reflexive*. Suppose it is not. Then there exists $x \in A$ such that $\neg(x \sim_i x)$. But by completeness of $\succsim_i$ it follows that $\neg(x \sim_i x)$ is equivalent to $x \succ_i x$, which contradicts the fact that $\succ_i$ is irreflexive. Hence, $\sim_i$ is reflexive. Next, we prove that the indifference relation $\sim_i$ is *transitive*. Consider any $x, y, z \in A$ such that $x \sim_i y$ and $y \sim_i z$. Using the definition of an indifference relation, we get $x \sim_i y$ and $y \sim_i z$ taken together is equivalent to $[x \succsim_i y$ and $y \succsim_i x]$ and $[y \succsim_i z$ and $z \succsim_i y]$. Equivalently, we have $[x \succsim_i y$ and $y \succsim_i z]$ and $[z \succsim_i y$ and $y \succsim_i x]$. In view of transitivity of $\succsim_i$ on A, this is equivalent to $[x \succsim_i z$ and $z \succsim_i x]$ giving $x \sim_i z$. Finally, we prove that the indifference relation $\sim_i$ is *symmetric*. If for some $x, y \in A$ we have $x \sim_i y$, then by definition we get $x \sim_i y$ is equivalent to $[x \succsim_i y$ and $y \succsim_i x]$, which is the same as $[y \succsim_i x$ and $x \succsim_i y]$ giving $y \sim_i x$.

(*c*) Finally, we prove that if $x \succ_i y$ and $y \succsim_i z$, then $x \succ_i z$. Assume it is not. Then there exists $x, y, z \in A$ such that $x \succ_i y$, $y \succsim_i z$, and $\neg(x \succ_i z)$ so that using completeness we have $z \succsim_i x$. By transitivity of $\succsim_i$ on A, $y \succsim_i z$ and $z \succsim_i x$ imply $y \succsim_i x$, which contradicts $x \succ_i y$. $\qquad\square$

4.3   THE ARROW IMPOSSIBILITY THEOREM

Let $\mathcal{Q}$ represent the set of all possible orderings on A and $\mathcal{P}$ represent the set of all possible strict relations on A such that $\mathcal{P} \subset \mathcal{Q}$. Formally, a preference relation $\succsim_i \in \mathcal{P}$ if it is reflexive ($x \succsim_i x$ for all $x \in A$), transitive ($x \succsim_i y, y \succsim_i z$ implies $x \succsim_i z$), and *total* (if $x \neq y$, then either $x \succsim_i y$ or $y \succsim_i x$ but not both).

Definition 4.1   A *social welfare function* defined on a given subset $D \subseteq \mathcal{Q}^n$ is a rule $F : D \to \mathcal{Q}$ that assigns a rational preference relation in $F(.) \in \mathcal{Q}$ for any profile of preference relation in the admissible domain $D \subseteq \mathcal{Q}^n$.

Definition 4.2   A social welfare function $F : D \to Q$ satisfies
unrestricted domain if $D = Q^n$.

If a social welfare function F satisfies unrestricted domain, then
we have $F : Q^n \to Q$ which is the Arrovian social welfare function
(as defined in Chapter 2). The next property is weak Pareto, which
requires that if all agents strictly prefer the alternative x over y, then
society must also strictly prefer x over y.

Definition 4.3   A social welfare function $F : D \to Q$ satisfies *weak
Pareto*, if for any $x, y \in A$ and any preference profile $\succsim = (\succsim_1$
$,\dots, \succsim_n) \in D$ such that $x \succ_i y$ for all $i \in N$, we have $x \succ y$.

Example 4.1   (The Borda rule) Consider the scoring rule F^s :
$Q^n \to Q$ given in Definition 2.1 of Chapter 2. Specifically consider
the Borda rule $F^{sB} : Q^n \to Q$, where $|A| = p$ and the score
vector is $s = (s_1 = p - 1, s_2 = p - 2, \dots, s_p = 0)$. Observe that
if for $\succsim = (\succsim_1, \dots, \succsim_n) \in Q$ we have $x \succ_i y$ for all $i \in N$, then
$r(x; \succsim_i) < r(y; \succsim_i)$ for all $i \in N$ implying $s_{r(x; \succsim_i)} > s_{r(y; \succsim_i)}$ for all
$i \in N$, which in turn implies that $s(x; \succsim) > s(y; \succsim)$. Hence, under
the Borda count, $x \succ y$. Thus, the Borda rule satisfies weak Pareto.

Next we introduce the axiom of independence of irrelevant
alternatives. Social preference orderings fulfill the independence-of-
irrelevant-alternatives postulate if the relative social ordering of
any two alternatives x and y depends absolutely on the individual
orderings between x and y and not on the individuals' concern
about the ranking of other alternatives. Let $\succsim_i|_{\{x,y\}}$ stand for the
preference ordering $\succsim_i$ of agent i when restricted to the set $\{x, y\}$
and $\succsim|_{\{x,y\}}$ stand for the preference ordering of the society under
some social welfare function F when restricted to the set $\{x, y\}$.

Definition 4.4   A social welfare function $F : D \to Q$ satisfies
independence of irrelevant alternatives if for any $\{x, y\} \subset A$ and any
$\succsim, \succsim' \in D$ such that $\succsim_i|_{\{x,y\}} = \succsim'_i|_{\{x,y\}}$ for all $i \in N$, we have $\succsim|_{\{x,y\}} = \succsim'|_{\{x,y\}}$.

Proposition 4.2   The plurality rule, the anti-plurality rule, and the
Borda rule violate independence of irrelevant alternatives.

Proof. To see that the plurality rule violates independence of irrelevant alternatives, consider the following example with three alternatives $A = \{x, y, z\}$ and nine agents $N = \{1, \ldots, 9\}$. In this example, we consider the profiles $\succsim = (\succsim_1, \ldots, \succsim_9)$ and $\succsim' = (\succsim_1', \ldots, \succsim_9')$ with the following specifications:

(i) The preference $\succsim$ is such that $x \succ_i y \succ_i z$ for all $i \in \{1, 2, 3, 4\}$, $y \succ_i x \succ_i z$ for all $i \in \{5, 6, 7\}$, and $z \succ_i y \succ_i x$ for all $i \in \{8, 9\}$.

(ii) The preference $\succsim'$ is such that $x \succ_i' z \succ_i' y$ for all $i \in \{1, 2, 3, 4\}$ and $y \succ_i' z \succ_i' x$ for all $i \in \{5, 6, 7, 8, 9\}$.

First note that under the plurality rule, $x\hat{F}^{sP}(\succsim)y\hat{F}^{sP}(\succsim)z$, that is, for the profile $\succsim$, we have x is strictly preferred to y and y is strictly preferred to z for society. Also note that we have $y\hat{F}^{sP}(\succsim')x\hat{F}^{sP}(\succsim')z$, that is, for the profile $\succsim'$, we have y is strictly preferred to x and x is strictly preferred to z for society under the plurality rule. Also observe that $\succsim_i|_{x,y} = \succsim_i'|_{x,y}$ for all $i \in \{1, \ldots, 9\}$, that is, the relative ranking between alternatives x and y has remained unchanged for all the agents while moving from the profile $\succsim$ to $\succsim'$. Yet we have $x\hat{F}^{sP}(\succsim)y$ and $y\hat{F}^{sP}(\succsim')x$, which is a violation of independence of irrelevant alternatives.

To see that the anti-plurality rule as well as the Borda rule violate independence of irrelevant alternatives, consider the following example with three alternatives $A = \{x, y, z\}$ and two agents $N = \{1, 2\}$. In this example, we consider the profiles $\succsim = (\succsim_1, \succsim_2)$ and $\succsim' = (\succsim_1', \succsim_2')$ with the following specifications:

(i) The preference $\succsim$ is such that $x \succ_1 z \succ_1 y$ and $y \succ_2 x \succ_2 z$

(ii) The preference $\succsim'$ is such that $x \succ_1' y \succ_1' z$ and $y \succ_2' z \succ_2' x$

Observe that under the anti-plurality rule, $x\hat{F}^{sA}(\succsim)y\overline{F}^{sA}(\succsim)z$, that is, for the profile $\succsim$, we have x is strictly preferred to y and y is indifferent to z for society. Also note that we have $y\hat{F}^{sA}(\succsim')x\overline{F}^{sA}(\succsim')z$, that is, for the profile $\succsim'$, we have y is strictly preferred to x and x is indifferent to z for society under the anti-plurality rule. Again, note that $\succsim_i|_{x,y} = \succsim_i'|_{x,y}$ for all $i \in \{1, 2\}$, that is, the relative ranking between alternatives x and y has remained unchanged for both the agents while moving from the profile $\succsim$ to $\succsim'$. Yet we have

$x\hat{F}^{sA}(\succsim)y$ and $y\hat{F}^{sA}(\succsim')x$ and we have a violation of independence of irrelevant alternatives.

Similarly, note that under the Borda count, $x\hat{F}^{sB}(\succsim)y\hat{F}^{sB}(\succsim)z$, that is, for the profile $\succsim$, we have x is strictly preferred to y and y is strictly preferred to z for society. Also note that we have $y\hat{F}^{sB}(\succsim'$ $)x\hat{F}^{sB}(\succsim')z$, that is, for the profile $\succsim'$, we have y is strictly preferred to x and x is strictly preferred to z for society under the Borda count. Given $\succsim_i|_{x,y} = \succsim'_i|_{x,y}$ for all $i \in \{1,2\}$, $x\hat{F}^{sB}(\succsim)y$, and $y\hat{F}^{sB}(\succsim')x$, we have a violation of independence of irrelevant alternatives.   □

We have seen in Proposition 4.2 that all the three important scoring rules fail to satisfy independence of irrelevant alternatives. Thus, independence of irrelevant alternatives is indeed a strong requirement. Can we rank alternatives by comparing pairs of alternatives and then derive a social preference? Will that lead to a binary social preference which is also an ordering? Can we use something like the pairwise majority voting? The answer is no since we have the Condorcet cycle, as explained in Chapter 2 (see Example 2.3).

The next definition is one of a dictatorial social welfare function and it is an instance of a social welfare function that satisfies unrestricted domain, weak Pareto, and independence of irrelevant alternatives.

Definition 4.5 A social welfare function $F : D \to Q$ is *dictatorial* if there exists an agent $d \in N$ such that for any $x, y \in A$ and for any profile $(\succsim_1, \ldots, \succsim_n) \in D$, $x \succ y$ whenever $x \succ_d y$.

One can verify that any dictatorial social welfare function can be defined on the entire domain (that is, without imposing any domain restriction). Hence, one can easily define a dictatorial social welfare function satisfying unrestricted domain. Moreover, for any profile $\succsim = (\succsim_1, \ldots, \succsim_n) \in Q^n$ such that for some $x, y \in A$, $x \succ_i y$ for all $i \in N$, any dictatorial social welfare function will prescribe $x \succ y$ for the society since for the dictator $d \in N$ we also have $x \succ_d y$. Hence, any dictatorial social welfare function also satisfies weak Pareto. Finally, for any dictatorial social welfare function F, if for any $\{x,y\} \subset A$ and any $\succsim, \succsim' \in D$ such that $\succsim_i|_{\{x,y\}} = \succsim'_i|_{\{x,y\}}$ for all $i \in N$, then we also have have $\succsim|_{\{x,y\}} = \succsim'|_{\{x,y\}}$ since for a dictatorial social welfare function with

$d \in N$ as the dictator, $\succsim|_{\{x,y\}} = \succsim_d|_{\{x,y\}}$, $\succsim'|_{\{x,y\}} = \succsim'_d|_{\{x,y\}}$, and by definition of independence of irrelevant alternatives we have $\succsim_d|_{\{x,y\}} = \succsim'_d|_{\{x,y\}}$. Hence, any dictatorial social welfare function satisfies independence of irrelevant alternatives. The argument provided in this paragraph till now shows that any dictatorial social welfare function is sufficient to obtain a social welfare function that satisfies unrestricted domain, weak Pareto, and independence of irrelevant alternatives.

The next theorem, better known as the Arrow's impossibility theorem (or the general possibility theorem), is due to Arrow (1950), and the theorem argues that a dictatorial social welfare function is also necessary to obtain a social welfare function that satisfies unrestricted domain, weak Pareto, and independence of irrelevant alternatives.

Theorem 4.1 Suppose the set of alternatives A has at least three elements. Every social welfare function $F : D \to Q$ that satisfies unrestricted domain, weak Pareto, and independence of irrelevant alternatives is dictatorial.

In words, let the number of alternatives be at least three. Then a social welfare function satisfying the postulates of unrestricted domain, weak Pareto, and independence of irrelevant alternatives comes to be dictatorial. Theorem 4.1 is known as the general possibility theorem due to Arrow. The impossibility version of the same theorem states that there is no social welfare function that satisfies unrestricted domain, weak Pareto, independence of irrelevant alternatives, and non-dictatorship. Here non-dictatorship means that a single agent's preference cannot represent a whole community, that is, the social welfare function needs to consider the wishes of multiple voters.

4.4 TWO PROOFS OF ARROW'S THEOREM

The first proof, which is due to Arrow (1950), uses two lemmas. The first lemma, better known as the field expansion lemma, argues that if a group can decide on the relative ordering of a pair of alternatives for the society when all members from the complement group oppose it, then the same group can decide the social ordering over all pairs of alternatives (no matter what the complement group says). The next lemma, better known as the group contraction lemma, argues that if a group can decide on the social ordering over all pairs of alternatives and if the group size is larger than unity, then so can some proper subset of the group. The field expansion lemma and the group contraction lemma along with weak Pareto give the result.

The other proof is due to Geanakoplos (2005) and this proof uses four steps. The first two steps mainly use the implications of weak Pareto and independence of irrelevant alternatives to identify an "extremely pivotal" agent. The remaining two steps of the proof then argue that this extremely pivotal agent is the dictator for society.

4.4.1 *Arrow's proof*

Let $G \subseteq N$. The coalition G is *almost decisive* over the ordered pair (x, y) (denoted by $\overline{D}_G(x, y)$) if for all profiles $(\succsim_1, \ldots, \succsim_n) \in \mathcal{Q}^n$ such that $x \succ_i y$ for all $i \in G$ and $y \succ_j x$ for all $j \in N \setminus G$, we have $x \succ y$ for society. Therefore, for a social welfare function F, if we can find a group G and a pair of alternatives $x, y \in A$ such that whenever all agents in the group G feel that x is strictly preferred to y and all members in the complement group $N \setminus G$ feel that y is strictly preferred to x and the social welfare function prescribes that x is strictly preferred to y for the society, then we say that the group G is almost decisive over the ordered pair (x, y). The coalition G is *decisive* over the ordered pair (x, y) (denoted by $D_G(x, y)$) if for all $(\succsim_1, \ldots, \succsim_n) \in \mathcal{Q}^n$ such that $x \succ_i y$ for all $i \in G$, we have $x \succ y$ for society (irrespective of the preference of any $j \in N \setminus G$ over x and y). Therefore, for a social welfare function F, if we can find a group G and a pair of alternatives $x, y \in A$ such that whenever all agents in the group G feel that x is strictly preferred to y and the social welfare function prescribes that x is strictly preferred to y for society (no matter what the relative preference between x and y is for the agents in the complement group $N \setminus G$), then we say that the group G is decisive over the ordered pair (x, y). Clearly, if a group

G is decisive over an ordered pair (x, y), then the same group G is almost decisive over the same pair, that is, $D_G(x, y) \Rightarrow \overline{D}_G(x, y)$.[1] However, the converse is not necessarily true.

We start with the field expansion lemma that demands the following. If a social welfare function fulfills the axioms unrestricted domain, weak Pareto, and independence of irrelevant alternatives, and if there is a coalition which is almost decisive over a pair of alternatives, then it is decisive over all pairs of alternatives.

Lemma 4.1 (The field expansion lemma)
Suppose the set of alternatives A has at least three elements. Consider any social welfare function $F : D \to Q$ that satisfies unrestricted domain, weak Pareto, and independence of irrelevant alternatives. If there exists a coalition G and an ordered pair (x, y) such that $\overline{D}_G(x, y)$, then we have $D_G(a, b)$ for all pair $a, b \in A$.

Proof. We prove the following seven exhaustive possibilities to complete the proof of the lemma:

F(1) $\overline{D}_G(x, y) \Rightarrow D_G(a, b)$, where a, b, x, y are all pairwise distinct

F(2) $\overline{D}_G(x, y) \Rightarrow D_G(x, a)$

F(3) $\overline{D}_G(x, y) \Rightarrow D_G(a, y)$

F(4) $\overline{D}_G(x, y) \Rightarrow D_G(a, x)$

F(5) $\overline{D}_G(x, y) \Rightarrow D_G(y, a)$

F(6) $\overline{D}_G(x, y) \Rightarrow D_G(x, y)$

F(7) $\overline{D}_G(x, y) \Rightarrow D_G(y, x)$

Proof of F(1): We want to prove that $\overline{D}_G(x, y) \Rightarrow D_G(a, b)$, where a, b, x, y are all pairwise distinct. Let $\succsim = (\succsim_1, \ldots, \succsim_n) \in Q^n$ be such that (I) $a \succ_i x \succ_i y \succ_i b$ for all $i \in G$, and (II) $y \succ_i x$, $a \succ_i x$ and $y \succ_i b$ for all $i \in N \setminus G$. Note that the construction of the profile $\succsim$ is such that we have not specified the relative ranking of the alternatives a and b for the agents in the set $N \setminus G$. Due to

---

[1] Given any two set A_1 and A_2, the notation $A_1 \Rightarrow A_2$ means that A_1 implies A_2; equivalently, it means that if A_1 holds, then A_2 also holds; or equivalently it also means that if $x \in A_1$, then $x \in A_2$.

unrestricted domain, we can always select such a profile. Since we have $\overline{D}_G(x, y)$ by assumption, $x \succ y$ for society. By weak Pareto, we get $a \succ x$ and $y \succ b$. Therefore, $a \succ x \succ y \succ b$ and by transitivity of social preference, we get $a \succ b$. Given independence of irrelevant alternatives and the fact that we have not specified the rankings of the coalition $N \setminus G$ over a and b in the above construction given by (I) and (II), we get $D_G(a, b)$.

Proof of F(2): We want to prove that $\overline{D}_G(x, y) \Rightarrow D_G(x, a)$. Let $\underset{\sim}{\succsim} = (\succsim_1, \ldots, \succsim_n) \in \mathcal{Q}^n$ be such that (I) $x \succ_i y \succ_i a$ for all $i \in G$, and (II) $y \succ_i x$ and $y \succ_i a$ for all $i \in N \setminus G$. In this construction we have not specified the relative ranking between x and a for the agents in $N \setminus G$. By unrestricted domain, such a profile is present in the domain. Since we have $\overline{D}_G(x, y)$ by assumption, $x \succ y$ for society. By weak Pareto, we get $y \succ a$. Applying transitivity of the social preference, we get $x \succ a$ no matter what the ranking between x and a is for the agents in $N \setminus G$. Thus, using independence of irrelevant alternatives, we get $D_G(x, a)$.

Proof of F(3): We want to prove that $\overline{D}_G(x, y) \Rightarrow D_G(a, y)$. Let $\underset{\sim}{\succsim} = (\succsim_1, \ldots, \succsim_n) \in \mathcal{Q}^n$ be such that (I) $a \succ_i x \succ_i y$ for all $i \in G$, and (II) $y \succ_i x$ and $a \succ_i x$ for all $i \in N \setminus G$. In this construction we have not specified the relative ranking between y and a for the agents in $N \setminus G$. Again from unrestricted domain, the above construction is feasible and by assumption, $\overline{D}_G(x, y) \Rightarrow x \succ y$. By weak Pareto, $a \succ x$ and hence by transitivity $a \succ y$, no matter what the ordering of the agents in $N \setminus G$ is over a and y. Thus, by independence of irrelevant alternatives, we get $D_G(a, y)$.

Proof of F(4): In this case, we want to show that $\overline{D}_G(x, y) \Rightarrow D_G(a, x)$. Given $\overline{D}_G(x, y)$, from F(3) we get $D_G(a, y)$. Further, from the definitions of almost decisiveness and decisiveness over any given ordered pair of alternatives, it follows that $D_G(a, y) \Rightarrow \overline{D}_G(a, y)$. From F(2), it follows that $\overline{D}_G(a, y) \Rightarrow D_G(a, x)$.

Proof of F(5): In this case, we want to prove that $\overline{D}_G(x, y) \Rightarrow D_G(y, a)$. Given $\overline{D}_G(x, y)$, from F(2) we get $D_G(x, a)$. From the definitions of almost decisiveness and decisiveness over any given ordered pair of alternatives, it follows that $D_G(x, a) \Rightarrow \overline{D}_G(x, a)$. Using F(3), we get $\overline{D}_G(x, a) \Rightarrow D_G(y, a)$.

Proof of F(6): In this case, we want to prove that $\overline{D}_G(x, y) \Rightarrow D_G(x, y)$. Given $\overline{D}_G(x, y)$, from F(3) we get $D_G(a, y)$. By definitions of almost decisiveness and decisiveness, $D_G(a, y) \Rightarrow \overline{D}_G(a, y)$. Using F(3), it follows that $\overline{D}_G(a, y) \Rightarrow D_G(x, y)$.

Proof of F(7): In this case, we want to prove that $\overline{D}_G(x, y) \Rightarrow D_G(y, x)$. From F(4), it follows that $\overline{D}_G(x, y) \Rightarrow D_G(a, x)$. From the definitions of almost decisiveness and decisiveness, $D_G(a, x) \Rightarrow \overline{D}_G(a, x)$. Finally, using F(3), we get $\overline{D}_G(a, x) \Rightarrow D_G(y, x)$. $\square$

The next lemma, better known as the group contraction lemma, specifies that if a social welfare function fulfills the axioms unrestricted domain, weak Pareto, and independence of irrelevant alternatives, and if there is a non-singleton decisive coalition, then some proper subset of the coalition is decisive as well.

Lemma 4.2 (The group contraction lemma)
Suppose the set of alternatives A has at least three elements. Consider any social welfare function $F : D \rightarrow Q$ that satisfies unrestricted domain, weak Pareto, and independence of irrelevant alternatives. If a coalition G is decisive and $|G| > 1$, then so is some proper subset of G.

Proof. Let G be a decisive group and G_1 and G_2 be two non-empty subsets of G such that $G_1 \cup G_2 = G$ and $G_1 \cap G_2 = \emptyset$. Consider the profile $\succsim = (\succsim_1, \ldots, \succsim_n) \in Q^n$ with the following properties:

(g1) $a \succ_i x \succ_i y$ for all $i \in G_1$,

(g2) $x \succ_i y \succ_i a$ for all $i \in G_2$, and

(g3) $y \succ_i a \succ_i x$ for all $i \in N \setminus G$.[2]

Since G is decisive, we have $x \succ y$. By completeness of social preference, either $a \succ y$ or $y \succsim a$. If $a \succ y$, then G_1 is almost decisive over (a, y), that is, $\overline{D}_{G_1}(a, y)$ and, by Lemma 4.1, the group G_1 is decisive over all pairs. If $y \succsim a$, then, given $x \succ y$, by applying transitivity we get $x \succ a$. Clearly, $\overline{D}_{G_2}(x, a)$ and, by Lemma 4.1, G_2 is decisive. $\square$

---

[2] It is possible that $N \setminus G = \emptyset$. However, even if $N \setminus G$ is an empty set, the reader can verify that the proof of Lemma 4.2 goes through.

$\succsim_1$	$\succsim_2$	$\cdots$	$\succsim_{n-1}$	$\succsim_n$		$\succsim'_1$	$\succsim'_2$	$\cdots$	$\succsim'_{n-1}$	$\succsim'_n$
b	$\vdots$	$\vdots$	b	$\vdots$		b	$\vdots$	$\vdots$	b	$\vdots$
$\vdots$	$a \sim_2 c$	$\vdots$	$\vdots$	a	$\leftarrow \succsim, \succsim' \rightarrow$	$\vdots$	c	$\vdots$	$\vdots$	c
a	$\vdots$	$\vdots$	c	$\vdots$		c	a	$\vdots$	c	$\vdots$
c	$\vdots$	$\vdots$	a	c		a	$\vdots$	$\vdots$	a	a
$\vdots$	b	$\vdots$	$\vdots$	b		$\vdots$	b	$\vdots$	$\vdots$	b

Figure 4.1   Profiles $\succsim = (\succsim_1, \ldots, \succsim_n)$ and $\succsim' = (\succsim'_1, \ldots, \succsim'_n)$

Proof of Theorem 4.1: Condition weak Pareto implies that the set N is decisive. Since N is finite, a repeated application of Lemma 4.2 implies that there must be a dictator. $\qquad\qquad\qquad\qquad\qquad$ $\square$

4.4.2   Geanakoplos' proof

The proof is due to Geanakoplos (2005). It uses four steps to derive Theorem 4.1.

Step 1: Let $b \in A$. Any profile $(\succsim_1, \ldots, \succsim_n) \in \mathcal{Q}^n$ in which every agent puts b at the very top or at the very bottom of his ranking of alternatives, society must do so as well.

Proof of Step 1: Assume it is not. Then the social welfare function $F(.)$ is such that there exists a profile $\succsim$ and a non-empty set $S \subset N$ with the property that $b \succ_i x$ for all $i \in S$ and all $x \in A \setminus \{b\}$, and $x \succ_i b$ for all $i \in N \setminus S$ and all $x \in A \setminus \{b\}$, and we have $a \succsim b \succsim c$ for some $a, c \in A \setminus \{b\}$. From $\succsim$, we construct the profile $\succsim'$ by moving c ahead of a (Ceteris Paribus). These profiles are shown in Figure 4.1. In Figure 4.1, each agent's preference is represented as a column with the property that alternatives more preferred appear earlier. For example, $\succsim_1$ in Figure 4.1 for the profile $\succsim$ shows that b is the top element followed by other elements and then a which is strictly preferred to c followed by other elements. Similarly, $\succsim_2$ in Figure 4.1 for the profile $\succsim$ shows that there are some elements preferred to a and c, when alternatives a and c are indifferent. Then there are some alternatives that are inferior to a and c followed by b as the least preferred alternative and so on. We will follow the same convention for the remaining figures of this chapter.

Observe that $\succsim_i |\{a,b\} = \succsim_i' |\{a,b\}$ for all $i \in N$. Since we have $a \succsim b$ for the profile $\succsim = (\succsim_1, \ldots, \succsim_n)$, by independence of irrelevant alternatives we get $a \succsim' b$ for the profile $\succsim' = (\succsim_1', \ldots, \succsim_n')$. Similarly, $\succsim_i |\{b,c\} = \succsim_i' |\{b,c\}$ for all $i \in N$, $b \succsim c$ for the profile $\succsim = (\succsim_1, \ldots, \succsim_n)$ and the application of independence of irrelevant alternatives gives $b \succsim' c$ for $\succsim' = (\succsim_1', \ldots, \succsim_n')$. Since we have $a \succsim' b$ and $b \succsim' c$, by applying transitivity we get $a \succsim' c$. But $a \succsim' c$ contradicts weak Pareto since for the profile $\succsim' = (\succsim_1', \ldots, \succsim_n')$ we have $c \succ_i' a$ for all $i \in N$. □

Step 2: Consider any $b \in A$ and any profile $\succsim^0 = (\succsim_1^0, \ldots, \succsim_n^0)$ such that for all $x \in A \setminus \{b\}$, $x \succ_i^0 b$ for all $i \in N$. There is an agent $n^* = n(b)$ who is "extremely" pivotal in the sense that by changing his preference at some profile, he can move the alternative b from the bottom of the social ranking to the top.

Proof of Step 2: Consider the profile $\succsim^0 = (\succsim_1^0, \ldots, \succsim_n^0)$ such that for all $x \in A \setminus \{b\}$, $x \succ_i^0 b$ for all $i \in N$. This is depicted in Figure 4.2 below.

$$\begin{array}{ccccc} \succsim_1^0 & \succsim_2^0 & \cdots & \succsim_{n-1}^0 & \succsim_n^0 \\ \vdots & \vdots & & \vdots & \vdots \\ b & b & \cdots & b & b \end{array}$$

Figure 4.2 **Profile** $\succsim^0 = (\succsim^0, \ldots, \succsim^0)$

By weak Pareto, for the profile $\succsim^0 = (\succsim_1^0, \ldots, \succsim_n^0)$ (given above), $x \succ^0 b$ for all $x \in A \setminus \{b\}$. Now, let individuals from 1 to n successively move b from the bottom of their rankings to the top, leaving the other relative rankings in place. Let n^* be the first agent whose change causes the social ranking to change. Note that we can always find such an n^* since when we reach the last individual, we will have b at the top of every individual's preference and hence, in that case, we must have $b \succ x$ for all $x \in A \setminus \{b\}$ due to weak Pareto. Let $\succsim^I$ be that profile for which the social ordering is $x \succ^I b$ for all $x \in A \setminus \{b\}$ where agents from 1 to $n^* - 1$ have b as the top element and the remaining agents have b as the bottom element. Let $\succsim^{II}$ be that profile (obtained from $\succsim^I$ by making only agent n^* move b from the bottom to the top) such that $b \succ^{II} x$ for all $x \in A \setminus \{b\}$.

The construction of these two profiles are given below in Figures 4.3 and 4.4.

$\succsim_1^I$	$\cdots$	$\succsim_{n^*-1}^I$	$\succsim_{n^*}^I$	$\succsim_{n^*+1}^I$	$\cdots$	$\succsim_n^I$
b		b	$\vdots$	$\vdots$		$\vdots$
$\vdots$		$\vdots$	b	b		b

Figure 4.3　**Profile** $\succsim^I = (\succsim^I, \ldots, \succsim^I)$

$\succsim_1^{II}$	$\cdots$	$\succsim_{n^*-1}^{II}$	$\succsim_{n^*}^{II}$	$\succsim_{n^*+1}^{II}$	$\cdots$	$\succsim_n^{II}$
b		b	b	$\vdots$		$\vdots$
$\vdots$		$\vdots$	$\vdots$	b		b

Figure 4.4　**Profile** $\succsim^{II} = (\succsim^{II}, \ldots, \succsim^{II})$

It follows that n^* is the pivotal agent as for profile $\succsim^I$, $x \succ^I b$ for all $x \in A \setminus \{b\}$ and for the profile $\succsim^{II}$, $b \succ^{II} x$ for all $x \in A \setminus \{b\}$. That $n^* = n(b)$ is extremely pivotal follows from Step 1. □

Step 3: Using Step 2, the extremely pivotal agent $n^* = n(b)$ is a dictator over any pair $a, c \in A$ not involving b.

Proof of Step 3: Construct profile $\succsim^{III}$ obtained from profile $\succsim^{II}$ by letting n^* move a above b, so that $\succsim_{n^*}^{III}$ is such that $a \succ_{n^*}^{III} c$. Profile $\succsim^{III}$ is depicted in Figure 4.5 below.

Observe that $\succsim_i^I| \ \{x, b\} = \succsim_i^{II}| \ \{x, b\} = \succsim_i^{III}| \ \{x, b\}$ for all $i \in N \setminus \{n^*\}$. Moreover, $\succsim_i^{III} |\{a, b\} = \succsim_i^I |\{a, b\}$ for all $i \in N$ and $a \succ^I b$. Hence, using independence of irrelevant alternatives, we get $a \succ^{III} b$. Similarly, note that $\succsim_i^{III} |\{b, c\} = \succsim_i^{II} |\{b, c\}$ for all $i \in N$ and $b \succ^{II} c$. Hence, by independence of irrelevant alternatives, we get $b \succ^{III} c$. Therefore, we get $a \succ^{III} b$ and $b \succ^{III} c$ and by applying transitivity of social preference we obtain $a \succ^{III} c$. Thus, $a \succ^{III} c$ given $a \succ_{n^*}^{III} c$. Hence, by independence of irrelevant alternatives, the social preference over $\{a, c\}$ must agree with n^*. □

Step 4: n^* is the dictator over every pair $a, b \in A$.

$\succsim_1^{III}$	$\succsim_2^{III}$	$\cdots$	$\succsim_{n^*-1}^{III}$	$\succsim_{n^*}^{III}$	$\succsim_{n^*+1}^{III}$	$\cdots$	$\succsim_n^{III}$
b	b		b	a	$\vdots$		$\vdots$
$\vdots$	$\vdots$		$\vdots$	b	$\vdots$		$\vdots$
$\vdots$	$\vdots$		$\vdots$	c	$\vdots$		$\vdots$
$\vdots$	$\vdots$		$\vdots$	$\vdots$	b		b

Figure 4.5   **Profile** $\succsim^{III} = (\succsim^{III}, \dots, \succsim^{III})$

Proof of Step 4: Take $c \in A \setminus \{b\}$. Do the same construction as in Step 2 so that there is an $n(c) \in N$ who is extremely pivotal. From Step 3 we know that $n(c)$ is a dictator over any $\alpha, \beta \in A \setminus \{c\}$, like for example for $a, b \in A \setminus \{c\}$. But n^* affects society's ranking over a, b while moving from profile $\succsim^I$ to $\succsim^{II}$ in Step 2. Thus, this dictator $n(c)$ over a, b must actually be n^*. ☐

What Arrow's impossibility theorem shows is that we should not expect a collectivity of agents to behave with the kind of consistency that we may hope from an agent.

4.5 EXERCISES

For explanations or definitions of the notation, see the main text of Chapter 4.

(E-4.1) Suppose $\succsim$ is a binary relation on A such that $\succ$ and $\sim$ are transitive. Then show that $\succsim$ is an ordering.

(E-4.2) Suppose the relation $\succsim$ on A is an order. Show that if $x \succsim y$ and $y \succ z$, then $x \succ z$.

(E-4.3) Suppose that there are three or more alternatives. Show that both the plurality rule $F^{sP} : \mathcal{Q}^n \to \mathcal{Q}$ and the anti-plurality rule $F^{sAP} : \mathcal{Q}^n \to \mathcal{Q}$ fail to satisfy weak Pareto.

(E-4.4) A social welfare function F satisfies *positive responsiveness* if the following holds: If $\succsim_i = \succsim_i' \ \forall \ i \in N \setminus \{j\}$ and either $(y \succ_j x$ and $x \succsim_j' y)$ or $(x \sim_j y$ and $x \succ_j' y)$, then $x \succsim y$ implies $x \succ' y$. Suppose there are three or more alternatives. Show that if a social welfare function $F : D \to Q$ satisfies unrestricted domain and positive responsiveness, then a group G is almost decisive over a pair (x, y) if and only if the same group G is decisive over the pair (x, y).

4.6   BIBLIOGRAPHICAL NOTES

- There are other papers that have provided alternative proofs of Arrow's impossibility theorem. This includes papers by Barberá (1980) and Dardanoni (2001).

- Arrow's impossibility theorem was used by Fishburn (1975) to characterize lexicographic preferences. An alternative proof of Fishburn's result was given by Mitra and Sen (2014) using the notion of extreme pivotal agent used by Geanakoplos (2005) in his first proof of Arrow's impossibility theorem.

- The proof of arrow's impossibility Theorem due to Geanakoplos (2005), which we have presented in this chapter, is only the first proof of his three proofs of Arrow's impossibility theorem (see Geanakoplos 2005).

REFERENCES

Arrow, K. J. 1950. "A Difficulty in the Concept of Social Welfare." *Journal of Political Economy* 58 (4): 328–346.

Barberá, S. 1980. "Pivotal Voters: A New Proof of Arrow's Theorem." *Economics Letters* 6 (1): 13–16.

Dardanoni, V. 2001. "A Pedagogical Proof of Arrow's Impossibility Theorem." *Social Choice and Welfare* 18 (1): 107–112.

Fishburn, P. C. 1975. "Axioms for Lexicographic Preferences." *Review of Economic Studies* 42 (3): 415–419.

Geanakoplos, J. 2005. "Three Brief Proofs of Arrow's Impossibility Theorem." *Economic Theory* 26 (July): 211–215.

Mitra, M., and D. Sen. 2014. "An Alternative Proof of Fishburn's Axiomatization of Lexicographic Preferences." *Economics Letters* 124 (2): 168–170.

RELAXING ARROW'S AXIOMS

5.1 INTRODUCTION

In this chapter, we explore the extent to which we can escape the dictatorship result if we relax some of Arrow's axioms. If we relax independence of irrelevant alternatives, then we get the Borda Count which is a well-defined social welfare function satisfying unrestricted domain and weak Pareto. This we have already discussed is Example 4.5 of Chapter 4. In Section 5.2, we relax weak Pareto and replace it by a weaker axiom of non-imposition and then we get the result due to Wilson (1972) that stipulates that a social welfare function satisfying unrestricted domain, independence of irrelevant alternatives, and non-imposition axioms must be null or dictatorial or inverse-dictatorial, given that the number of alternatives is not less than three. Both inverse-dictatorial and null social welfare functions are quite uninteresting. Inverse-dictatorship requires that there exists an agent i whose strict preference over every pair of alternatives is reversed for the society under all profiles in the domain. Like inverse-dictatorial social welfare function, the null social welfare function is also uninteresting since the society is always indifferent across all alternatives for all possible profiles in the domain.

In Section 5.3, we relax transitivity of social preferences and then either we end up in oligarchy or we end up violating the no veto power. Specifically, the oligarchy result, due to Weymark (1984), specifies that a social quasi-ordering that satisfies unrestricted domain, weak Pareto, and independence of irrelevant alternatives must be oligarchic, given that the number of alternatives is not less than three and the set of individuals is finite. In this context, we also derive the Liberal Paradox due to Sen (1970b) that shows that there is no social weak quasi-ordering that satisfies unrestricted domain, weak Pareto, and a very weak form of liberalism. Finally, in Section 5.4, we relax the axiom of unrestricted domain and assume single-peaked preferences and then we can escape Arrow's dictatorship conclusion. A set of individuals is said to have single-peaked preferences over a set of possible alternatives if the alternatives can be ordered along a line such that the following two conditions hold: (i) each agent has a best (or most preferred) alternative in the set, and (ii) for each agent, alternatives that are further from his or her best alternative are preferred less. The result in this context is due to Black (1948), who proved that if the domain of preferences satisfies single-peakedness, then pairwise majority voting cycles (Condorcet cycle) cannot occur, and the most preferred alternative of the median individual is a maximal element for the society obtained through pairwise majority voting across all alternatives.

5.2 **RELAXING WEAK PARETO**

If we relax weak Pareto, then what is a "satisfactory" replacement? Wilson (1972) suggested non-imposition which is defined below. In this section, we show that by relaxing weak Pareto and using a weaker notion of non-imposition we do not gain much. We begin by specifying some important definitions which are self explanatory.

Definition 5.1 A social welfare function $F : D \rightarrow Q$ satisfies *non-imposition* if for all $x, y \in A$, there exists a profile $\succsim = (\succsim_1, \ldots, \succsim_n) \in D$ such that $x \succsim y$.

Non-imposition rules out the possibility that F is such that there exists alternatives $x, y \in A$ so that for every profile $\succsim \in D$, we have $y \succ x$. Observe that if a social welfare function satisfies unrestricted domain and weak Pareto, then it satisfies non-imposition but the converse is not true.

Definition 5.2 A social welfare function $F : D \to Q$ is *inverse-dictatorial* if there exists an agent $i \in N$ such that for all $x, y \in A$ and all profiles $\succsim = (\succsim_1, \ldots, \succsim_n) \in D$, we have the following: if $x \succ_i y$, then $y \succ x$.

Observe that inverse-dictatorial social welfare function fails to satisfy weak Pareto but satisfies independence of irrelevant alternatives. Moreover, if an inverse-dictatorial social welfare function also satisfies unrestricted domain, then it also satisfies non-imposition.

Definition 5.3 A social welfare function $F : D \to Q$ is *null* if for all $x, y \in A$ and for all profiles $\succsim = (\succsim_1, \ldots, \succsim_n) \in D$, $x \sim y$.

The null social welfare function fails to satisfy weak Pareto but does satisfy independence of irrelevant alternatives. Moreover, if the null social welfare function also satisfies unrestricted domain, then it also satisfies non-imposition.

The next result is due to Wilson (1972).

Theorem 5.1 (Wilson 1972) Suppose the set of alternatives A has at least three elements. A social welfare function $F : D \to Q$ that satisfies unrestricted domain, independence of irrelevant alternatives, and non-imposition must either be null or dictatorial or inverse-dictatorial.

Let $F : D \to Q$ be a social welfare function satisfying the independence of irrelevant alternatives and non-imposition. For any $x, y \in A$, we write $PO(x, y)$ if for all profiles $\succsim = (\succsim_1, \ldots, \succsim_n) \in D$ such that $x \succ_i y$ for all $i \in N$, we have $x \succ y$. For any $x, y \in A$, we write $APO(x, y)$ if for all profiles $\succsim = (\succsim_1, \ldots, \succsim_n) \in D$ such that $x \succ_i y$ for all $i \in N$, we have $y \succ x$. The following three self-explanatory lemmas will be useful for proving Theorem 5.1.

Lemma 5.1 Suppose the set of alternatives A has at least three elements and suppose that the social welfare function F : $D \to Q$ satisfies unrestricted domain, independence of irrelevant alternatives, and non-imposition. For all $a, b, x, y \in A$, $PO(a, b)$ implies that $PO(x, y)$.

Proof. There are several cases to consider like in the field expansion lemma. We only prove $PO(a, b)$ implies that $PO(a, y)$, where $b \neq y$. Pick an arbitrary profile $\succsim \in D$, where $a \succ_i b$ and $a \succ_i y$ for all $i \in N$. We will show that $a \succ y$. Since F satisfies non-imposition, there exists a profile $\succsim' \in D$ such that $b \succsim' y$. Construct the profile $\succsim''$ such that for all $i \in N$, $a \succ_i'' b$, $a \succ_i'' y$, and $\succsim_i''|_{\{b,y\}} = \succsim_i'|_{\{b,y\}}$. This construction is clearly feasible due to unrestricted domain. Since $PO(a, b)$, we have $a \succ'' b$. On the other hand, independence of irrelevant alternatives implies $b \succsim'' y$. Since the social ordering is transitive we have $a \succ'' y$ (given $a \succ'' b$ and $b \succsim'' y$) and by independence of irrelevant alternatives, we get $a \succ y$. □

Lemma 5.2 Suppose the set of alternatives A has at least three elements and suppose that the social welfare function F : $D \to Q$ satisfies unrestricted domain, independence of irrelevant alternatives, and non-imposition. For all $a, b, x, y \in A$, $APO(a, b)$ implies that $APO(x, y)$.

Proof. Like in the previous lemma, there are several cases to consider and we only prove $APO(a, b)$ implies $APO(a, y)$, where $b \neq y$. Pick an arbitrary profile $\succsim \in D$, where $a \succ_i b$ and $a \succ_i y$ for all $i \in N$. We will show that $y \succ a$. Since F satisfies non-imposition, there exists a profile $\succsim'$ such that $y \succsim' b$. Construct the profile $\succsim''$ such that for all $i \in N$, $a \succ_i'' b$, $a \succ_i'' y$, and $\succsim_i''|_{\{b,y\}} = \succsim_i'|_{\{b,y\}}$. Given unrestricted domain, this selection is clearly feasible. Since $APO(a, b)$, we have $b \succ'' a$. On the other hand, independence of irrelevant alternatives implies $y \succsim'' b$. Since the social ordering is transitive, we have $y \succ'' a$ and by independence of irrelevant alternatives, we get $y \succ a$. □

Lemma 5.3 Suppose the set of alternatives A has at least three elements. If the social welfare function F : $D \to Q$ satisfies unrestricted domain, independence of irrelevant alternatives, and non-imposition, then one of the following statements must hold:

(W1) F is null.

(W2) $PO(x, y)$ holds for some pair $x, y \in A$.

(W3) $APO(x, y)$ holds for some pair $x, y \in A$.

Proof. Suppose that neither (W1) nor (W2) nor (W3) hold. Since (W1) does not hold, there exists $x, y \in A$ and a profile $\succsim \in D$ such that $x \succ y$ holds. Pick z distinct from both x and y and let $\succ'$ be a profile such that $x \succ_i' z$ and $y \succ_i' z$ for all $i \in N$ and $\succsim_i'|_{\{x,y\}} = \succsim_i|_{\{x,y\}}$. Again, this is clearly feasible. Since neither $PO(x, z)$ nor $APO(x, z)$ hold, we must have $x \sim' z$. Similarly, since neither $PO(y, z)$ nor $APO(y, z)$ hold, we must have $y \sim' z$. Since F is transitive, we have $x \sim' y$. Applying the independence of irrelevant alternatives, we have $x \sim y$, which is a contradiction to our assumption that $x \succ y$. $\qquad\square$

Proof of Theorem 5.1: Suppose F is not null. Applying Lemma 5.3, either $PO(x, y)$ must hold for some $x, y \in A$ or $APO(x, y)$ must hold for some pair $x, y \in A$. Suppose the former holds. Then, by Lemma 5.1, weak Pareto holds and the existence of a dictator follows from Arrow's impossibility theorem and hence F is dictatorial. If the latter holds, then, by Lemma 5.2, $APO(x, y)$ holds for all $x, y \in A$ and the proof of Arrow's theorem can be modified in a straightforward manner to show that F is inverse-dictatorial. $\qquad\square$

Theorem 5.1 (due to Wilson 1972) shows that if we drop weak Pareto and replace it with a very mild axiom of non-imposition, then we do not gain much since we either get dictatorship or inverse-dictatorship, or we get that F has to be null. Like dictatorship, inverse-dictatorship or null social welfare functions are also not desirable for a society. Therefore, if we really have to come out of the dictatorship conclusion and get something democratic for society, then relaxing weak Pareto is not the correct path.

5.3   RELAXING TRANSITIVITY OF (SOCIAL) BINARY RELATIONS

Rationality (or ordering) of social preference (or individual preference) requires that the "at least as good as" relation $\succsim$ on the set of alternatives A is reflexive, complete, and transitive, that is, $\succsim \in Q$. We now relax transitivity of the social preference $\succsim$. In particular, we assume that $\succsim$ is a binary relation (that is, $\succsim$ is reflexive and complete) and we replace transitivity either by quasi-transitivity so that we get a (social) quasi-ordering or by acyclicity so that we get a (social) weak quasi-ordering. Recall that Q^q is the set of all possible quasi-transitive (social) binary relations and Q^a is the set of all possible acyclic (social) binary relations.

Proposition 5.1   If there are at least three alternatives in the set A, then we have the following:

(O1) If a binary relation $\succsim \in Q$, then $\succsim \in Q^q$.

(O2) If a binary relation $\succsim \in Q^q$, then $Q \in Q^a$.

Proposition 5.1 has two statements. The first statement, that is, (O1), specifies that if a binary relation $\succsim$ is an ordering (social ordering), then it is also a quasi-ordering (social quasi-ordering). The second statement, that is, (O2), specifies that if a binary relation $\succsim$ is a quasi-ordering (social quasi-ordering), then it is a weak quasi-ordering (weak social quasi-ordering).

Proof of Proposition 5.1:
Proof of (O1): Suppose it is not. Then there exists an ordering $\succsim \in Q$ such that $\succsim \notin Q^q$. That is, for the ordering $\succsim$, there exists $x, y, z \in A$ such that $x \succ y$, $y \succ z$, and $\neg(x \succ z)$. Since $\succsim$ is complete, we have $z \succsim x$ (from $\neg(x \succ z)$). But given $\succsim$ is an ordering, $z \succsim x$ and $x \succ y$ implies $z \succ y$, which contradicts $y \succ z$.
Proof of (O2): Suppose it is not. Then there exists a quasi-ordering $\succsim \in Q^q$ such that $\succsim \notin Q^a$. That is, for the quasi-ordering $\succsim$, there exists $x_1, \ldots, x_k \in A$ such that $x_1 \succ x_2$, $x_2 \succ x_3, \ldots x_{k-1} \succ x_k$ and $x_k \succ x_1$. By repeatedly applying quasi-transitivity, we get $x_1 \succ x_{k-1}$ and, given $x_{k-1} \succ x_k$ and

$x_k \succ x_1$, we have a violation of quasi-transitivity of strict preference. This is a contradiction since $\succsim \in \mathcal{Q}^a$. □

From Proposition 5.1 it is clear that the set of all orderings is a strict subset of the set of all quasi-orderings, which in turn is a strict subset of the set of all weak quasi-orderings, that is, $\mathcal{Q} \subset \mathcal{Q}^q \subset \mathcal{Q}^a$.

5.3.1 *Quasi-transitivity social binary relations*

What happens if we require that the social binary relation is quasi-transitive instead of transitive? Recall that a social quasi-ordering F^q is a mapping from any domain $D(\subseteq \mathcal{Q}^n)$ to the set of all quasi-transitive binary relation $\mathcal{Q}^q$. Can we find social quasi-ordering F^q that satisfies unrestricted domain, weak Pareto, independence of irrelevant alternatives, and is not dictatorial? The answer is yes.

Example 5.1 Consider $F_N^{OL} : \mathcal{Q}^n \to \mathcal{Q}^q$ such that for all $x, y \in A$; $[x \succ_i y \ \forall \ i \in N]$ implies $x \succ y$ and we have $x \sim y$ otherwise. It is easy to check that F_N^{OL} satisfies unrestricted domain, weak Pareto, independence of irrelevant alternatives, and is not dictatorial. However, this F_N^{OL} is not a social welfare function since it is quasi-transitive but not transitive. To see this, consider $N = \{1, 2\}$ and $A = \{x, y, z\}$. Let $\succsim_1: x \succ_1 z \succ_1 y$ and $\succsim_2: y \succ_2 x \succ_2 z$. Given F^q, we get $x \sim y, y \sim z$, and $x \succ z$, and the transitivity of indifference is violated. Observe that F_N^{OL} is the special case of oligarchic binary relation with oligarchic group N and hence it is a social quasi-ordering (see Chapter 2).

Before going to our next theorem, we provide another way of defining the oligarchic social quasi-ordering.

Definition 5.4 A social quasi-ordering $F_G^{OL} : D \to \mathcal{Q}^q$ is *oligarchic* if there exists a non-empty coalition $G \subseteq N$ such that

(1) G is decisive (that is, for any profile $\succsim \in D$ such that $x \succ_i y$ $\forall i \in G$, we have $x \hat{F}_G^{OL}(\succsim)y$).

(2) All members of G have a *veto power* (that is, if $\succsim \in D$ is such that $x \succ_i y$ for any $i \in G$, then $x F_G^{OL}(\succsim)y$).

Observe that if $|G| = 1$ we have *dictatorship*, and if $G = N$ we have strict preference only over Pareto outcomes (that is, Example 5.1 above). The next theorem is due to Weymark (1984).

Theorem 5.2 Suppose there are at least three alternatives in A and suppose that the set of agents N is finite. Then any social quasi-ordering $F^q : D \to Q^q$ satisfying unrestricted domain, weak Pareto, and independence of irrelevant alternatives must be oligarchic.

The proof of this theorem uses the following lemmas.

Lemma 5.4 Let $\succsim$ be a binary relation over a finite set A of alternatives with $|A| \geq 3$. The following statements are equivalent:

(i) The binary relation is quasi-transitive, that is, $\succsim \in Q^q$.
(ii) For all $x, y, z \in A$ such that $x \succ y$ and $y \succsim z$, we get $x \succsim z$.

Proof.   Suppose (i) is true but (ii) is not. Then there exists $x, y, z \in A$ such that $x \succ y$, and $y \succsim z$ imply $z \succ x$ (since $\succsim$ is complete $\neg(x \succsim z)$ implies that $z \succ x$). Given $z \succ x$ and $x \succ y$, from quasi-transitivity we get $z \succ y$, which contradicts $y \succsim z$. For the other part, suppose that condition (ii) holds but $\succsim \notin Q^q$. Then there exists $x, y, z \in A$ such that $x \succ y$, $y \succ z$, and $z \succsim x$. Since (ii) holds, $y \succ z$ and $z \succsim x$ imply $y \succsim x$ and we have a contradiction to $x \succ y$.   □

Individual i is *almost semi-decisive* over the ordered pair (x, y), if $x \succ_i y$ and $y \succ_j x$ for all $j \in N \setminus \{i\}$ implies that $x \succsim y$. To prove Theorem 5.2 we will need the following lemma.

Lemma 5.5 (The veto-field expansion lemma)
Suppose there are at least three alternatives in A, the set of agents N is finite, and suppose that the social quasi-ordering $F^q : D \to Q^q$ satisfies unrestricted domain, weak Pareto, and independence of irrelevant alternatives. If agent i is almost semi-decisive over some ordered pair (x, y), then i has a veto over all possible ordered pairs (a, b).

Sketch of the Proof. Suppose that a, b, x, y are all pairwise distinct. Consider a profile $(\succsim_1, \ldots, \succsim_n) \in Q^n$ and any $i \in N$ such that:

(i) $a \succ_i x \succ_i y \succ_i b$, and

(ii) $a \succ_j x$ and $y \succ_j b$ for all $j \in N \setminus \{i\}$.

Due to unrestricted domain, constructions of profiles of the form given by (i) and (ii) are admissible. Observe that the profiles given by conditions (i) and (ii) are such that agent i prefers a over b though the relative ordering between a and b for every agent $j \in N \setminus \{i\}$ is not specified and hence can be anything.

Given that i is almost semi-decisive over (x, y), $x \succsim y$. By weak Pareto, $a \succ x$ and $y \succ b$. Now, $a \succ x$ and $x \succsim y$ imply $a \succsim y$ (due to Lemma 5.4). So we have $a \succsim y$ and $y \succ b$. Using arguments similar to that applied in Lemma 5.4 we can prove that $a \succsim y$ and $y \succ b$ imply $a \succsim b$. Applying independence of irrelevant alternatives, we get i has veto over the ordered pair (a, b). The remaining steps of this proof are very similar to the field expansion lemma (that is, Lemma 4.10) and is hence omitted. □

It is easy to verify that the field expansion lemma (that is, Lemma 4.10) goes through with quasi-transitivity.

Proof of Theorem 5.2: By Lemma 4.10 (that is, the field expansion lemma) and weak Pareto, it follows that there exists a *smallest* decisive coalition. Let it be called G^S. (If $|G^S| = 1$ we have dictatorship which implies oligarchy with one individual.) If cardinality of the set G^S is greater than unity, then we want to show that every $i \in G^s$ has veto power. Consider the profile $\succsim = (\succsim_1, \ldots, \succsim_n) \in \mathcal{Q}^n$ and any $i \in G^s$ such that we have

(i) $x \succ_i y \succ_i z$,

(ii) $y \succ_j z \succ_j x$ for all $j \in G^s \setminus \{i\}$, and

(iii) $z \succ_l x \succ_l y$ for all $l \in N \setminus \{G^s\}$.

Since G^s is decisive, we have $y \succ z$. If $y \succ x$, then $\overline{D}_{G \setminus \{i\}}(y, x)$ implies $D_{G \setminus \{i\}}(a, b)$ for all $a, b \in A$ (by the field expansion lemma), which would violate the fact that G^s is the smallest decisive coalition. Therefore, by completeness of the social binary relation, we must have $x \succsim y$. Now by quasi-transitivity, $x \succsim y$ and $y \succ z$ imply $x \succsim z$. Thus, agent i is almost semi-decisive over the ordered pair (x, z). From the veto-field expansion lemma (that is, Lemma 5.5), we get i has a veto power over all pairs. The same argument applies for any $i \in G^s$. Thus, the smallest decisive group G^s is an oligarchy.   □

Theorem 5.2 due to Weymark (1984) shows that if we relax social ordering to social quasi-ordering and require the social quasi-ordering to satisfy the three Arrovian axioms of unrestricted domain, weak Pareto, and independence of irrelevant alternatives, then we end up with oligarchy, which is the dictatorship of a few and is hence undesirable.

5.3.2   *Acyclic social binary relations*

Suppose that the social binary relation is acyclic instead of being quasi-transitive. Then we have the following result which states that a binary relation over a finite set of alternatives with at least three elements is acyclic if and only if the maximal set corresponding to every non-empty subset of the set of alternatives and the binary relation is non-empty.

Proposition 5.2 Let $\succsim$ be a binary relation over a finite set A of alternatives with at least three elements and let $\mathcal{A}$ denote the set of all possible non-empty subsets of A. The following statements are equivalent:

(i) The binary relation $\succsim$ is acyclic, that is, $\succsim \in \mathcal{Q}^a$.

(ii) For each non-empty set $S \in \mathcal{A}$, $M(S; \succsim) \neq \emptyset$.

Proof.   (i) $\Rightarrow$ (ii). Suppose $\succsim \in \mathcal{Q}^a$ and consider $S \in \mathcal{A}$. We show that $M(S; \succsim) \neq \emptyset$. If everything in S is indifferent, then there in no problem since then $M(S; \succsim) = S$ and we are done. Consider $x_1 \in S$. If $x_1 \in M(S; \succsim)$, then again we are done. However, if $x_1 \notin M(S; \succsim)$, then there exists $x_2 \in S$ with $x_2(\neq x_1)$ such that $x_2 \succ x_1$. If $x_2 \in M(S; \succsim)$, then again we are done. However, if $x_2 \notin M(S; \succsim)$, then there exists x_3 such that $x_3 \succ x_2$. Here $x_3 \neq x_1$ because if $x_3 = x_1$, then we have $x_3 = x_1 \succ x_2 \succ x_1$, which is a violation of acyclicity. Moreover, $\neg(x_1 \succ x_3)$ because if $x_1 \succ x_3$, then given $x_3 \succ x_2$ and $x_2 \succ x_1$, $x_1 \succ x_3$ leads to a violation of acyclicity. Therefore, if $x_3 \notin M(S; \succsim)$, then there exists x_4 distinct from x_1 and x_2 such that $x_4 \succ x_3$. Since A is finite, S has to be finite, then this process of non-inclusion cannot continue forever and hence there exists some $\tilde{x} \in S$ such that $\tilde{x} \in M(S; \succsim)$. So a maximal element always exists.

(ii) $\Rightarrow$ (i). Assume not, that is, let $M(S; \succsim) \neq \emptyset$ for all $S \in \mathcal{A}$ and $\succsim \notin \mathcal{Q}^a$. Then there exists a positive integer k and a set $S^* = \{x_1, \ldots, x_k\} \in \mathcal{A}$ such that $x_1 \succ x_2 \succ \ldots \succ x_k \succ x_1$. Clearly $M(S^*; \succsim) = \emptyset$ and we have a violation of our assumption that $M(S; \succsim) \neq \emptyset$ for all $S \in \mathcal{A}$. □

Recall that a weak social quasi-ordering F^a is a mapping from any domain $D(\subseteq \mathcal{Q}^n)$ to the set of all acyclic binary relation $\mathcal{Q}^a$, that is, $F^a : D \to \mathcal{Q}^a$. The next example, taken from Mas-Colell et al. (1995), is an instance of a non-dictatorial social weak quasi-ordering.

Example 5.2 Consider $N = \{1, 2\}$, $A = \{x, y, z\}$, and define F^a : $\mathcal{Q}^2 \to \mathcal{Q}^a$ as follows. For any $v, w \in A$, we say that $v \succsim w$ if either $v \succsim_1 w$ or $v = y, w = x$, and $v \succ_2 w$. Thus, the social preference agrees with the preference of agent 1 with one qualification: agent 2 can veto the possibility that $x \succ y$. Specifically, if $y \succ_2 x$, then $y \succsim x$. Therefore, if $x \succ_1 y$ and $y \succ_2 x$, then $x \sim y$. If $y \succ_1 x$ and $y \succ_2 x$, then $y \succ x$. One can verify that this F^a satisfies acyclicity but fails to satisfy quasi-transitivity. For example, let $\succsim_1$: $x \succ_1 z \succ_1 y$ and $\succsim_2$: $\bullet \succ_2 y \bullet \succ_2 x \succ_2 \bullet$, where any dot in the preference of agent 2 can be replaced by z. Note that $x \succ z$ since $x \succ_1 z$ and $z \succ y$ since $z \succ_1 y$. Therefore, quasi-transitivity requires that $x \succ z$ and $z \succ y \Rightarrow x \succsim y$. However, this is not the case here since $y \succ_2 x \Rightarrow y \succsim x$ and $x \succ_1 y \Rightarrow x \succsim y$. Therefore, $x \sim y$. However, acyclicity is not violated since $x \succ z$ and $z \succ y$ and acyclicity implies that $\neg(y \succ x) \Rightarrow x \succsim y$. Since we have $x \sim y$, acyclicity is satisfied.

The next result, which is due to Mas-Colell and Sonnenschein (1972), says that if the number of individuals in the society is at least four having preferences on at least three or more alternatives and if a weak social quasi-ordering satisfies the axioms unrestricted domain, weak Pareto, independence of irrelevant alternatives, and positive responsiveness, then someone has a veto. Recall that positive responsiveness was formally defined in Exercise (E-4.4) of Chapter 4.

Proposition 5.3 If the number of agents in N is at least four, the number of elements in the set of alternatives A is at least three and if the weak social quasi-ordering $F^a : D \to Q^a$ satisfies unrestricted domain, weak Pareto, independence of irrelevant alternatives, and positive responsiveness, then someone has a veto.

Given the results of this section so far, we find that relaxing transitivity does not help as either we continue to have oligarchy (when the social binary relation is quasi-transitive) or we continue to have an agent with veto power (when the social binary relation is acyclic). We do not prove Proposition 5.3 and instead in the next subsection we provide a more popular impossibility result on liberalism.

5.3.3 *Paretian liberal: An impossibility result with acyclicity*

A common objection to the method of majority decision is that it is illiberal, that is, given other things in society, if you prefer to have pink walls rather than white then society should permit you to have this, even if a majority of the community would like to see your walls white. Similarly, whether you should sleep on your back or on your belly is a matter in which society should permit you absolute freedom, even if a majority of the community is nosey enough to feel that you must sleep on your back. One can formalize this concept of individual liberty in an extremely weak form and examine its consequences. The liberal paradox was discovered by Sen (1970b) and it shows that no social system can simultaneously (*a*) be committed to a minimal sense of freedom, (*b*) always result in weak Pareto efficiency, and (*c*) be capable of functioning in any society whatsoever (unrestricted domain).

Suppose the set of all agents is $N = \{1, \dots, n\}$ and assume that every agent $i \in N$ has a strict preference ordering on the set of alternatives A which is finite and has at least three alternatives. Let $\Pi(A) = \{S \subset A \mid |S| = 2\}$ be the set of all two-element subsets of A. A *right-system* is an assignment of n non-identical sets that belong to $\Pi(A)$ to the agents in N. $RS = \{S_1, \dots, S_n\}$ is thus a right system if $S_i \in \Pi(A)$ for every $i \in N$ and $S_i \neq S_j$ for every $i, j \in N$ such that $i \neq j$. An agent i is called *decisive with respect to the set* $S = \{x, y\}$ that belongs to $\Pi(A)$, if $x \succ_i y$ implies that $x \succ y$, and $y \succ_i x$ implies that $y \succ x$. A right-system is *effective* if every individual is decisive with respect to the two alternatives assigned to him.

Definition 5.5 (Liberalism)
There exists a right-system $RS = \{S_1, \ldots, S_n\}$, such that every agent $i \in N$ is decisive with respect to S_i.

Liberalism requires that for each agent $i \in N$, there is at least one pair of alternatives, say (x, y), such that if this agent prefers x to y, then society should prefer x to y, and if he prefers y to x, then society should prefer y to x. The intention is to permit each agent the freedom to determine at least one social choice, for example, having his own walls pink rather than white, other things remaining the same for him and the rest of society.

In fact, one can weaken the condition of liberalism further. Such freedom may not be given to all, but to a proper subset of individuals. However, to make sense, the subset must have more than one member, since if it includes only one then we might have a dictatorship. Hence, we demand such freedom for at least two agents.

Definition 5.6 (Minimal liberalism)
There are at least two agents such that for each of them there is at least one pair of alternatives over which he is decisive.

Proposition 5.4 There is noweak social quasi-ordering $F^a : D \to Q^a$ that satisfies unrestricted domain, weak Pareto, and minimal liberalism.

Proof. Let us prove the result for two agents, that is, for $N = \{1, 2\}$. In this case, $RS = \{S_1, S_2\}$ and $S_1 \neq S_2$. The proof of the general case is analogous. We can have two possibilities, that is, $S_1 \cap S_2 = \emptyset$ and $S_1 \cap S_2 \neq \emptyset$. We show that in either case we have a violation of acyclicity.

If the first possibility holds, then assume without loss of generality that $S_1 = \{x, y\}$ and $S_2 = \{w, z\}$. Given unrestricted domain, construct the following preferences: $w \succ_1 x \succ_1 y \succ_1 z$ and $y \succ_2 z \succ_2 w \succ_2 x$. Minimal liberalism implies that $x \succ y$ and $z \succ w$ for society. Moreover, weak Pareto implies $w \succ x$ and $y \succ z$

for society. But $w \succ x$, $x \succ y$, $y \succ z$, and $z \succ w$ demonstrate a violation of acyclicity.[1]

If the second possibility holds, then assume without loss of generality that $S_1 = \{x, y\}$ and $S_2 = \{y, w\}$, and, given unrestricted domain, construct the preferences $w \succ_1 x \succ_1 y$ and $y \succ_2 w \succ_2 x$. Minimal liberalism implies that $x \succ y$ and $y \succ w$. Moreover, weak Pareto implies that $w \succ x$. But $x \succ y$, $y \succ w$, and $w \succ x$ again demonstrate a violation of acyclicity.[2]   □

5.4 DOMAIN RESTRICTION: SINGLE-PEAKED PREFERENCES

We first define a domain restriction (specifically, restrictions on individual preferences), which is known as single-peaked preferences.

Definition 5.7 An alternative $x \in A$ is a *weak Condorcet winner* under $\succsim$ if and only if $N(x, y; \succsim) \geq N(y, x; \succsim)$ for all $y \in A \setminus \{x\}$.

Definition 5.8 An alternative $x \in A$ is a *strong Condorcet winner* under $\succsim$ if and only if $N(x, y; \succsim) > N(y, x; \succsim)$ for all $y \in A \setminus \{x\}$.

Therefore, an alternative x is a weak Condorcet winner (strong Condorcer winner) if it at least ties (wins) with all other alternatives in a pairwise majority voting. Clearly, if an alternative is a strong Condorcet winner, then it is also a weak Condorcet winner but the converse is not true.

Definition 5.9 A binary relation $\geq$ on the set of alternatives A is a *linear order* on A if it is *transitive* ($x \geq y$, $y \geq z$ implies that $x \geq z$) and *total* ($x, y \in A$, $x \neq y$, we have either $x \geq y$ or $y \geq x$ but not both).

---

[1] If $|N| > 2$, then let $S_1 = \{x, y\}$ and $S_2 = \{w, z\}$, $w \succ_1 x \succ_1 y \succ_1 z$, $y \succ_2 z \succ_2 w \succ_2 x$ and for any $j \in N \setminus \{1, 2\}$, select any ordering $\succ_j$ such that $w \succ_j x$ and $y \succ_j z$. The proof goes through.

[2] If $|N| > 2$, then let $S_1 = \{x, y\}$, $S_2 = \{y, w\}$, $w \succ_1 x \succ_1 y$, $y \succ_2 w \succ_2 x$ and for any $j \in N \setminus \{1, 2\}$, select any ordering $\succsim_j$ such that $w \succ_j x$. The proof goes through.

The simple example of a linear order occurs when A is a subset of the real line ($A \subset \mathbb{R}$) and $\geq$ is the natural "greater than equal to" order of the real line.

Definition 5.10 Let $\geq$ be a linear order over A. The ordering $\succsim_i \in Q$ is *single peaked* if there exists $x^* \in A$ such that for all $y, z \in A$, $[x^* \geq y > z \text{ or } z > y \geq x^*] \Rightarrow y \succ_i z$.

Let $Q_\geq$ be the set of all single-peaked preferences with respect to $\geq$. We assume that $\geq$ is fixed. We shall denote the peak of a single-peaked ordering $\succsim_i$ as $\tau(\succsim_i)$. We have the following observations in this context:

(1) Let $A = [0, 1]$ denote the fraction of the government's budget that is spent on defence (or on education). According to voter i, the optimal fraction is 0.25. If i's preference is single peaked, then i prefers 0.3 over 0.45 and 0.1 over 0.001. Note that single-peakedness places no restrictions on alternatives on different "sides" of the peak, that is, the voter can either prefer 0.05 to 0.4 or vice-versa.

(2) Let $A = [a, b] \subset \mathbb{R}$ and $\geq$ is the greater than or equal to ordering of the real numbers. Then a continuous rational preference relation $\mathcal{R}$ on A is single peaked with respect to the order $\geq$ if and only if it is strictly convex, that is, if and only if, for every $z \in A$, we have $\alpha x + (1 - \alpha)y \succ z$ whenever $x \succsim z, y \succsim z, x \neq y$, and $\alpha \in (0, 1)$.

(3) Take $N = \{1, 2, 3\}$ and $A = \{x, y, z\}$. Assume the preference under the Condorcet paradox, that is, $\succsim_1: x \succ_1 y \succ_1 z, \succsim_2: z \succ_2 x \succ_2 y$, and $\succsim_3: y \succ_3 z \succ_3 x$. For the linear order $x < y < z$, agent 2's preference fails to be single peaked. One can verify that social preferences under the Condorcet paradox fail to satisfy single-peakedness for all possible linear orders $\geq$.

(4) Let $|A| = m$ and let $\mathcal{P}_\geq (\subset Q_\geq)$ denote the set of all *strict single-peaked preferences*, given the linear order $\geq$ on A. Then one can show that $|\mathcal{P}_\geq| = 2^{m-1}$. In an exercise you are asked to prove this result.

Definition 5.11 Let $\succsim = (\succsim_1, \ldots, \succsim_n) \in Q_\geq^n$ be a profile of single-peaked preferences. The *median voter* in the profile $\succsim$ is the voter h such that $|\{i \in N : \tau(\succsim_h) \geq \tau(\succsim_i)\}| \geq \frac{n}{2}$ and $|\{i \in N : \tau(\succsim_i) \geq \tau(\succsim_h)\}| \geq \frac{n}{2}$.

The median voter exists for all profiles, although the identity of the median voter may not always be unique. However, if n is odd, then the *median peak* is unique. The next result is known as the *median voter theorem* due to Duncan Black (see Black 1948). Black's theorem demonstrates rigorously that given any linear order on the set of alternatives A, for every profile the maximal set associated with the entire set of alternatives A is non-empty and that it always includes the peak of the median voter.

Theorem 5.3 Fix a linear order $\geq$ on A. For any single-peaked profile $\succsim \in \mathcal{Q}^n_\geq$, the maximal set on A is non-empty, that is, $M(A; Q^{maj}(\succsim)) \neq \emptyset$. In particular, the peak of the median voter is a maximal element on A, that is, $\tau(\succsim_h) \in M(A; Q^{maj}(\succsim))$.

Proof. Pick any arbitrary $\succsim \in \mathcal{Q}^n_\geq$. We show that $\tau(\succsim_h) Q^{maj}(\succsim) b$ for all $b \in A$. We consider two cases.

  Case 1: Let $b \in A$ be such that $\tau(\succsim_h) > b$. Take any $i \in N$ such that $\tau(\succsim_i) \geq \tau(\succsim_h)$. Since $\succsim_i \in \mathcal{Q}_\geq$ and $\tau(\succsim_i) \geq \tau(\succsim_h) > b$, we have $\tau(\succsim_h) \succ_i b$. Since $|\{i \in N \mid \tau(R_i) \geq \tau(R_h)\}| \geq \frac{n}{2}$ and since h is the median voter, it follows that $\tau(\succsim_h) Q^{maj}(\succsim) b$.

  Case 2: Let $b \in A$ be such that $\tau(\succsim_h) < b$. Take any $i \in N$ such that $\tau(\succsim_i) \leq \tau(\succsim_h)$. Since $\succsim_i \in \mathcal{Q}_\geq$ and $b > \tau(\succsim_h) \geq \tau(\succsim_i)$, we have $\tau(\succsim_h) \succ_i b$. Since $|\{i \in N \mid \tau(\succsim_h) \geq \tau(\succsim_i)\}| \geq \frac{n}{2}$ and since h is the median voter, it follows that $\tau(\succsim_h) Q^{maj}(\succsim) b$.

  Cases 1 and 2 cover all possibilities and the result follows. $\square$

The median voter theorem guarantees the existence of a weak Condorcet winner whenever the preferences of all agents are single peaked with respect to a given linear ordering $\geq$. The median voter theorem also guarantees acyclicity of social preference. However, the median voter theorem *cannot* guarantee transitivity of social preference. This is shown in the following example.

Example 5.3 Let $N = \{1, 2\}$, $A = \{x, y, z\}$, and let the linear order $\geq$ be $x < y < z$. Consider $\succsim = (\succsim_1, \succsim_2) \in \mathcal{Q}^2_\geq$ such that $\succsim_1: x \succ_1 y \succ_1 z$ and $\succsim_2: y \succ_2 z \succ_2 x$. Note that $1 = N(x, y; \succsim) = N(y, x; \succsim) \Rightarrow x \sim y$ and $2 = N(y, z; \succsim) > N(z, y; \succsim) = 0 \Rightarrow y \succ z$. Transitivity would require that $x \succ z$. However, $1 = N(x, z; \succsim) = N(z, x; \succsim) \Rightarrow x \sim z$ and we have a violation of transitivity. Observe that acyclicity is preserved, since $M(\{x,y\};\succsim) = \{x,y\}$, $M(\{x,z\};\succsim) = \{x,z\}$, $M(\{y,z\};\succsim) = \{y\}$ and $M(\{x,y,z\};\succsim) = \{x,y\}$.

Under what condition do we have transitivity of social binary preference relation with individual preferences satisfying single-peakedness? The next proposition provides the conditions under which the pairwise majority voting relation becomes transitive.

Proposition 5.5 Assume that n is odd and, given a linear order $\geq$ on A, all agents have strict single-peaked preferences. Then for every strict preference profile $\succ = (\succ_1, \ldots, \succ_n) \in \mathcal{P}_{\geq}^n$, the pairwise majority voting relation $\hat{Q}^{maj}(\succ)$ yields transitivity.

Proof. Given that n is odd and that the voter's preference does not have indifference, for any $x, y \in A$ and any $\succ \in \mathcal{P}_{\geq}^n$, either $x\hat{Q}^{maj}(\succ)y$ holds or $y\hat{Q}^{maj}(\succ)x$ holds. Pick any $x, y, z \in A$ and a profile $\succ \in \mathcal{P}_{\geq}^n$ and assume that $x\hat{Q}^{maj}(\succ)y$ and $y\hat{Q}^{maj}(\succ)z$. One can easily verify that each $\succ_i$ induces single-peaked preferences over $\{x, y, z\}$. Applying Theorem 5.3 to the set $\{x, y, z\}$, it follows that $M(\{x,y,z\};\succ) \neq \emptyset$. Therefore, $z\hat{Q}^{maj}(\succ)x$ is ruled out, and by completeness and no indifference we have $x\hat{Q}^{maj}(\succ)z$. Hence, we have established that if $x\hat{Q}^{maj}(\succ)y$ and $y\hat{Q}^{maj}(\succ)z$, then $x\hat{Q}^{maj}(\succ)z$, implying that $\hat{Q}^{maj}(\succ)$ is transitive. $\square$

What comes out of this chapter is that unrestricted domain is the key axiom that needs to be relaxed in order to come out of the dictatorship conclusion in a convincing way.

5.5 EXERCISES

For explanations or definitions of the notation, see the main text of Chapter 5.

(E-5.1) Give a complete proof of Lemma 5.1, Lemma 5.2, and Lemma 5.5.

(E-5.2) Show that if $\succsim \in \mathcal{Q}^q$, then for all $x, y, z \in A$ such that $x \succsim y$ and $y \succ z$, we get $x \succsim z$.

(E-5.3) Given the relation $\succsim$ on A with $|A| \geq 4$ and any set S taken from $\mathcal{A}$ (the set of all possible subsets of A), the maximal set associated with the set S and the preference relation $\succsim$ on A is $M(S; \succsim) = \{x \in S \mid \not\exists y \in S \text{ such that } y \succ x\}$. A binary relation $\succsim$ satisfies *acyclicity of triples* if for every triple $x, y, z \in A$ such that $x \succ y$ and $y \succ z$, we have $\neg(z \succ x)$. Show that acyclicity over triples is not sufficient to ensure $M(S; \succsim) \neq \emptyset$ for all $S \in \mathcal{A}$.

(E-5.4) Let $|A| = m$ and let $\mathcal{P}_{\geq}$ denote the set of all strict single-peaked preferences given the linear order $\geq$ on A. Show that $|\mathcal{P}_{\geq}| = 2^{m-1}$.

5.6 BIBLIOGRAPHICAL NOTES

- Theorem 5.1 (due to Wilson [1972]) on relaxing weak Pareto is an impossibility result like the Arrow impossibility theorem. A comparison of Arrow and Wilson's impossibility theorems can be found in Campbell and Kelly (2003).

- In this chapter, we have discussed three papers that deal with relaxing transitivity of social binary relation. These are Sen (1970a), Mas-Colell and Sonnenschein (1972), and Weymark (1984). Other papers in this context are Sen (1969b) and Blair and Pollak (1982).

- There are many papers that deal with single-peaked preferences. A characterization of single-peaked domains was provided by Ballester and Haeringer (2011).

REFERENCES

Ballester, M. A., and G. Haeringer. 2011. "A Characterization of the Single-peaked Domain." *Social Choice and Welfare* 36 (February): 305–322.

Black, D. 1948. "On the Rationale of Group Decision-Making." *Journal of Political Economy* 56 (1): 23–34.

Blair, D. H., and R. A. Pollak. 1982. "Acyclic Collective Choice Rules." *Econometrica* 50 (4): 931–943.

Campbell, D. E., and J. S. Kelly. 2003. "On the Arrow and Wilson Impossibility Theorems." *Social Choice and Welfare* 20 (2): 273–281.

Mas-Colell, A., and H. Sonnenschein. 1972. "General Possibility Theorems for Group Decisions." *Review of Economic Studies* 39 (2): 185–192.

Mas-Colell, A., M. D. Whinston, and J. R. Green. 1995. *Microeconomic Theory*. New York: Oxford University Press.

Sen, A. K. 1969. "Quasi-transitivity, Rational Choice and Collective Decisions." *Review of Economic Studies* 36 (3): 381–393.

———. 1970a. *Collective Choice and Social Welfare*. Amsterdam, The Netherlands: Elsevier.

———. 1970b. "The Impossibility of a Paretian Liberal." *Journal of Political Economy* 78 (1): 152–157.

Weymark, J. A. 1984. "Arrow's Theorem with Social Quasi-ordering." *Public Choice* 42 (3): 235–246.

Wilson, R. 1972. "Social Choice Theory without the Pareto Principle." *Journal of Economic Theory* 5 (3): 478–486.

ARROW'S THEOREM WITH UTILITIES

6

6.1 INTRODUCTION

Arrow's theorem is based on both *non-measurability* (utility of an individual cannot be measured) and *non-comparability* (the welfare of two different individuals cannot be compared). The non-measurability is implicit in Arrow's use of orderings to represent individual preferences and non-comparability is implied by the controversial *irrelevance of individual alternatives* axiom. If either of these assumptions is relaxed, then Arrow's theorem does not hold.

Sen (1970) was the first to propose a framework for exploring the consequences of relaxing non-measurability and non-comparability. Instead of assuming the set of all preference ordering as a primitive (as in Arrow), he assumed it to be the set of all possible *utility functions*. A *profile* is a list of utility functions, one for each agent. A *social welfare functional* associates a utility function to each profile.

In this framework, Arrow's theorem holds if the utility functions are only ordinally measurable and interpersonally non-comparable. Arrow's impossibility theorem is robust in the sense that weakening the requirement that social preferences are orderings, while preserving non-measurability and non-comparability, leaves little room for sensible social binary relations. Sen (1974, 1977a, 1986a) has provided a taxonomy of different measurability and comparability assumptions. In this chapter, we study Arrow's theorem under these measurability and comparability assumptions.

Why should we care about measurability and comparability assumptions? d'Aspremont and Gevers (2002) argue that there is a distinction between the problem of determining the "relationship that collective decisions or preferences ought to have with individual preferences" and the separate problem where "an ordinary citizen attempts to take the standpoint of an ethical observer in order to formulate social evaluation judgements." The first problem is appropriate when looking at the design of constitutions, for instance. When designing a constitution, we will be concerned with the abilities of voters to manipulate the voting process because voting decisions typically involve groups. We also want to make minimal assumptions on measurability and comparability because preferences cannot be measured.

However, when an ordinary citizen takes the viewpoint of an ethical observer, she can make assumptions about measurability and comparability in order to determine her own voting strategy, or to recommend a voting process for society. d'Aspremont and Gevers (2002) also observe that much of the discussion of social welfare prior to Arrow was concerned with the second problem.

In addition to demonstrating the Arrow theorem, this chapter makes detailed investigations on the implications of additional concepts of measurability and comparability of individual utilities on forms of social evaluation functional. The presentation of the chapter relies substantially on Blackorby, Donaldson, and Weymark (1984).

6.2 THE FRAMEWORK AND ASSUMPTIONS

Let $N = \{1, \ldots, n\}$ be the set of individuals with $n \geq 2$ and let the set of alternatives be $A = \{a, b, c, \ldots, x, y, z, \ldots\}$. We assume at the outset that this set contains at least three elements. Each person $i \in N$ has a utility function $u_i : A \to \mathbb{R}$. Let $\mathcal{U}$ denote all such utility functions. An n-tuple of utility functions $u = (u_1, \ldots, u_n)$ is a *profile of utility functions*, or a profile, for short. As before, let $\mathcal{R}$ be the set of all orderings on A and $D \subseteq \mathcal{U}^n$ be the set of all admissible profiles. The *social evaluation functional* (SEF) is a mapping from D to $\mathcal{R}$, where $F(u)$ is the *social ordering* on A when the utility profile is u. We write $\succsim_u = F(u)$ with the corresponding indifference and strict preference relations $\sim_u$ and $\succ_u$, respectively. We start with the following basic properties. The first property is that all utility functions are admissible.

Definition 6.1 (Unrestricted domain)
$D = \mathcal{U}^n$.

The second property requires that if everyone is indifferent between a pair of alternatives, then society must be as well. This property prevents the imposition of the preferences of an outsider and is called Pareto indifference.

Definition 6.2 (Pareto indifference)
For all $a, b \in A$ and all $u \in D$, if $u(a) = u(b)$ (that is, $u_i(a) = u_i(b)$ for all $i \in N$), then $a \sim_u b$.

The next property requires the social ordering over any pair of alternatives to be independent of the utility information of other alternatives.

Definition 6.3 (Binary independence of irrelevant alternatives)
For all $u, u' \in D$, if for any $a, b \in A$, $u(a) = u'(a)$ and $u(b) = u'(b)$, then $\succsim_u |_{a,b} = \succsim u' |_{a,b}$, that is, $x \succsim_u y \Leftrightarrow x \succsim_{u'} y$ and $y \succsim_u x \Leftrightarrow y \succsim_{u'} x$.

The properties unrestricted domain, Pareto indifference, and binary independence of irrelevant alternatives taken together are called *welfarism* and have strong implications for F. Welfarism requires that the SEF must ignore all non-utility features of the alternatives (like names) and concentrate on the vector of utilities associated with any such alternatives. This property is known as strong neutrality (SN).

Definition 6.4 (Strong neutrality)
For all $a, b, x, y \in A$ and $u, u' \in D$, if $u(a) = u'(x)$ and $u(b) = u'(y)$, then $\succsim_u|_{a,b} = \succsim_{u'}|_{x,y}$, that is, $a \succsim_u b \Leftrightarrow x \succsim_{u'} y$ and $b \succsim_u a \Leftrightarrow y \succsim_{u'} x$.

The following proposition, given unrestricted domain, specifies Pareto indifference and binary independence of irrelevant alternatives as necessary and sufficient conditions for SN (Sen 1977a). Variants of this result were proved by Guha (1972), Blau (1976), and d'Aspremont and Gevers (1977).

Proposition 6.1 If an SEF $F : \mathcal{D} \to \mathcal{Q}$ satisfies unrestricted domain, then F satisfies Pareto indifference and binary independence of irrelevant alternatives if and only if F satisfies SN.

Proof. (i) The first step is to prove that SN implies Pareto indifference and binary independence of irrelevant alternatives. In the statement of SN, the alternatives and the utilities are not required to be distinct. Hence, by setting $x = a$ and $y = b$, it is obvious that SN imply binary independence of irrelevant alternatives. Similarly, by setting $u = u'$, $x = a$, and $y = b$, it is obvious that SN imply Pareto indifference.

(ii) The second step is to prove that Pareto indifference and binary independence of irrelevant alternatives imply SN. For this case, there are many possibilities. We only prove the result for two possibilities.

Case 1: Consider all distinct $a, b, x, y \in A$ and consider profiles $u, u' \in \mathcal{U}^n$ such that $u_i(a) = u'_i(x)$ and $u_i(b) = u'_i(y)$ for all $i \in N$. To prove SN, we have to show that $\succsim_u|_{a,b} = \succsim_{u'}|_{x,y}$. Construct a profile u'' such that $u''_i(a) = u''_i(x) = u_i(a) = u'_i(x)$ and $u''_i(b) = u''_i(y) = u_i(b) = u'_i(y)$ for all $i \in N$. By binary independence of irrelevant alternatives, $\succsim_u|_{a,b} = \succsim_{u''}|_{a,b}$ and $\succsim_{u'}|_{x,y} = \succsim_{u''}|_{x,y}$. By Pareto indifference, $a \sim_{u''} x$ so that the transitivity of $\succsim_{u''}$ implies $\succsim_{u''}|_{a,b} = \succsim_{u''}|_{x,b}$. Moreover, by Pareto indifference, $b \sim_{u''} y$ so that the transitivity of $\succsim_{u''}$ implies $\succsim_{u''}|_{x,b} = \succsim_{u''}|_{x,y}$. Hence we get $\succsim_u|_{a,b} = \succsim_{u''}|_{a,b} = \succsim_{u''}|_{x,b} = \succsim_{u''}|_{x,y} = \succsim_{u'}|_{x,y}$ implying $\succsim_u|_{a,b} = \succsim_{u'}|_{x,y}$.

Case 2: Consider the case where $a, b, y \in A$ and the profiles $u, u' \in \mathcal{U}^n$ are such that $u_i(a) = u'_i(a)$ and $u_i(b) = u'_i(y)$ for all $i \in N$. To prove SN, we have to show that $\succsim_u|_{a,b} = \succsim_{u'}|_{a,y}$. Construct a profile $\bar{u}$ such that $\bar{u}_i(a) = u_i(a) = u'_i(a)$ and $\bar{u}_i(b) = \bar{u}_i(y) = u_i(b) = u'_i(y)$ for all $i \in N$. By binary independence of irrelevant alternatives, $\succsim_u|_{a,b} = \succsim_{\bar{u}}|_{a,b}$ and $\succsim_{u'}|_{a,y} = \succsim_{\bar{u}}|_{a,y}$. By Pareto indifference, $b \sim_{\bar{u}} y$ so that the transitivity of $\succsim_{\bar{u}}$ implies $\succsim_{\bar{u}}|_{a,b} = \succsim_{\bar{u}}|_{a,y}$. Hence $\succsim_u|_{a,b} = \succsim_{u'}|_{a,y}$. □

It is particularly important to note that SN demands not only non-utility information be disregarded within a single utility profile but also across profiles. This has the rather remarkable implication that when F satisfies the welfarism axioms (that is, unrestricted domain, Pareto indifference, and binary independence of irrelevant alternatives), all of the orderings $\succsim_u$ can be represented by a single ordering $\succsim^*$ of $\mathbb{R}^n$, the space of utility n-tuple.

Proposition 6.2 If an SEF F satisfies unrestricted domain, then F satisfies Pareto indifference and binary independence of irrelevant alternatives if and only if there exists an ordering $\succsim^*$ on $\mathbb{R}^n$ such that for all $a, b \in A$ and for all profiles u, $\succsim_u|_{a,b} = \succsim^*|_{u(a),u(b)}$.

Proof. Let $\succsim^*$ be an ordering on $\mathbb{R}^n$ with $\succ^*$ being the asymmetric part of $\succsim^*$ and $\sim^*$ being the symmetric part of $\succsim^*$. Construct an SEF F as follows: For all profiles u and alternatives $a, b \in A$, $\succsim_u|_{a,b} = \succsim^*|_{u(a),u(b)}$. The transitivity of $\succsim_u$ is a direct consequence of the transitivity of $\succsim^*$. For any $a, b \in N$ and any $u \in \mathcal{U}^n$ such that $u(a) = u(b)$, we have $u(a) \sim^* u(b)$ and hence we have $a \sim_u b$ implying that $\succsim_u$ satisfies Pareto indifference. Consider any $a, b \in A$ and let $u, u' \in \mathcal{U}^n$ be such that $u(a) = u'(a)$ and $u(b) = u'(b)$. Then $\succsim_u|_{a,b} = \succsim^*|_{u(a),u(b)} = \succsim^*|_{u'(a),u'(b)} = \succsim_{u'}|_{a,b}$. Hence, we have $\succsim_u|_{a,b} = \succsim_{u'}|_{a,b}$ implying binary independence of irrelevant alternatives.

Let $F : \mathcal{U}^n \to \mathcal{Q}$ satisfy binary independence of irrelevant alternatives and Pareto indifference. We define $\succsim^*$ as follows. Consider two arbitrary points $\alpha, \beta \in \mathbb{R}^N$. By unrestricted domain, there exists a pair of alternatives $a, b \in A$ and some $u \in \mathcal{U}^n$ such that $u(a) = \alpha$ and $u(b) = \beta$. Define $\succsim^*|_{\alpha,\beta} = \succsim_u|_{a,b}$. Since F satisfies unrestricted domain, Pareto indifference, and binary independence of irrelevant alternatives, by Proposition 6.1, it also satisfies SN. This implies that the ranking of vectors α and β according to $\succsim^*$ does not depend on the alternatives a, b and profile u chosen in the construction (that is, it does not depend on the fact that u is such that $u(a) = \alpha$ and $u(b) = \beta$). Hence, $\succsim^*$ is well defined. Moreover, $\succsim^*$ is transitive because $\succsim_u$ is transitive for all $u \in \mathcal{U}^n$. □

6.3 **MEASURABILITY AND COMPARABILITY**

SN implies that all the relevant information for the social ordering of alternatives a and b is contained in the utility n-tuples $u(a)$ and

$u(b)$. Arrow further assumes that the individual preferences are ordinal and that they are non-comparable across agents. Therefore, all usable information is contained in the profile of individual preference orderings $\succsim = (\succsim_1, \ldots, \succsim_n) \in \mathcal{Q}^n$ implicit in the profile $u \in \mathcal{U}^n$.

We consider a general framework for considering alternative assumptions about the measurability and comparability of utilities. Measurability assumptions specify what transformations may be applied to an individual's utility function without altering the individually usable information. Comparability assumptions specify how much of this information may be used interpersonally. It is convenient to consider measurability and comparability conditions simultaneously. Different measurability and comparability assumptions are obtained by partitioning the domain D into information sets and requiring all utility profiles in the same information set to be mapped by the SEF F into the same ordering of A. For example, in Arrow's framework if $u, u' \in D(\subseteq \mathcal{U}^n)$ and u_i' is an increasing transform of u_i for each $i \in N$, then $F(u) = F(u')$ (they yield the same ordering of A). Formally, we suppose that D has been partitioned into a set of information sets $S = \{S_t \mid t \in T\}$, where S_t is an information set for each $t \in T$ and T indexes the elements of the partition. We require the SEF to be constant on each information set.

Definition 6.5 (Information invariance)
For all $u, u' \in D$, if $u, u' \in S_t$ for some t, then $F(u) = F(u')$.

We call a vector of increasing functions $\phi = (\phi_1, \ldots, \phi_n) : \mathbb{R}^n \to \mathbb{R}^n$ an *invariance transform* if the following holds: For any $u \in D$, if $u'(a) = \phi(u(a)) = (\phi_1(u_1(a)), \ldots, \phi_n(u_n(a)))$ for all $a \in A$, then $u, u' \in S_t$ for some $t \in T$. Thus, u and u' are informationally equivalent. Let Φ be the class of such information-preserving transformations (which is an alternative way of describing S). The idea is as follows. Divide the set of all profiles $\mathcal{U}^n$ into equivalence classes. Two profiles u, u' belong to the same equivalence class if there exists $\phi \in \Phi$ such that $u' = \phi(u)$. An SEF F is invariant with respect to Φ if $F(u) = F(u')$. In other words, two profiles in the same equivalence class have the same "information" permissible for aggregation from the viewpoint of F. Observe that the finer the partition of $\mathcal{U}^n$ into equivalence classes or partitions, the greater is the information that is being allowed for aggregation.

In the presence of the welfarism axioms (that is, unrestricted domain, Pareto indifference, and binary independence of irrelevant alternatives) and information invariance, any partition S of $\mathcal{U}^n$ will impose structure on the social welfare ordering $\succsim^*$ on $\mathbb{R}^n$.

Definition 6.6 (Information invariance for $\succsim^*$)
For all $\alpha, \beta, \alpha'', \beta'' \in \mathbb{R}^n$, if $\alpha'' = \phi(\alpha)$ and $\beta'' = \phi(\beta)$ for some $\phi \in \Phi$, then $\succsim^*|_{\alpha,\beta} = \succsim^*|_{\alpha'',\beta''}$.

Information invariance for $\succsim^*$ says that if one pair of utility n-tuples is obtained from another pair of utility n-tuples by an invariance transformation, then the social rankings of the pairs are identical. Thus, if the class of invariance transformations is shrunk, there will be fewer such pairs that must be ranked identically on informational grounds, which implies greater usable information and hence fewer restrictions imposed on the social welfare ordering. Consequently, as usable utility information is increased, the number of social welfare orderings compatible with a given list of properties will also increase.

Definition 6.7 An SEF F is *ordinally measurable and non-comparable* if Φ consists of all n-tuples of increasing functions $\phi = (\phi_1, \ldots, \phi_n)$.

In ordinal measurability and non-comparability, only ordinal information is being allowed for aggregation. This is the Arrovian case. To illustrate this, suppose we need to compare two utility profiles $u = (2,2)$ and $u' = (4,1)$ with respect to the ordering $\succsim^*$. Person 1 is better off in u' than in u, whereas person 2 is better off in u than in u'. Given that ϕ_i's can be different across persons, in this two-person economy we may choose $\phi_1(t) = t^2$ and $\phi_2(t) = 3t - 1$. Under these transformations, u and u' are transformed into $(4,5)$ and $(16,2)$ respectively. Then under ordinal measurability and non-comparability, $(2,2) \succsim^* (4,1)$ is equivalent to $(4,5) \succsim^* (16,2)$.

Definition 6.8 An SEF F is *cardinally measurable and non-comparable* if Φ consists of all n-tuples of affine functions, that is, $\phi = (\phi_1, \ldots, \phi_n) \in \Phi$ if and only if for all $i \in N$, $\phi_i(t) = k_i + l_i t$ with $l_i > 0$.

In cardinal measurability and non-comparability, we allow for independent affine transformations of utilities for individuals. In this case it is possible to make intrapersonal comparisons of utility losses or gains of the form $(u_i(x) - u_i(y))$, but cross-personal comparisons of such gains and losses are not possible. This is because the scale factor l_i and the translation factor k_i vary across persons.

Definition 6.9 An SEF F is *ordinally measurable and fully comparable* if there exists an increasing function $\phi_0 : \mathbb{R} \to \mathbb{R}$ such that an invariance transform $\phi = (\phi_1, \ldots, \phi_n) \in \Phi$ if and only if $\phi_i = \phi_0$ for all $i \in N$.

Under this informational restriction only an identical ordinal transformation can be used. Consequently, cross-person comparisons of utility levels are allowed. More precisely, we can make statements of the form $u_i \geq u_j$ if and only if $\phi_0(u_i) \geq \phi_0(u_j)$.

Definition 6.10 An SEF F is *cardinally measurable and fully comparable* if there exists an affine function $\phi_0(t) = k + lt$ with $l > 0$ such that $\phi = (\phi_1, \ldots, \phi_n) \in \Phi$ if and only if $\phi_i = \phi_0$ for all $i \in N$.

Under this informational constraint the use of a common affine transformation is permissible. It enables us to compare utility differences and utility levels across persons.

Definition 6.11 An SEF F is *cardinally measurable unit comparable* if Φ consists of all n-tuples of affine transformations in which the scale factors are assumed to be the same but the translation factors are different, that is, $\phi = (\phi_1, \ldots, \phi_n) \in \Phi$ if and only if for all $i \in N$, $\phi_i(t) = k_i + lt$ with $l > 0$.

Evidently, in this situation one can compare utility differences, but not utility levels, across persons.

We will also "consider a situation where the ability to discriminate is at least as great is possible" under ordinal measurability and full comparability of utilities. This is referred to as level-plus comparability. Let us denote the class of invariance transformations associated with the ordinally measurable fully comparable utilities by Φ_{OF}.

Definition 6.12 A class of information preserving transformations Φ satisfies the level-plus comparability assumption if $\Phi \subseteq \Phi_{OF}$.

In all the above cases we have discussed so far, the information invariance transformations place some restrictions on the social welfare ordering. If no restriction is imposed by a transformation of this type, then the only permissible transformation is the identity mapping $\phi_0(t) = t$. In this situation all utility numbers have complete numerical significance. This is the case of perfect measurability and full comparability of utilities.

6.4 ARROW'S THEOREM

One can impose other axioms on the ordering $\succsim^*$ on $\mathbb{R}^n$ to establish a version of Arrow's theorem.

Definition 6.13 (Weak Pareto)
For all $\alpha, \beta \in \mathbb{R}^n$, if $\alpha_i > \beta_i$ for all $i \in N$, then $\alpha \succ^* \beta$.

That is, of two utility profiles if everybody strictly prefers the former over the latter, then the society declares the former as socially better.

Definition 6.14 (Dictatorship)
$\succsim^*$ is a *dictatorship* if and only if there is an individual $k \in N$ such that for all $\alpha, \beta \in \mathbb{R}^n$, if $\alpha_k > \beta_k$, then $\alpha \succ^* \beta$.

Thus, under dictatorship there is someone whose strict preferences dictate the social ordering.

Theorem 6.1 Assume that the SEF F satisfies the welfarism axioms. Then the social welfare ordering $\succsim^*$ satisfies information invariance with respect to ordinally measurable, non-comparable utilities, and weak Pareto if and only if it is a dictatorship.

Proof. We first provide the proof for the two-person case. For this, refer to Figure 6.1. Fix a utility tuple $\bar{u} = (\bar{u}_1, \bar{u}_2) \in \mathbb{R}^2$. Based on $\bar{u}$ we define four open regions of $\mathbb{R}^2$ as follows:

- Region I: $R(I) = \{(u_1, u_2) \in \mathbb{R}^2 \mid u_1 > \bar{u}_1, u_2 > \bar{u}_2\}$
- Region II: $R(II) = \{(u_1, u_2) \in \mathbb{R}^2 \mid u_1 < \bar{u}_1, u_2 > \bar{u}_2\}$
- Region III: $R(III) = \{(u_1, u_2) \in \mathbb{R}^2 \mid u_1 < \bar{u}_1, u_2 < \bar{u}_2\}$
- Region IV: $R(IV) = \{(u_1, u_2) \in \mathbb{R}^2 \mid u_1 > \bar{u}_1, u_2 < \bar{u}_2\}$.

utility of person 2

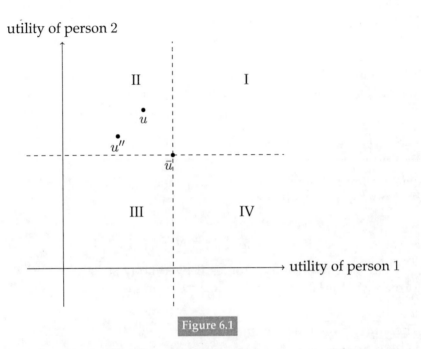

Figure 6.1

By weak Pareto it follows that all points in Region I are preferred to $\bar{u}$ and $\bar{u}$ is preferred to all points in Region III.

Next, we show that either $u \succ^* \bar{u}$ for all $u \in R(II)$ or $\bar{u} \succ^* u$ for all $u \in R(II)$. We first establish that all points in Region II must be ranked in the same way against $\bar{u}$. That is, for all $u, u'' \in R(II)$, $\succsim^*|_{u,\bar{u}} = \succsim^*|_{u'',\bar{u}}$. Consider any $u, u'' \in R(II)$ such that $u \gg u''$ (that is, $u_i > u_i''$ for all i). For each individual $i \in \{1, 2\}$, let the affine invariance transform be $\phi_i(t) = \{(\bar{u}_i - u_i'')/(\bar{u}_i - u_i)\}.t + \{(u_i'' - u_i)/(\bar{u}_i - u_i)\}.\bar{u}_i$. Observe that $\phi_i(\bar{u}_i) = \bar{u}_i$ and $\phi_i(u_i) = u_i''$ for $i \in \{1, 2\}$ implying $\phi(\bar{u}) = \bar{u}$ and $\phi(u) = u''$. By ordinal measurability and non-comparability, $\succsim^*|_{u,\bar{u}} = \succsim^*|_{\phi(u),\phi(\bar{u})} = \succsim^*|_{u'',\bar{u}}$ implying $\succsim^*|_{u,\bar{u}} = \succsim^*|_{u'',\bar{u}}$. In the construction of $u, u'' \in R(II)$, we have $u \gg u''$ and by weak Pareto this means that $u \succ^* u''$. Hence, there cannot be any $u' \in R(II)$ such that $u' \sim^* \bar{u}$ because if it were the case then $u \sim^* \bar{u}$ and $\bar{u} \sim^* u''$ and by transitivity of $\succsim^*$ we have $u \sim^* u''$, which contradicts $u \succ^* u''$. Therefore, either $u \succ^* \bar{u}$ for all $u \in R(II)$ or $\bar{u} \succ^* u$ for all $u \in R(II)$. A similar argument shows that either $u' \succ^* \bar{u}$ for all $u' \in R(IV)$ or $\bar{u} \succ^* u'$ for all $u' \in R(IV)$.

Next, we establish that the ranking of points in Region II relative to $\bar{u}$ must be opposite to that of points in Region IV, that is, (a) if $u \succ^* \bar{u}$ for all $u \in R(II)$, then $\bar{u} \succ^* u'$ for all $u' \in R(IV)$, and (b) if $\bar{u} \succ^* u$ for all $u \in R(II)$, then $u' \succ^* \bar{u}$ for all $u' \in R(IV)$. Suppose we are in case (a), that is, $u \succ^* \bar{u}$ for all $u \in R(II)$. Consider any $u \in R(II)$ and, for each $i \in \{1, 2\}$, let the affine invariance transform be $\phi_i(t) = t + (\bar{u}_i - u_i)$. Observe that $\phi_1(u_1) = \bar{u}_1$, $\phi_1(\bar{u}_1) = \bar{u}_1 + (\bar{u}_1 - u_1) := c_1 > \bar{u}_1$ and $\phi_2(u_2) = \bar{u}_2$, $\phi_1(\bar{u}_2) = \bar{u}_2 + (\bar{u}_2 - u_2) := c_2 < \bar{u}_2$. Therefore, $c = (c_1, c_2) \in R(IV)$. Observe that given $u \succ^* \bar{u}$, by ordinal measurability and non-comparability, we have $\phi(u) \succ^* \phi(\bar{u}) = \bar{u} \succ^* c$. The proof of case (b) is similar. Hence, we have established that the ranking of points in Region II relative to $\bar{u}$ must be opposite to that of points in Region IV.

Assume that $u \succ^* \bar{u}$ for all $u \in R(II)$ and $\bar{u} \succ^* u'$ for all $u' \in R(IV)$. Therefore, $u \succ^* \bar{u}$ for all $u \in R(I) \cup R(II)$ and $\bar{u} \succ^* u'$ for all $u' \in R(III) \cup R(IV)$. Consider any point $\alpha \in \{u \in \mathbb{R}^2 \mid u_1 = \bar{u}_1, u_2 > \bar{u}_2\}$. For any such α, there exists $u \in R(II)$ such that $\alpha \gg u$ implying $\alpha \succ^* u$ (by weak Pareto). Given $\alpha \succ^* u$ and given $u \succ^* \bar{u}$ (by assumption), applying transitivity of $\succsim^*$ we get $\alpha \succ^* \bar{u}$. Therefore, any point belonging to the set $\{u \in \mathbb{R}^2 \mid u_1 = \bar{u}_1, u_2 > \bar{u}_2\}$ is preferred to $\bar{u}$. Similarly, one can show that $\bar{u}$ is preferred to any point $\beta \in \{u \in \mathbb{R}^2 \mid u_1 = \bar{u}_1, u_2 < \bar{u}_2\}$. Hence, we have (A) all points in $\{u \in \mathbb{R}^2 \mid u_2 > \bar{u}_2\}$ are preferred to $\bar{u}$ and $\bar{u}$ is preferred to all points in $\{u \in \mathbb{R}^2 \mid u_2 < \bar{u}_2\}$. Similarly, assume that $u \succ^* \bar{u}$ for all $u \in R(IV)$ and $\bar{u} \succ^* u'$ for all $u' \in R(II)$. One can similarly show that (B) all points in $\{u \in \mathbb{R}^2 \mid u_1 > \bar{u}_1\}$ are preferred to $\bar{u}$ and $\bar{u}$ is preferred to all points in $\{u \in \mathbb{R}^2 \mid u_1 < \bar{u}_1\}$. We say that the *pseudo-indifference curve* through $\bar{u}$ is horizontal if possibility (A) holds and the pseudo-indifference curve is vertical if possibility (B) holds. If the pseudo-indifference curve is horizontal (respectively vertical) for some $\bar{u}$, it must be horizontal (respectively vertical) for all $\bar{u} \in \mathbb{R}^2$. If this was false, the two pseudo-indifference curves would intersect, contradicting the transitivity of $\succsim^*$. We can now complete the proof of the two-person case. If all pseudo-indifference curves are horizontal, then person 2 is the dictator; if they are vertical, then person 1 is the dictator.

The reverse implication, that is, a dictatorship satisfies the invariance requirement and weak Pareto, is easy to verify. This completes the diagrammatic graphical proof of the Arrow theorem for the two-person case.

For $n > 2$, we can prove the theorem as follows. Consider a move away from $\bar{u} \in \mathbb{R}^n$, where person k is made better off and all the rest worse off. Because of information invariance and the weak Pareto property, if this move is ranked better than $\bar{u}$, then (due to ordinal measurability and non-comparability) all moves from $\bar{u}$ where k is better off must be ranked better than $\bar{u}$. By applying arguments similar to the two-person case (with appropriate affine transformations), this rule must be the same for all $\bar{u}$ and k must be the dictator. Consequently, all such moves (that makes one person better off and others worse off) must be ranked worse than the starting point if dictatorship has to be avoided. But this is not possible if $\succsim^*$ is to be transitive. To illustrate, let $n = 3$ and $\bar{u} = (2, 2, 2)$. Then $u^1 = (3, 1, 1)$ is worse than $\bar{u}$, $u^2 = (2.5, 2.5, 0.5)$ should be worse than u^1, and $\bar{u} = (2, 2, 2)$ should be worse than u^2. Thus, we have $\bar{u} \succ^* u^1$, $u^1 \succ^* u^2$ and $u^2 \succ^* \bar{u}$ and we have a violation of transitivity. Consequently, there must be a dictator. $\square$

Observe that we did not use the full power of ordinally measurability and non-comparablity of F while proving Theorem 6.1. We only used affine transformations. Note that these affine transformations are independent since the scale and translation terms vary across persons. Thus, this result is valid even for F that satisfies cardinal measurability and non-comparability. Hence, we have the following result.

Corollary 6.1 Assume that the SEF F satisfies the welfarism axioms. Then the social welfare ordering $\succsim^*$ satisfies information invariance with respect to cardinally measurable, non-comparable utilities, and weak Pareto if and only if it is a dictatorship.

The ordering $\succsim^*$ that we have constructed in Theorem 6.1 for the two-person case is not complete. For instance, if all the pseudo-indifference curves are vertical, we know the following: for $u, u' \in \mathbb{R}^2$ such that $u_1 > u'_1$, we have $u \succ^* u'$. But we say nothing in the case $u_1 = u'_1$. In order to characterize $\succsim^*$, we need additional axioms.

Definition 6.15 *Continuity*: For all $\alpha \in \mathbb{R}^n$, the set $\{\beta \in \mathbb{R}^n \mid \beta \succsim^* \alpha\}$ is closed and the set $\{\beta \in \mathbb{R}^n \mid \alpha \succsim^* \beta\}$ is also closed.

According to continuity, minor changes in utilities do not change the nature of ordering between two utility tuples.[1]

Definition 6.16 *Strong dictatorship*: $\succsim^*$ satisfies strong dictatorship if and only if there is an individual $k \in N$ such that for all $\alpha, \beta \in \mathbb{R}^n$, if $\alpha_k \geq \beta_k$ then $\alpha \succsim^* \beta$.

That is, a person is referred to as a strong dictator if his preferences dictate the society's preferences.

Proposition 6.3 Assume that the SEF F satisfies the welfarism axioms. Then the social welfare ordering $\succsim^*$ that satisfies information invariance with respect to ordinal measurability and non-comparability of utilities, weak Pareto, and continuity is a strong dictatorship.

6.5 POSITIONAL DICTATORSHIPS

Given a vector of utilities u, let $r(u)$ be the person who is rth best off. In a *positional dictatorship*, the dictatorship power is given, not to a particular individual but to a particular position.

Definition 6.17 $\succsim^*$ is a *positional dictatorship* if and only if there exists $r, 1 \leq r \leq n$, such that for $\bar{u}, \bar{\bar{u}} \in \mathbb{R}^n$, if $\bar{u}_{r(\bar{u})} > \bar{\bar{u}}_{r(\bar{\bar{u}})}$, then $\bar{u} \succ^* \bar{\bar{u}}$.

To understand this, let $u = (3, 1, 9)$. Then $1(u) = 3$ since person 3 has the highest utility here. Likewise, $2(u) = 1$ and $3(u) = 2$. Ties can be broken arbitrarily. For instance, if $u = (3, 3, 9)$, then $2(u) = 1$ and $3(u) = 2$ or, $2(u) = 2$ and $3(u) = 1$.

---

[1] A closed set is defined in Chapter 9, n7.

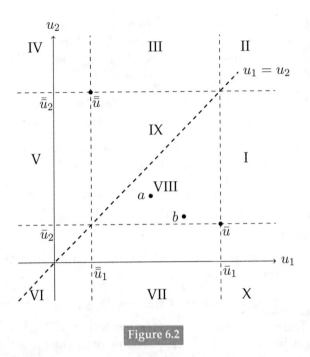

Figure 6.2

Theorem 6.2 If the SEF F satisfies the welfarism axioms, then the social welfare ordering $\succsim^*$ satisfies information invariance with ordinally measurable, fully comparable utilities, weak Pareto, and anonymity if and only if it is a positional dictatorship.

Proof. Let $\bar{u}$ be the reference point. By anonymity, $\bar{\bar{u}} = (\bar{u}_2, \bar{u}_1)$ is indifferent to $\bar{u}$. By weak Pareto, Regions I and II are preferred to $\bar{u}$ and Regions II and III are preferred to $\bar{\bar{u}}$. By transitivity, Region III is preferred to $\bar{u}$ also. Similarly, Regions V, VI, and VIII are worse than $\bar{u}$ and $\bar{\bar{u}}$ (refer to Figure 6.2).

Any u in Region VIII is distinguished by five inequalities: (i) $u_1 > u_2$, (ii) $u_1 < \bar{u}_1$, (iii) $u_2 > \bar{u}_2$, (iv) $u_1 > \bar{u}_2$, and (v) $u_2 < \bar{u}_1$. In addition, $\bar{u}_1 > \bar{u}_2$. Since only utilities can be compared, these inequalities exhaust the information. To see this in terms of invariance, compare points a and b. Since these are both in Region VIII, $\bar{u}_1 > a_1 > a_2 > \bar{u}_2$ and $\bar{u}_1 > b_1 > b_2 > \bar{u}_2$. We can find a single increasing transform mapping $\bar{u}$ into itself and a to b (see Figure 6.3). Therefore, the ranking of a against $\bar{u}$ must be the same as the ranking of b against $\bar{u}$.

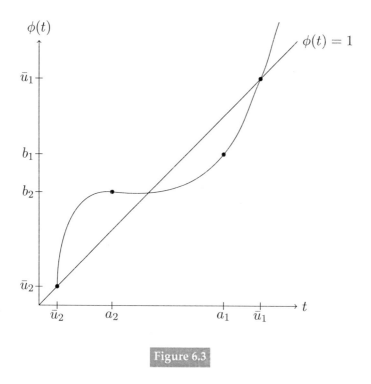

Figure 6.3

Since $\succsim^*$ is an ordering we must have (a) u $\succ^*$ $\bar{u}$, (b) $\bar{u}$ $\succ^*$ u, or (c) u $\sim^*$ $\bar{u}$. The last case is eliminated by the argument in Theorem 6.1.

By anonymity, every point in Region IX is indifferent to a point in Region VIII, and hence, by transitivity, points in this region must be ranked the same way with respect to $\bar{u}$ as points in Region VIII.

An argument similar to that of Theorem 6.1 shows that all points in Region X (and by anonymity, Region IV) are ranked identically with respect to $\bar{u}$, and in the opposite way to points in Regions VIII and IX. By weak Pareto and transitivity, if two adjacent regions have the same ranking, then so does their common boundary.

It follows that by specifying the ranking in Region VIII, the social welfare ordering must be one of the two positional dictatorships: in one, the lower rank (person 2) dictates, and in the other, the higher rank (person 1) dictates. Points on the dotted line through $\bar{u}$ can be ranked in any manner with respect to $\bar{u}$.

It may be worthwhile to note that whichever rank dictates for a reference point $\bar{u}$ must dictate for all choices of $\bar{u}$. To see this, suppose that the lower rank dictates for $\bar{u}$, but the higher rank dictates for another reference point $\hat{u}$. Then transitivity and weak Pareto cannot be consistent with this since the dotted lines through $\bar{u}$ and $\hat{u}$ cross.

To complete the proof, we note that it is easy to verify that a positional dictatorship satisfies the invariance requirement, weak Pareto, and anonymity.   □

Remark 6.1 If one adds *continuity* to the set of assumptions, then the dotted lines turn into *indifference curves*, one of which represents *maximin* and the other, *maximax*.

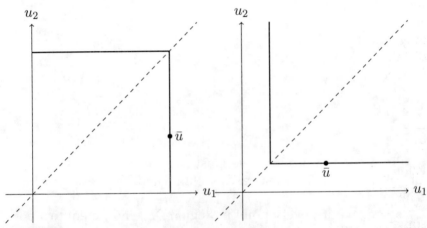

Figure 6.4   The left figure represents *maximax* preferences while the right figure corresponds to *maximin* preferences

Note that the right figure above corresponds to the preference of the lower rank and the left figure corresponds to that of the higher rank.

Remark 6.2 One might think that replacing continuity with *strong Pareto* will give *lexicographic positional dictatorships* ("leximin" and "leximax" in the right and left panels respectively of Figure 6.4). Gevers (1979) shows that this is not true for $n > 2$. The problem is that if the dictating person has the same utility in u and $\bar{u}$, then the utility level relative to those of the other individuals can be used to determine the ranking between u and $\bar{u}$, but this is disallowed in Arrow's framework.

d'Aspremont and Gevers (1977) impose a separability axiom to prevent the above possibility. The axiom says that if some individuals are indifferent between two alternatives, then the ranking of the two alternatives is independent of the utility levels that the indifferent individuals enjoy. We can then apply Theorem 6.2 sequentially to find a sequence of positional dictators who rule "lexicographically."

Remark 6.3 Dropping anonymity gives more social welfare orderings. A *rank-ordered set* is the set of all n-tuples which have the same rank ordering. If $n = 2$, then there are two rank-ordered sets: $Z_1 = \{u \in \mathbb{R}^2 | u_1 \geq u_2\}$ and $Z_2 = \{u \in \mathbb{R}^2 | u_2 \geq u_1\}$. There is now a dictator within each rank-ordered set. When $n = 2$, the only additional rules obtained by dropping anonymity are the two dictatorial rules (see Figure 6.4), but if $n > 2$, there are more rules (which includes the dictatorial rules).

6.6 LEXIMIN

While all the rules discussed so far (dictatorial, positional dictatorship) are variants of dictatorial rules, it is not clear who will be the dictator. In order to say something about this, we need something like an equity criterion. The following criterion is due to Hammond (1976) . It is defined for *two-person situations*, that is, when we have two utility vectors where all but two agents have the same utility in both vectors.

Axiom 6.1 (Hammond equity)
For all $i, j \in N$, and for all $\bar{u}, \bar{\bar{u}} \in \mathbb{R}^n$, if $\bar{u}_k = \bar{\bar{u}}_k$ for all $k \neq i, j$, and $\bar{\bar{u}}_i > \bar{u}_i > \bar{u}_j > \bar{\bar{u}}_j$, then $\bar{u} \succ^* \bar{\bar{u}}$.

To understand this, note that all but agents i and j have the same utility in $\bar{u}$ and $\bar{\bar{u}}$. Now, if $\bar{u}_i + \bar{u}_j = \bar{\bar{u}}_i + \bar{\bar{u}}_j$, then Hammond equity amounts to ordering vectors according to stochastic dominance (applied to two agents at a time). The above criterion is more general than simple stochastic dominance, though it is in the same spirit. It is straightforward to see that Hammond equity involves interpersonal comparability.

We use Hammond equity to establish a basis for the lexicographic maximin or the *leximin rule*. First, we formally define this rule.

Definition 6.18 $\succsim^*$ is the *leximin rule* if and only if for all $\bar{u}, \bar{\bar{u}} \in \mathbb{R}^n$, $\bar{u} \succ^* \bar{\bar{u}}$ if and only if there exists $k \in N$ such that $\bar{u}_{k(u)} > \bar{\bar{u}}_{k(u)}$ and $\bar{u}_{j(u)} = \bar{\bar{u}}_{j(u)}$ for all $j > k$.

This rule therefore first compares the worst-off agents in both vectors. If the worst-off agent in $\bar{u}$ has a higher utility than the worst-off agent in $\bar{\bar{u}}$, then $\bar{u}$ is superior to $\bar{\bar{u}}$. If the worst-off agent in the two vectors gets the same utility, then we move to the second worst-off agent and so on, sequentially.

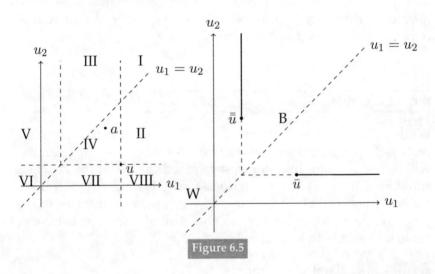

Figure 6.5

Theorem 6.3 If the SEF F satisfies the welfarism axioms, then the social welfare ordering $\succsim^*$ satisfies information invariance with level-plus comparability, Hammond equity, strong Pareto, and anonymity if and only if $\succsim^*$ is the lexicographic maximin (leximin) rule.

Proof. Refer to the left diagram in Figure 6.5, where $\bar{u}$ is the reference point. Recall that transitivity and the Pareto principle imply that if any two regions are ranked the same way with respect to $\bar{u}$, then their common boundary is also ranked the same way.

By the strong Pareto principle, Regions I and II and their boundaries are better than $\bar{u}$ while Regions VI and VII and their boundaries are worse. Now suppose a is a point in Region IV. Note that person 2 is better off compared to $\bar{u}$ while person 1 is worse off. By the Hammond equity principle, a is better than $\bar{u}$; hence, all points in Region IV are better than $\bar{u}$. Hammond equity principle also implies that $\bar{u}$ is superior to all points in Region VIII.

Anonymity implies that Region III is better than $\bar{u}$ and Region V worse. Furthermore, $\bar{\bar{u}} = (\bar{u}_2, \bar{u}_1)$ is indifferent to $\bar{u}$ and points on the dotted line below $\bar{\bar{u}}$ worse than $\bar{u}$ and points above $\bar{\bar{u}}$ better than $\bar{u}$. Putting everything together, we get the lexicographic maximin rule as illustrated in the right diagram of Figure 6.4.

It is easy to check that leximin implies the assumptions of the theorem. $\qquad\square$

6.7 UTILITARIANISM

Definition 6.19 *Generalized Utilitarianism*: $\succsim^*$ is a generalized utilitarian ordering if and only if there exists $\alpha \in \mathbb{R}^n_+, \alpha_i > 0$ for some i, such that $\bar{u} \succsim^* \bar{\bar{u}}$ if and only if $\sum_i \alpha_i \bar{u}_i \geq \sum_i \alpha_i \bar{\bar{u}}_i$, where $\mathbb{R}^n_+$ is the non-negative part of the n dimensional Euclidean space with the origin deleted.

Theorem 6.4 If the SEF F satisfies the welfarism axioms, then the social welfare ordering $\succsim^*$ satisfies information invariance with cardinally measurable, unit-comparable utilities, weak Pareto, and continuity if and only if it is a generalized utilitarian rule.

Proof. The proof of sufficiency is straightforward, so we will focus on the necessity part. In Figure 6.6, let the origin be the reference point. By weak Pareto, all points in the interior of the first quadrant are strictly superior and all points in the interior of the third

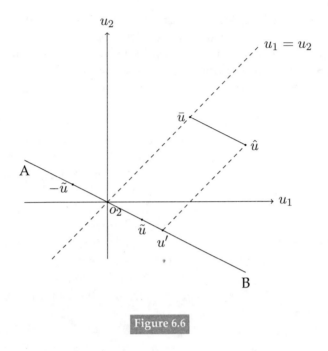

Figure 6.6

quadrant are strictly inferior to o_2. By continuity, there is a point $u' \neq o_2$ in the fourth quadrant which is indifferent to o_2.[2] By the information assumption, $\lambda u' \sim^* o_2$ for all $\lambda > 0$. This establishes that all points on $o_2 B$ are indifferent to o_2.

Next, by subtracting $\tilde{u}$ from o_2 and $\tilde{u}$ and invoking information invariance with cardinally measurable, unit-comparable utilities, we conclude that $o_2 \sim^* -\tilde{u}$ and $\tilde{u} \sim^* o_2$. By transitivity, $\tilde{u} \sim^* -\tilde{u}$, and it now follows that all points on AB are indifferent to one another. Observe that this line can be represented as $\sum_{i \in N} \alpha_i u_i = 0$.

The next step is to extend this logic for all points $\hat{u}$. Let $\bar{u} = (t, t)$ be a point on the 45° line such that $\sum_{i \in N} \alpha_i \hat{u}_i = \sum_{i \in N} \alpha_i \bar{u}_i$. Let $u' = \hat{u} - (t, t)$; also, note that $o_2 = \bar{u} - (t, t)$. Since, $u' \sim^* o_2$, information invariance implies that $\hat{u} \sim^* \bar{u}$. Applying information invariance again, we conclude that all points such that $\sum_{i \in N} \alpha_i u_i$ is a constant are indifferent to one another.

---

[2] Note that u' may be on the boundary of the fourth quadrant.

Weak Pareto requires that α_i values are non-negative for all i, with at least one of them being positive and that $\sum_{i\in N}\alpha_i u_i > \sum_{i\in N}\alpha_i u_i^*$ implies that u is preferred to u^* by the generalized utilitarian rule. □

6.8 EXERCISES

For explanations or definitions of the notation, see the main text of Chapter 6.

(E-6.1) (a) Design a non-dictatorial SEF that satisfies the postulates of unrestricted domain and independence of irrelevant alternatives, but not weak Pareto.

(b) Rigorously discuss the measurability and comparability assumptions of the underlying utility functions.

(E-6.2) In question number (E-6.1) (a), discuss the implication of anonymity on the SEF.

(E-6.3) (a) Illustrate the following notions of measurability and comparability in terms of a social welfare ordering by giving numerical examples:

(i) ordinal measurability full comparability,
(ii) cardinal measurability non-comparability,
(iii) cardinal measurability unit comparability, and
(iv) cardinal measurability full comparability.

(b) Make a systematic comparison, in terms of information restrictions, between

(i) ordinal measurability non-comparability and ordinal measurability full comparability;
(ii) cardinal measurability non-comparability and cardinal measurability unit comparability;
(iii) cardinal measurability unit comparability and cardinal measurability full comparability.

(E-6.4) Answer question number (E-6.1) (a) by replacing "non-dictatorial" by "dictatorial".

(E-6.5) Utility functions are said to be translation scale measurable and fully comparable if the information preserving transformation is of the type $\phi(t) = a + t$, where a is a scalar (see Section 6.3 for explanation of the notation). Design a SEF that satisfies the welfarism axioms, weak Pareto, non-dictatorship, and anonymity; and whose underlying utility functions are translation scale measurable fully comparable.

6.9 BIBLIOGRAPHICAL NOTES

- The welfarism theorem, a key result on SEF, was presented in Sen (1977a, 1982). See also d'Aspremont and Gevers (1977), Sen (1977b, 1982), Hammond (1979), and Roberts (1980).

- SN has been analyzed by Guha (1972), Blau (1976), d'Aspremont and Gevers (1977), and Sen (1977). Excellent discussions on welfarism and SN are available in the informative survey of d'Aspremont and Gevers (2002).

- In-depth discussions on measurability and comparability of utilities are available in Sen (1974), Sen (1977a, 1982), d'Aspremont and Gevers (1977, 2002), and Blackorby, Donaldson, and Weymark (1984).

- Corollary 6.1, which establishes the existence of a dictatorial SEF under cardinal measurability non-comparability of utilities, was demonstrated by Sen (1970). Variants of the positional dictatorship theorem were proved by Gevers (1979) and Roberts (1980).

- The leximin theorem was demonstrated by Hammond (1976). Results related to leximin can be found in Sen (1977a, 1982), Strasnick (1976a, 1976b), d'Aspremont and Gevers (1977), Deschamps and Gevers (1978), and Hammond (1979). D'Aspremont and Gevers (1977) presented a characterization of the utilitarian ordering.

- Blackorby, Bossert, and Donaldson (1995) reviewed and discussed axiomatizations of utilitarian and generalized utilitarian SEF (see also Sen 1977b; Maskin 1978).

• The problem of social evaluation under risk and uncertainty was addressed by Ben-Porath, Gilboa, and Schmeidler (1977). This issue is discussed in greater detail in Chapter 9 of this monograph.

REFERENCES

Ben-Porath, E., I. Gilboa, and D. Schmeidler. 1977. "On the Measurement of Inequality under Uncertainty." *Journal of Economic Theory* 75 (1): 194–204.

Blackorby, C., D. Donaldson, and J. A. Weymark. 1984. "Social Choice with Inter-personal Utility Comparisons: A Diagrammatic Introduction." *International Economic Review* 25 (2): 327–356.

Blackorby, C., W. Bossert, and D. Donaldson. 1995. "Intertemporal Population Ethics: Critical-Level Utilitarian Principles." *Econometrica* 65 (6): 1303–1320.

Blau, J. H. 1976. "Neutrality, Monotonicity, and the Right of Veto: A Comment." *Econometrica* 44 (3): 603.

d'Aspremont, C., and L. Gevers. 1977. "Equity and the Informational Basis of Collective Choice." *Review of Economic Studies* 44 (2): 199–209.

———. 2002. "Social Welfare Functionals and Interpersonal Comparability." In *Handbook of Social Choice and Welfare*, edited by K. Arrow, A. K. Sen, and K. Suzumura, 1:459–541. Amsterdam, The Netherlands: North-Holland.

Deschamps, R., and L. Gevers. 1978. "Leximin and Utilitarian Rules: A Joint Characterization." *Journal of Economic Theory* 17 (2): 143–163.

Gevers, L. 1979. "On Interpersonal Comparability and Social Welfare Orderings." *Econometrica* 47 (1): 75–90.

Guha, A. S. 1972. "Neutrality, Monotonicity, and the Right of Veto." *Econometrica* 40 (5): 821–826.

Hammond, P. J. 1976. "Equity, Arrow's Conditions, and Rawls' Difference Principle." *Econometrica* 44 (4): 793–804.

———. 1979. "Equity in Two-Person Situations: Some Consequences." *Econometrica* 47 (5): 1127–1135.

Maskin, E. 1978. "A Theorem on Utilitarianism." *Review of Economic Studies* 45 (1): 93–96.

Roberts, K. W. S. 1980. "Price Independent Welfare Prescriptions." *Journal of Public Economics* 13 (3): 277–297.

Sen, A. K. 1970. *Collective Choice and Social Welfare.* Amsterdam, The Netherlands: Elsevier.

———. 1974. "Informational Bases of Alternative Welfare Approaches." *Journal of Public Economics* 3 (4): 387–403.

———. 1977a. "On Weights and Measures: Informational Constraints in Social Welfare Analysis." *Econometrica* 45 (7): 1539–1572.

———. 1977b. "Social Choice Theory: A Re-examination." *Econometrica* 45 (1): 53–88.

———. 1982. *Choice, Welfare and Measurement.* Oxford: Blackwell.

———. 1986. "Information and Invariance in Normative Choice." In *Social Choice and Public Decision Making: Essays in Honor of Kenneth J. Arrow,* edited by W. P. Heller, R. Starr R, and D. A. Starrett, 1:29–55. Cambridge: Cambridge University Press.

Strasnick, S. 1976a. "Social Choice and the Derivation of Rawls' Difference Principle." *Journal of Philosophy* 73 (4): 85–99.

———. 1976b. "The Problem of Social Choice: Arrow to Rawls." *Philosophy and Public Affairs* 5 (3): 241–273.

HARSANYI'S SOCIAL AGGREGATION THEOREM

7

7.1 INTRODUCTION

In the earlier chapters, it has been assumed that social states are characterized by complete certainty in the sense that they are fully observable by the individuals under consideration. Consequently, each state may be regarded as a certain prospect. An individual can therefore order alternative social states using his preferences without any ambiguity. Thus, the decisions taken by the individuals are taken in an environment of certainty. But when states are affected by uncertainty, the decision criterion may be of a different type. To understand this, consider two farmers for whom the extent of rainfall has a very high impact on their crop outputs from their respective lands. Rainfall conditions may be subdivided into the following categories: (i) flood, (ii) optimum, (iii) hardly sufficient, (iv) less than hardly sufficient, and (v) drought. Each of these categories represents a circumstance of nature. In such a situation, each farmer maximizes his expected (von Neumann–Morgenstern) utility function. A natural question that arises in this context is the following: how are the individual utilities aggregated to arrive at a social utility? John C. Harsanyi (1955) made an excellent recommendation along this line. Harsanyi assumed at that outset that individual and social preferences fulfill the expected utility axioms and these preferences are portrayed by von Neumann–Morgenstern utility functions. The set of alternatives on which individual and social preferences are defined is constituted by the lotteries bred from a finite set of well-defined basic prospects. By including a Pareto principle within the framework, Harsanyi demonstrated that social utility function can be expressed as an affine combination of individual utility functions. In other words, given that the origin of the social utility function has been appropriately normalized, social utility comes to be a weighted sum of individual utilities. This relationship is referred to as the Harsanyi social aggregation theorem (Weymark 1991, 1994).

In Harsanyi's social aggregation theorem, individual and social preferences are defined on the set of lotteries generated from a finite set of basic prospects. These preferences are expected to satisfy expected utility hypothesis and are represented by von Neumann–Morgenstern utility functions. The only link between the individual and social preferences is the requirement that the society should be indifferent between a pair of lotteries when all individuals are indifferent between them. This consideration is called Pareto indifference. Harsanyi concluded that social utility is an affine combination of the individual utility functions, that is, social utility is a weighted sum of individual utilities. This affine relationship between the individual and social utility functions is Harsanyi's aggregation theorem.

7.2 THE MODEL

Let $X = \{x_0, x_1, \ldots, x_m\}$ be the set of certain prospects, where $m \geq 1$. A lottery $p = (p_0, p_1, \ldots, p_m)$ offers each sure prospect x_i with probability $Pr(x_i) = p_i$ for each $i = 0, 1, \ldots, m$. For any two vectors (lotteries) p, q, (i) $p \geq q$ means $p_i \geq q_i$ for all i, (ii) $p > q$ means $p_i \geq q_i$ for all i and $p_k > q_k$ for some k, and (iii) $p >> q$ means $p_i > q_i$ for all i. O_m is the m-coordinated vector of zeros, I_k is the k-dimensional identity matrix, that is, the $k \times k$ matrix each of whose diagonal entries is 1 and off-diagonal entries is 0. The set of all lotteries is denoted by

$$\mathcal{L} = \left\{ p \in \mathbb{R}^{m+1} \mid p_i \geq 0, \forall i \text{ and } \sum_{k=0}^{m} p_k = 1 \right\}. \quad (7.1)$$

Here $\mathbb{R}^{m+1}$ represents the $(m+1)$-dimensional Euclidean space. We use the terms "lottery," "prospect," and "alternative" synonymously. Consequently, it is not necessary to treat sure prospects separately from lotteries as the certain alternative x_i is equivalent to the lottery $e^i = (e_0^i, e_1^i, \ldots, e_m^i)$, where $e_j^i = 1$ if $i = j$ and $e_j^i = 0$ if $i \neq j$. In other words, X is equivalent to the lottery set $\{e^0, e^1, \ldots, e^m\}$, where e^i offers x_i as the prize with certainty. When $m = 2$, the set $\mathcal{L}$ is a simplex with vertices given by $\{e^0, e^1, e^2\}$. For $p \in \mathcal{L}$, let $\tilde{p} = (p_1, \ldots, p_m)'$. Evidently, p is also uniquely determined by $\tilde{p}$.

We consider a society of n individuals where n is finite. A ranking of the lotteries in $\mathcal{L}$ for any person j is given by a weak preference relation "at least as good as" $\succsim_j$, and $\succ_j$ and $\sim_j$ are respectively the strict and indifference parts of $\succsim_j$. Formally, for all $p, q \in \mathcal{L}$ (a) $p \succ_j q$, if and only if $p \succsim_j q$ and not $q \succsim_j p$, and (b) $p \sim_j q$, if and only if $p \succsim_j q$ and $q \succsim_j p$.

Remark 7.1 *Consequentialist premise*: Suppose we fix the set of certain alternatives $X = \{x_0, x_1, \ldots, x_m\}$. Given T lotteries $L_t = (p_0^t, p_1^t \ldots, p_m^t) \in \mathcal{L}$, $t = 1, \ldots, T$ and associated probabilities $Pr(L_t) = \alpha_t \geq 0$ with the property that $\sum_{t=1}^{T} \alpha_t = 1$, a *compound lottery* $(L_1, \ldots, L_t; \alpha_1, \ldots, \alpha_T)$ is the risky alternative that yields the lottery L_t with probability α_t for $t = 1, \ldots, T$. For example, let $X = \{x_0, x_1, x_2\}$ and let $L_1 = (p_0^1 = \frac{1}{3}, p_1^1 = \frac{1}{2}, p_2^1 = \frac{1}{6})$ and $L_2 = (p_0^2 = \frac{1}{4}, p_1^2 = \frac{1}{4}, p_2^2 = \frac{1}{2})$, where $p_i^t = Pr(x_i \mid L_t)$ for all $i = 0, 1, \ldots, m$ and all $t = 1, \ldots, T$. Suppose the compound lottery is $(L_1, L_2; \alpha_1, \alpha_2)$ with $\alpha_1 = \frac{1}{10}$ and $\alpha_2 = \frac{9}{10}$. From this compound lottery, we can calculate the reduced lottery $p = (p_0, p_1, p_2)$, where $p_0 = Pr(L_1).Pr(x_0 \mid L_1) + Pr(L_2).Pr(x_0 \mid L_2) = \alpha_1 p_0^1 + \alpha_2 p_0^2 = 31/120$, $p_1 = Pr(L_1).Pr(x_1 \mid L_1) + Pr(L_2).Pr(x_1 \mid L_2) = \alpha_1 p_1^1 + \alpha_2 p_1^2 = 33/120$, and $p_2 = Pr(L_1).Pr(x_2 \mid L_1) + Pr(L_2).Pr(x_2 \mid L_2) = \alpha_1 p_2^1 + \alpha_2 p_2^2 = 56/120$. Thus, for the compound lottery $(L_1, L_2; \alpha_1, \alpha_2)$, we have calculated the corresponding *reduced lottery* $p = (p_0 = 31/120, p_1 = 33/120, p_2 = 56/120)$ that generates the same distribution over the alternatives $X = \{x_0, x_1, x_2\}$. In general, for any compound lottery $(L_1, \ldots, L_T; \alpha_1, \ldots, \alpha_T)$, we can calculate the corresponding *reduced lottery* $p = (p_0, p_1, \ldots, p_m)$ that generates the same ultimate distribution over the alternatives X, where for each alternative x_i, $p_i = \sum_{t=1}^{T} Pr(L_t).Pr(x_i \mid L_t) = \sum_{t=1}^{T} \alpha_t p_i^t$ and hence $p = \sum_{t=1}^{T} \alpha_t L_t$. We can have two or more compound lotteries leading to the same reduced lottery. For example, consider $X = \{x_0, x_1, x_2\}$ and two compound lotteries $(L_1, L_2, L_3; \alpha_1, \alpha_2, \alpha_3)$ and $(L_1', L_2'; \alpha_1', \alpha_2')$, where $L_1 = (1, 0, 0)$, $L_2 = (0, 1, 0)$, $L_3 = (0, 0, 1)$, $L_1' = (\frac{1}{2}, \frac{1}{2}, 0)$, $L_2' = (\frac{1}{2}, 0, \frac{1}{2})$, and $\alpha_1 = \frac{1}{2}$, $\alpha_2 = \alpha_3 = \frac{1}{4}$, $\alpha_1' = \alpha_2' = \frac{1}{2}$. Observe that $(\frac{1}{2}, \frac{1}{4}, \frac{1}{4}) = \sum_{t=1}^{3} \alpha_t L_t = \sum_{t=1}^{2} \alpha_t' L_t'$. The theoretical analysis to follow rests on a basic *consequentialist premise that states that for any risky alternative, only reduced lottery over a final set of alternatives X is of relevance to each individual.* Hence, based on this premise, we can limit our attention to the set of all lotteries $\mathcal{L}$.

The following axioms are known as the expected utility axioms in the literature: (i) $\succsim_j$ is an ordering, that is, $\succsim_j$ is reflexive, complete, and transitive, (ii) $\succsim_j$ is continuous, that is, for any $L, L', L'' \in \mathcal{L}$, the sets $\{\alpha \in [0, 1] \mid \alpha L + (1 - \alpha) L' \succsim_j L''\} \subset [0, 1]$ and $\{\alpha \in [0, 1] \mid L'' \succsim_j \alpha L + (1 - \alpha) L'\} \subset [0, 1]$ are closed, and (iii) $\succsim_j$ satisfies independence, that is, for all $L, L', L'' \in \mathcal{L}$ and $\alpha \in (0, 1)$, we have $L \succsim_j L'$ if and only if $\alpha L + (1 - \alpha) L'' \succsim_j \alpha L' + (1 - \alpha) L''$. According to independence, among three lotteries L, L', and L^*, if L is preferred to L', then a mixture of L and L^* is also preferred to the same mixture of L' and L^*. Continuity implies that if a mixture $\alpha L + (1 - \alpha) L'$, $0 \leq \alpha \leq 1$, of two lotteries L and L', which is again a lottery, is strictly preferred to another lottery L'', then for any other lottery L''' close to the mixture, L''' is also strictly preferred to L''. A utility function U_j defined on $\mathcal{L}$ represents $\succsim_j$ if for all $p, q \in \mathcal{L}$, $U_j(p) \geq U_j(q)$ if and only if $p \succsim_j q$. Whether U_j represents $\succsim_j$ or not depends solely on the ordering properties of U_j.

A von Neumann–Morgenstern utility function is a function V_j defined on $\mathcal{L}$ with the property that for any $p \in \mathcal{L}$,

$$V_j(p) = \sum_{i=0}^{m} p_i V_j(e^i). \tag{7.2}$$

In $V_j(p)$, $V_j(e^i)$ is the utility number assigned to receiving x_i with certainty. As a result, with a von Neumann–Morgenstern utility function, the utility assigned to a lottery becomes the lottery's expected utility. The function V_j is linear in p.

Suppose that V_j represents $\succsim_j$, that is, $V_j(p) \geq V_j(q)$ if and only if $p \succsim_j q$. Now let

$$V_j'(p) = \alpha_j + \beta_j V_j(p), \ \beta_j > 0. \tag{7.3}$$

V_j' is an affine transformation of V_j. Since V_j' is an increasing transformation of V_j, V_j' is also a utility function representing the same preference $\succsim_j$. Now, $\alpha_j + \beta_j V_j(p) = \sum_{i=0}^{m} p_i[\alpha_j + \beta_j V_j(e^i)]$, which is equivalent to $V_j'(p) = \sum_{i=0}^{m} p_i V_j'(p)$. Thus, V_j' is also a von Neumann–Morgenstern utility function. In fact, we have the expected utility theorem that states the following.

Theorem 7.1 If the preference relation $\succsim_j$ on the set of lotteries $\mathcal{L}$ satisfies the expected utility axioms, then there exists a von Neumann–Morgenstern utility function V_j representing $\succsim_j$. Furthermore, V_j' is also a von Neumann–Morgenstern utility function representing the same $\succsim_j$, if and only if V_j' is an affine transformation of V_j.

As an example, let $X = \{x_0, x_1, x_2\}$ and let $e^2 \succ_j e^0$, $e^0 \succ_j e^1$, and $e^0 \sim_j (0, 2/3, 1/3)$, that is, x^2 is preferred to x_0, x_0 is preferred to x_1, and x_0 is indifferent to a lottery that yields x_1 with probability $2/3$ and x_2 with probability $1/3$. For this preference $\succsim_j$, we illustrate the associated utility function by setting $V_j(p) = 35p_0 + 30p_1 + 45p_2$ for all $p \in \mathcal{L}$. This is a von Neumann–Morgenstern utility function representing $\succsim_j$. In this case, we have $V_j(e^0) = 35$, $V_j(e^1) = 30$, and $V_j(e^2) = 45$. These numbers cannot be found independently. For example, as before, fix the values assigned to e^1 and e^2 at 35 and 30 respectively. Because $e^0 \sim_j (0, 2/3, 1/3)$, we have $V_j(e^0) = V_j(0, 2/3, 1/3)$ or $V_j(e^0) = (2/3)V_j(e^1) + (1/3)V_j(e^2) = (2/3).30 + (1/3).45 = 35$. All other von Neumann–Morgenstern utility functions representing $\succsim_j$ are obtained using (7.3). For instance, by setting $\alpha_j = -10$ and $\beta_j = 2$, it follows that $V_j'(p) = 60p_0 + 50p_1 + 80p_2$ is also a von Neumann–Morgenstern utility representation of $\succsim_j$.

Each person is assumed to have a von Neumann–Morgenstern utility function V_j, $j = 1, \ldots, n$, on $\mathcal{L}$, that is, a utility function V_j that satisfies

$$V_j(p) = \sum_{i=0}^{m} p_i V_j(e_i) \tag{7.4}$$

for all $p \in \mathcal{L}$. Society is also assumed to have a von Neumann–Morgenstern utility function V on $\mathcal{L}$ that satisfies

$$V(p) = \sum_{i=0}^{m} p_i V(e_i) \tag{7.5}$$

for all $p \in \mathcal{L}$.

According to Harsanyi's aggregation equation, the social utility function is an affine combination of individual utility functions. Analytically, Harsanyi's aggregation equation says that there exists $\lambda = (\lambda_1, \ldots, \lambda_n) \in \mathbb{R}^n$ and $\mu \in \mathbb{R}$ such that for all $p \in \mathcal{L}$,

$$V(p) = \sum_{j=1}^{n} \lambda_j V_j(p) + \mu. \tag{7.6}$$

The different versions of the Harsanyi's aggregation theorem specify that the individual and social utility functions are related by a Pareto principle. Let us consider three alternative Pareto Principles.

- *Pareto Indifference*: For all $p, q \in \mathcal{L}$, if $V_j(p) = V_j(q)$ for all $j = 1, \ldots, n$, then $V(p) = V(q)$.

- *Semistrong Pareto*: For all $p, q \in \mathcal{L}$, if $V_j(p) \geq V_j(q)$ for all $j = 1, \ldots, n$, then $V(p) \geq V(q)$.

- *Strong Pareto*: For all $p, q \in \mathcal{L}$, if $V_j(p) \geq V_j(q)$ for all $j = 1, \ldots, n$, then $V(p) \geq V(q)$ and if, furthermore, there exists an individual k such that $V_k(p) > V_k(q)$, then $V(p) > V(q)$.

Pareto indifference argues that society is indifferent between a pair of lotteries whenever everyone in society is so. Likewise, semistrong Pareto demands society to weakly prefer one lottery to another if everyone weakly prefers the former lottery to the latter. Strong

Pareto buttresses semistrong Pareto by further requiring society to strictly prefer one lottery to a second if everyone weakly prefers the first to the second and at least one person strictly prefers the former to the latter. Clearly, Pareto indifference is implied by semistrong Pareto, which in turn is implied by strong Pareto.

7.2.1 *Harsanyi's social aggregation with Pareto indifference*

According to the original version of Harsanyi's social aggregation theorem, if Pareto indifference is satisfied, then the social utility function V must be an affine combination of individual utility functions.

Theorem 7.2 Suppose, V_j, $j = 1, \ldots, n$ and V are von Neumann–Morgenstern utility functions on $\mathcal{L}$. If Pareto indifference is satisfied, then there exists $\lambda = (\lambda_1, \ldots, \lambda_n)' \in \mathbb{R}^n$ and $\mu \in \mathbb{R}$ such that (7.6) is satisfied for all $p \in \mathcal{L}$.

Remark 7.2 Statement of Theorem 7.2 is a rephrasing of Harsanyi's theorem (see Harsanyi 1955) by Fishburn (1984). The proof for Theorem 7.2, which we present below following Weymark (1994), is a minor modification of the proof of Border (1981). For alternative proofs, see Domotor (1979), Fishburn (1984), Border (1985), Coulhan and Mongin (1989), and Hammond (1992).

Proof of Theorem 7.2: For all $p \in \mathcal{L}$, define $\bar{V}_j(p) := V_j(p) - V_j(e_0)$ for $j = 1, \ldots, n$ and $\bar{V}(p) = V(p) - V(e_0)$, where $V(e_0)$ is the value of V in (7.5) when x_0 is chosen with probability 1. Note that

$$\bar{V}_j(e_0) = \bar{V}(e_0) = 0 \ \forall \, j = 1, \ldots, n. \tag{7.7}$$

To establish (7.6), it is sufficient to show the existence of a $\lambda \in \mathbb{R}^n$ such that for all $p \in \mathcal{L}$,

$$\bar{V}(p) = \sum_{j=1}^{n} \lambda_j \bar{V}_j(p). \tag{7.8}$$

Specifically, $\bar{V}(p) = \sum_{j=1}^{n} \lambda_j \bar{V}_j(p)$ means $V(p) - V(e_0) = \sum_{j=1}^{n} \lambda_j(V_j(p) - V_j(e_0))$, or, equivalently, $V(p) = \sum_{j=1}^{n} \lambda_j V_j(p) + V(e_0) - \sum_{j=1}^{n} \lambda_j V_j(e_0)$, or, equivalently, $V(p) = \sum_{j=1}^{n} \lambda_j V_j(p) + \mu$, where $\mu := V(e_0) - \sum_{j=1}^{n} \lambda_j V_j(e_0)$. Consequently, (λ, μ) will solve (7.6) with $\mu := V(e_0) - \sum_{j=1}^{n} \lambda_j V_j(e_0)$. Let $\bar{v}_j = [\bar{V}_j(e_1), \ldots, \bar{V}_j(e_m)]'$ for $j = 1, \ldots, n$ and $\bar{v} = [\bar{V}(e_1), \ldots, \bar{V}(e_m)]'$. It then follows from (7.4), (7.5), and (7.7) that

$$\bar{V}_j(p) = \tilde{p}'\bar{v}_j \ \forall \ j = 1, \ldots, n, \text{ and } \bar{V}(p) = \tilde{p}'\bar{v}, \qquad (7.9)$$

where $\tilde{p}'$ denotes the transpose of $\tilde{p}$. Specifically, note that for any $j = 1, \ldots, n$,

$$\tilde{p}'\bar{v}_j = \sum_{i=1}^{m} p_i(V_j(e_i) - V_j(e_0))$$

$$= \sum_{i=1}^{m} p_i V_j(e_i) - \sum_{i=1}^{m} p_i V_j(e_0)$$

$$= \sum_{i=0}^{m} p_i V_j(e_i) - p_0 V_j(e_0) - \sum_{i=1}^{m} p_i V_j(e_0)$$

$$= V_j(p) - \left\{ p_0 + \sum_{i=1}^{m} p_i \right\} V_j(e_0)$$

$$= V_j(p) - V_j(e_0)$$

$$= \bar{V}_j(p).$$

Similarly, one can also show that $\bar{V}(p) = \tilde{p}'\bar{v}$. Because of the linearity of von Neumann–Morgenstern utilitiy functions in probabilities, to establish (7.8) it is sufficient to demonstrate that there exists $\lambda \in \mathbb{R}^n$ such that

$$\bar{v} = \sum_{j=1}^{n} \lambda_j \bar{v}_j. \qquad (7.10)$$

That is,

$$\begin{pmatrix} \bar{V}(e_1) \\ \vdots \\ \bar{V}(e_m) \end{pmatrix} = \lambda_1 \begin{pmatrix} \bar{V}_1(e_1) \\ \vdots \\ \bar{V}_1(e_m) \end{pmatrix} + \lambda_2 \begin{pmatrix} \bar{V}_2(e_1) \\ \vdots \\ \bar{V}_2(e_m) \end{pmatrix} + \ldots + \lambda_n \begin{pmatrix} \bar{V}_n(e_1) \\ \vdots \\ \bar{V}_n(e_m) \end{pmatrix}.$$

$$(7.11)$$

Note that for any $i = 1, \ldots, m$, $\bar{V}(e_i) = \sum_{j=1}^{n} \lambda_j \bar{V}_j(e_i)$ means that x_i is chosen with probability 1 by all persons $j = 1, \ldots, n$. Consider the following matrix:

$$A = \begin{bmatrix} \bar{V}_1(e_1) & \bar{V}_2(e_1) & \dots & \bar{V}_n(e_1) \\ \vdots & \vdots & \dots & \vdots \\ \bar{V}_1(e_m) & \bar{V}_2(e_m) & \dots & \bar{V}_n(e_m) \end{bmatrix}.$$

Therefore, A is an $m \times n$ matrix whose j-th column is $\bar{v}_j$. Consider the system of equations

$$[y_1', y_2']_{1 \times 2m} \cdot \begin{bmatrix} A \\ -A \end{bmatrix}_{2m \times n} = O_n', \tag{7.12}$$

and

$$[y_1', y_2']_{1 \times 2m} \cdot \begin{bmatrix} \bar{v} \\ -\bar{v} \end{bmatrix}_{2m \times 1} = 1, \tag{7.13}$$

where $y_1, y_2 \in \mathbb{R}^m$. We first show that Pareto indifference is satisfied if and only if there is no non-negative solution to (7.12) and (7.13). Assume first that (y_1', y_2') is a non-negative solution to (7.12) and (7.13). By choosing $c > 0$ and sufficiently large, we get $\sum_{i=1}^m y_{1i} \leq c$ and $\sum_{i=1}^m y_{2i} \leq c$. Letting $\tilde{p} = (y_{11}/c, y_{12}/c, \dots, y_{1m}/c)$ and $\tilde{q} = (y_{21}/c, y_{22}/c, \dots, y_{2m}/c)$, the corresponding vectors p and q are included in $\mathcal{L}$. It follows from (7.12), that $\tilde{p}'\bar{v}_j = \tilde{q}'\bar{v}_j$ for all $j = 1, \dots, n$, or, equivalently, $\bar{V}_j(p) = \bar{V}_j(q)$ for all $j = 1, \dots, n$. From (7.13) it follows that $y_1'\bar{v} = y_2'\bar{v} + 1$ from which it follows that $(1/c)y_1'\bar{v} = (1/c)y_2'\bar{v} + (1/c)$, or, $p'\bar{v} = q'\bar{v} + (1/c)$, which implies that $\bar{V}(p) > \bar{V}(q)$ and we have a violation of Pareto indifference. Conversely, suppose that Pareto indifference is violated, that is, there exists $p, q \in \mathcal{L}$ such that $\bar{V}_j(p) = \bar{V}_j(q)$ for all $j = 1, \dots, n$ and $\bar{V}(p) > \bar{V}(q)$. Let $d := \bar{V}(p) - \bar{V}(q) > 0$. But then $y_1 = (p_1/d, \dots, p_m/d)'$ and $y_2 = (q_1/d, \dots, q_m/d)'$ is a non-negative solution to (7.12) and (7.13).

By assumption Pareto indifference is satisfied and hence there is no non-negative solution to (7.12) and (7.13). By a theorem of alternatives due to Gale (1960) (Gale's Theorem 7.1)[1] there exists

---

[1] For a formal statement, see Appendix.

a solution λ (which is an $n \times 1$ column vector) to

$$\begin{bmatrix} A \\ -A \end{bmatrix} \lambda \geq \begin{bmatrix} \bar{v} \\ -\bar{v} \end{bmatrix}. \tag{7.14}$$

The inequality in (7.14) can be rewritten as $A\lambda \geq \bar{v}$ and $A\lambda \leq \bar{v}$, or, equivalently, $A\lambda = \bar{v}$. The latter equation is simply (7.11) and we are done. $\qquad\square$

Harsanyi's proof of Theorem 7.2 (see Harsanyi 1955) employs an assumption that is not included in the assumption of the theorem. It follows from the proof of Theorem 7.2 that this additional assumption is not required for Harsanyi's result. However, Harsanyi's extra assumption implies that the coefficients in the aggregation equation (7.6) are unique. Let us call Harsanyi's implicit axiom "Independent Prospects." Formally, *Independent Prospects* requires that for each $j = 1, \ldots, n$, there exists $p^j, q^j \in \mathcal{L}$ such that $V_k(p^j) = V_k(q^j)$ for all $k \neq j$ and $V_j(p^j) \neq V_j(q^j)$. Independent Prospects represents preference diversity. It claims that we can vary any individual's utility without affecting the utility of any other individual. Equivalently, for each individual it is necessary to get a pair of lotteries for which that individual is not indifferent and for which everyone else is indifferent. Obviously, this assumption rules out the constancy of utility functions. With von Neumann–Morgenstern utility functions, this assumption can only be fulfilled if the number of individuals is less than the number of sure prospects.

For von Neumann–Morgenstern utility functions on the set of lotteries $\mathcal{L}$, Independent Prospects is equivalent to the requirement that the individual utility functions are affinely independent. The utility functions $(V_j)_{j=1}^{n}$ are *affinely independent* if and only if the solution $(\lambda', \mu)'$ to

$$\sum_{j=1}^{n} \lambda_j V_j(p) + \mu = 0 \tag{7.15}$$

for all p is $\lambda_1 = \ldots = \lambda_n = \mu = 0$.

Lemma 7.1   Suppose V_j, $j = 1, \ldots, n$ are von Neumann–Morgenstern utility functions on $\mathcal{L}$. Then Independent Prospects is verified if and only if the utility functions are affinely independent.

Proof. First, assume that utility functions are affinely dependent. This implies that there exists a solution to (7.15) with $\lambda_k \neq 0$ for some k. Without loss of generality, let $\lambda_k = -1$. Solving (7.15) gives

$$V_k(p) = \sum_{j \neq k} \lambda_j V_j(p) + \mu \tag{7.16}$$

for all $p \in \mathcal{L}$. For any $p, q \in \mathcal{L}$ for which $V_j(p) = V_j(q)$ for all $j \neq k$, we get from (7.16) that $V_k(p) = V_k(q)$. Thus, it is not possible to have Independent Prospects (since Independent Prospects requires the existence of $p, q \in \mathcal{L}$ for which $V_j(p) = V_j(q)$ for all $j \neq k$ and $V_k(p) \neq V_k(q)$).

Second, assume that Independent Prospects is violated. This means that there exists an individual k such that for all $p, q \in \mathcal{L}$, if $V_j(p) = V_j(q)$ for all $j \neq k$, then $V_k(p) = V_k(q)$. This condition is a rephrasing of Pareto indifference with V_k as the social utility function and V_j for all $j \neq k$ as the individual utility functions. It then follows from Theorem 7.2 that there exists λ_j, for all $j \neq k$ and μ such that condition (7.16) holds for all $p \in \mathcal{L}$. Hence, (7.15) has a solution with $\lambda_k = -1$. In words, the utility functions are affinely dependent. $\square$

Theorem 7.2 does not say that the solution $(\lambda', \mu)'$ to (7.6) is unique. Inclusion of Independent Prospects to the assumptions of Theorem 7.2 is equivalent to assuming that (7.6) has a unique solution.

Corollary 7.1 Suppose that the assumptions of Theorem 7.2 are satisfied. Then there exists a unique solution $(\lambda', \mu)'$ to (7.6) if and only if Independent Prospects is satisfied.

Proof. First, assume that Independent Prospects is violated, which means that the utility functions are affinely dependent. That is, there exists an individual k such that (7.16) possesses a solution. By Theorem 7.2, there exists a vector $(\alpha', \beta)'$ such that for all $p \in \mathcal{L}$,

$$V(p) = \sum_{j=1}^{n} \alpha_j V_j(p) + \beta. \tag{7.17}$$

Substituting (7.16) into (7.17) yields

$$V(p) = \sum_{j=1}^{n} \theta_j V_j(p) + \delta \qquad (7.18)$$

for all $p \in \mathcal{L}$, where $\theta_k = 0$, $\theta_j = \alpha_j + \alpha_k \lambda_j$ for all $j \neq k$, and $\delta = \beta + \alpha_k \mu$.[2] Multiplying both sides of (7.16) by ρ and then substituting it in (7.18) yields

$$V(p) = \sum_{j \neq k} [(\theta_j - \rho \lambda_j) V_j(p)] + \rho V_k(p) + \delta - \rho \mu \qquad (7.19)$$

for all $p \in \mathcal{L}$.[3] By varying ρ, it is possible to obtain a one-parameter family of solutions to (7.6).

Next, suppose Independent Prospects is satisfied. Hence, for each j, there exists $p^j, q^j \in \mathcal{L}$ such that $V_j(p^j) \neq V_j(q^j)$ and $V_k(p^j) = V_k(q^j)$ for all $k \neq j$. Using p^j and q^j in (7.6) implies

$$V(p^j) - V(q^j) = \lambda_j [V_j(p^j) - V_j(q^j)]. \qquad (7.20)$$

Since $V_j(p^j) \neq V_j(q^j)$, (7.20) implies uniqueness of λ_j. Since the selection of j was arbitrary, it follows that λ_j is unique for all $j = 1, \ldots, n$. By uniqueness of the vector λ in (7.6), μ must be unique as well. □

---

[2] Specifically,

$$V(p) = \sum_{j=1}^{n} \alpha_j V_j(p) + \beta,$$

or, $V(p) = \sum_{j \neq k} \alpha_j V_j(p) + \alpha_k V_k(p) + \beta,$

or, $V(p) = \sum_{j \neq k} \alpha_j V_j(p) + \alpha_k \left\{ \sum_{j \neq k} \lambda_j V_j(p) + \mu \right\} + \beta,$

or, $V(p) = \sum_{j \neq k} \{\alpha_j + \alpha_k \lambda_j\} V_j(p) + \alpha_k \mu + \beta,$

or, $V(p) = \sum_{j \neq k} \theta_j V_j(p) + \delta.$

[3] From (7.16), it follows that $\rho V_k(p) - \rho \sum_{j \neq k} \lambda_j V_j(p) - \rho \mu = 0$. Therefore, $V(p) = \sum_{j=1}^{n} \theta_j V_j(p) + \delta$ gives

$$V(p) = \sum_{j=1}^{n} \theta_j V_j(p) + \delta + \rho V_k(p) - \rho \sum_{j \neq k} \lambda_j V_j(p) - \rho \mu$$

or, $V(p) = \sum_{j \neq k} (\theta_j - \rho \lambda_j) V_j(p) + \theta_k V_k(p) + \rho V_k(p) + \delta - \rho \mu$

or, $V(p) = \sum_{j \neq k} (\theta_j - \rho \lambda_j) V_j(p) + \rho V_k(p) + \delta - \rho \mu$ (since $\theta_k = 0$).

7.2.2 *Harsanyi's social aggregation with semistrong Pareto*

As we have noted, Theorem 7.2 does not impose any restrictions on the signs of the weights $\lambda_j, j = 1, \ldots, n$. Replacement of Pareto indifference by semistrong Pareto implies that (7.6) has a solution with non-negative λ.

Theorem 7.3 Suppose $V_j, \ j = 1, \ldots, n$ and V are von Neumann–Morgenstern utility functions on $\mathcal{L}$. If semistrong Pareto is satisfied, then there exists $\lambda \geq 0_n$ and μ such that (7.6) is satisfied for all $p \in \mathcal{L}$. Furthermore, the vector $(\lambda', \mu)'$, which solves (7.6), is unique if and only if Independent Prospects is satisfied.

Proof. By the argument put forward in the proof of Theorem 7.2, it is sufficient to establish that there exists a vector $\lambda \geq 0_n$ which solves (7.10). Let A be the matrix defined below (7.11), that is,

$$A = \begin{bmatrix} \bar{V}_1(e_1) & \bar{V}_2(e_1) & \ldots & \bar{V}_n(e_1) \\ \vdots & \vdots & \ldots & \vdots \\ \bar{V}_1(e_m) & \bar{V}_2(e_m) & \ldots & \bar{V}_n(e_m) \end{bmatrix}.$$

Therefore, A is an $m \times n$ matrix whose j-th column is $\bar{v}_j$. Consider the system of inequalities

$$[y_1', y_2']_{1 \times 2m} \cdot \begin{bmatrix} A \\ -A \end{bmatrix}_{2m \times n} \geq O_n', \tag{7.21}$$

and

$$[y_1', y_2']_{1 \times 2m} \cdot \begin{bmatrix} -\bar{v} \\ \bar{v} \end{bmatrix}_{2m \times 1} \geq 1, \tag{7.22}$$

where $y_1, y_2 \in \mathbb{R}^m$. We now demonstrate that semistrong Pareto holds if and only if there is no non-negative solution to (7.21) and (7.22).

First, suppose $(y_1', y_2')'$ is a non-negative solution to (7.21) and (7.22). By defining $\tilde{p}$ and $\tilde{q}$ as in the proof of Theorem 7.2, it follows from (7.21) that $\bar{V}_j(p) \geq \bar{V}_j(q)$ for all $j = 1, \ldots, n$. From (7.22) we have $\tilde{q}'\bar{v} \geq \tilde{p}'\bar{v} + 1/c$ which implies $\bar{V}(q) > \bar{V}(p)$ and we have a violation of semistrong Pareto. Next, suppose that semistrong Pareto is violated, that is, there exists $p, q \in \mathcal{L}$ satisfying $\bar{V}_j(p) \geq$

$\bar{V}_j(q)$ and $\bar{V}(q) > \bar{V}(p)$. Now, define $d = \bar{V}(q) - \bar{V}(p) > 0$. It then follows that $y_1 = (p_1/d, \ldots, p_m/d)'$ and $y_2 = (q_1/d, \ldots, q_m/d)'$ is a non-negative solution to (7.21) and (7.22). By assumption semistrong Pareto holds, so there is no non-negative solution to (7.21) and (7.22). Equivalently, there is no non-negative solution to

$$[y_1', y_2']_{1 \times 2m} \begin{bmatrix} -A & \bar{v} \\ A & -\bar{v} \end{bmatrix}_{2m \times (n+1)} \leq [O_n', -1]. \tag{7.23}$$

By another theorem of alternatives due to Gale (see Gale [1960]; Gale's Theorem 7.2), there exists a non-negative solution y, with $(n + 1)$ coordinates to

$$\begin{bmatrix} -A & \bar{v} \\ A & -\bar{v} \end{bmatrix} y \geq O_{2m}, \tag{7.24}$$

and

$$[0_n', -1]y < 0. \tag{7.25}$$

From (7.25), $y_{n+1} > 0$ and without loss of generality we can set it equal to 1. Setting $\lambda_j = y_j$ for all $j = 1, \ldots, n$, (7.24) then implies that $A\lambda = \bar{v}$, which is a solution to (7.10) with a non-negative λ.

The uniqueness part follows from Corollary 7.1.   □

7.2.3 *Harsanyi's social aggregation with strong Pareto*

Once we extend semistrong Pareto to strong Pareto in Theorem 7.3, it follows that (7.6) has a solution with strictly positive vector of weights.

Lemma 7.2   Suppose V_j, $j = 1, \ldots, n$ and V are von Neumann–Morgenstern utility functions on $\mathcal{L}$. If strong Pareto and Independent Prospects hold jointly, then there exists a vector $(\lambda', \mu)'$ with $\lambda >> 0_n$ such that (7.6) is satisfied for all $p \in \mathcal{L}$ and, furthermore, this is the only vector which solves (7.6).

Proof.   Observe that the proof of Lemma 7.2 only makes use of the second part of the strong Pareto axiom, namely the condition that $V(p) > V(q)$ if $V_j(p) \geq V_j(q)$ for all $j = 1, \ldots, n$ with $V_k(p) > V_k(q)$ for some k. We refer to this condition as SP*.

By the argument put forward in the proof of Theorem 7.2, it is sufficient to establish that there exists a unique solution λ to (7.10) with $\lambda \gg 0_n$. Let A be the matrix defined below (7.11), that is,

$$A = \begin{bmatrix} \bar{V}_1(e_1) & \bar{V}_2(e_1) & \dots & \bar{V}_n(e_1) \\ \vdots & \vdots & \dots & \vdots \\ \bar{V}_1(e_m) & \bar{V}_2(e_m) & \dots & \bar{V}_n(e_m) \end{bmatrix}.$$

Consider the system of inequalities

$$[y_1', y_2']_{1 \times 2m} \cdot \begin{bmatrix} A \\ -A \end{bmatrix}_{2m \times n} > O_n', \tag{7.26}$$

and

$$[y_1', y_2']_{1 \times 2m} \cdot \begin{bmatrix} -\bar{v} \\ \bar{v} \end{bmatrix}_{2m \times 1} \geq 0. \tag{7.27}$$

We now show that SP* is verified if and only if there is no non-negative solution to (7.26) and (7.27).

First, assume that $(y_1', y_2')'$ is a non-negative solution to (7.26) and (7.27). By defining $\tilde{p}$ and $\tilde{q}$ as in the proof of Theorem 7.2, it follows from (7.26) that $\bar{V}_j(p) \geq \bar{V}_j(q)$ for all $j = 1, \dots, n$ and $\bar{V}_k(p) > \bar{V}_k(q)$ for some k. It then follows from (7.27) that $\bar{V}(q) \geq \bar{V}(p)$ and we have a violation of SP*.

Next, suppose that SP* is violated, that is, there exists $p, q \in \mathcal{L}$ satisfying $\bar{V}_j(p) \geq \bar{V}_j(q)$ for all j, $\bar{V}_k(p) > \bar{V}_k(q)$ for some k, and $\bar{V}(q) \geq \bar{V}(p)$. But then $y_1 = \tilde{p}$ and $y_2 = \tilde{q}$ is a non-negative solution to (7.26) and (7.27).

By assumption SP* is satisfied, so there is no non-negative solution to (7.26) and (7.27). By Tucker's theorem of alternatives (see Tucker 1956), there exists $z_1 \gg 0_n$ and $z_2 \geq 0$ such that

$$\begin{bmatrix} A \\ -A \end{bmatrix} z_1 + \begin{bmatrix} -\bar{v} \\ \bar{v} \end{bmatrix} z_2 = 0_{2m}. \tag{7.28}$$

If $z_2 = 0$, (7.28) implies that $Az_1 = 0_m$ with $z_1 \gg 0$. Setting $\lambda_j = z_{1j}/z_{11}$ for all $j = 1, \dots, n$, it follows that $-\bar{V}_1(p) = \sum_{j=2}^n \bar{V}_j(p)$ for all $p \in \mathcal{L}$, which is a violation of Independent Prospects. Hence, $z_2 > 0$ and, without loss of generality, it is set at 1. Letting $\lambda_j = z_{1j}$ for all $j = 1, \dots, n$, (7.28) implies that $A\lambda = \bar{v}$, which is (7.10) with strictly positive λ. The uniqueness of the solution vector $(\lambda', \mu)'$ follows from Corollary 7.1. $\qquad \square$

7.3 APPENDIX

Let $A = (a_{ij})$ be an $m \times n$ matrix, let $x = (\zeta_i)$ be an m-vector, and let $y = (\eta_i)$ be an n-vector. The product xA is an n-vector and the product Ay is an m-vector. Also let $b = (\beta_j)$ is an n-vector and $c = (c_j)$ is an m-vector.

Gale's Theorem 7.1 (Solutions of linear inequalities)
Exactly one of the following alternatives hold: either the inequality $Ay \geq c$ has a solution or the equations $xA = 0'_n$ and $xc = 1$ have a non-negative solution.

Gale's Theorem 7.2 (Non-negative solutions of linear inequalities)
Exactly one of the following alternatives hold: either the inequality $xA \leq b$ has a non-negative solution or the inequalities $Ay \geq 0_m$ and $by < 0$ have a non-negative solution.

7.4 ILLUSTRATIVE EXAMPLES

In this section, we present two illustrative examples that represent some different features of the Harsanyi aggregation theorem (see Weymark 1991). Harsanyi's theorem (that is, Theorem 7.2) says that social utility V must be an affine combination of individual utilities V_js'. The theorem does not say that the weights λ_js' must be positive (see 7.6) or even non-negative across individuals. Nor does it claim that only one vector of coefficients $(\lambda_1, \ldots, \lambda_n, \mu)$ satisfies (7.6).

Example 7.1 Suppose $m = 3$ and $n = 2$ so that there are three certain alternatives and two persons. Suppose that the von Neumann–Morgenstern utility functions are $V_1(p) = 15p_0 + 10p_1 + 20p_2$, $V_2(p) = 5p_0 + 15p_1 + 25p_2$, and $V(p) = 10p_0 + 10p_1 + 20p_2$ for all $p \in \mathcal{L}$. In general, Harsanyi's theorem specifies that $V(p) = \sum_{i=1}^{n} \lambda_i V_i(p) + \mu$ holds for any $p \in \mathcal{L}$. In particular, it holds for any lottery from the set $\{e^0, e^1, \ldots, e^m\}$, each of which offers a certain alternative with probability one. In our example, by considering each of the three sure prospects e^0, e^1, e^2 in turn, substituting from V_1, V_2, and V in the sum given by (7.6) yields $10 = 15\lambda_1 + 5\lambda_2 + \mu$, $10 = 10\lambda_1 + 15\lambda_2 + \mu$, and $20 = 20\lambda_1 + 25\lambda_2 + \mu$. It is easy to verify that $\lambda_1 = 2/3$, $\lambda_2 = 1/3$, and $\mu = -(5/3)$ solves these three equations. This solution is unique. The linearity of the utility functions guarantees that these values for $(\lambda_1, \lambda_2, \mu)$ solves (7.6) for all $p \in \mathcal{L}$.

Example 7.2 Suppose $m = 3$ and $n = 2$ so that there are three certain alternatives and two persons. Suppose that the von Neumann–Morgenstern utility functions are $V_1(p) = 10p_0 + p_1 + p_2$, $V_2(p) = p_0 + 10p_1 + 10p_2$, and $V(p) = 99p_0$ for all $p \in \mathcal{L}$. They yield three equations: $99 = 10\lambda_1 + \lambda_2 + \mu$ and $0 = \lambda_1 + 10\lambda_2 + \mu$ and $20 = 20\lambda_1 + 25\lambda_2 + \mu$.[4] The general solution to these three equations is $\lambda_2 = \lambda_1 - 11$ and $\mu = -\lambda_1 - 10\lambda_2$ and there are infinite number of values for $(\lambda_1, \lambda_2, \mu)$ that solves these two conditions. By setting $\lambda_1 = 12$, $\lambda_2 = 1$, and $\mu = -22$ and using Harsanyi's theorem, we get (I) $V(p) = 12V_1(p) + V_2(p) - 22$ for all $p \in \mathcal{L}$. Similarly, by setting $\lambda_1 = 10$, $\lambda_2 = -1$, and $\mu = 0$ and by Harsanyi's theorem, we get (II) $V(p) = 10V_1(p) - V_2(p)$ for all $p \in \mathcal{L}$. As the function V is same in both (I) and (II), we find that V can be thought of as an affine combination of the V_is' with each person being assigned some positive weights or as an affine combination of the V_is' with one person being assigned a negative weight. Furthermore, if $\lambda_1 < 0$, then both persons have negative weights. This creates a problem in the interpretation of the Harsanyi's theorem as a theorem about weighted utilitarianism.

Remark 7.3 *Independent Prospects and unique coefficients*: In Example 7.1, the unique solution is $(\lambda_1, \lambda_2, \mu) = (2/3, 1/3, -(5/3))$. If $V_2(p)$ is replaced by $V_2'(p) = -5p_0 - 15p_1 - 25p_2$ in Example 7.1, keeping $V_1(p)$ and $V(p)$ unchanged, then also we have a unique solution to (7.6) and it is given by $(\lambda_1, \lambda_2, \mu) = (-2/3, -1/3, -(5/3))$. This follows from the fact $V_2'(p)$ is simply the negative of $V_2(p)$. As a consequence, there is no solution to (7.6) that gives a non-negative weight to each person's utility function. The essential difference between this case and Example 7.1 is that the selections in Example 7.1 satisfies semistrong Pareto but the latter, with $V_2'(p)$ replacing $V_2(p)$, does not.

---

[4] Note that both e^1 and e^2 result in the same equation $20 = 20\lambda_1 + 25\lambda_2 + \mu$.

7.5 **EXERCISES**

For explanations or definitions of the notation, see the main text of Chapter 7.

(E-7.1) Give numerical examples of individual and social utility functions to illustrate (*a*) Pareto Indifference, (*b*) Semistrong Pareto, and (*c*) Strong Pareto.

(E-7.2) Show that the Pareto indifference is implied by semistrong Pareto, which in turn is implied by strong Pareto. In Lemma 7.2 of the main text, can we replace strong Pareto by weak Pareto? Demonstrate your claim rigorously.

(E-7.3) In Lemma 7.2 of the main text, can we replace strong Pareto by weak Pareto? Demonstrate your claim rigorously.

(E-7.4) Suppose there are three certain alternatives and two persons. Suppose that the von Neumann–Morgenstern utility functions are $V_1(p) = 20p_0 + 15p_2 + 25p_2$, $V_2(p) = 10p_0 + 30p_1 + 50p_2$, and $V(p) = 15p_0 + 15p_1 + 20p_2$ for all reduced lotteries $p = (p_0, p_1, p_2)$. Determine $(\lambda_1, \lambda_2, \lambda_3) \in \mathbb{R}^3$ and $\mu \in \mathbb{R}$ such that Harsanyi's aggregation theorem is satisfied for all reduced lotteries $p = (p_0, p_1, p_2)$. Is your solution unique?

(E-7.5) Prove or disprove the following: if a preference ordering $\succsim$ satisfies the expected utility axioms, then all utility representations of $\succsim$ must be von Neumann–Morgenstern utility functions.

(E-7.6) (*a*) Give a numerical example to illustrate how utility functions become affinely dependent when Independent Prospects is violated.

(*b*) Construct an example to verify that affinely dependent utility functions lead to violation of Independent Prospects.

(E-7.7) Suppose there are three certain alternatives and two persons. Suppose that the von Neumann–Morgenstern utility functions are $V_1(p) = 15p_0 + p_1 + p_2$, $V_2(p) = p_0 + 10p_1 + 10p_2$, and $V(p) = 99p_0 + 99p_1$ for all reduced lotteries $p = (p_0, p_1, p_2)$. Determine $(\lambda_1, \lambda_2, \lambda_3) \in \mathbb{R}^3$ and $\mu \in \mathbb{R}$ such that Harsanyi's aggregation theorem is satisfied for all reduced lotteries $p = (p_0, p_1, p_2)$.

(E-7.8) Try to show that any increasing transformation of a von Neumann–Morgenstern utility function may not preserve the expected utility property. Identify a transformation that preserves the property and show that the underlying certainty equivalent remains invariant under this transformation. (For definition of certainty equivalent, see Chapter 8, Section 8.6.)

7.6 BIBLIOGRAPHICAL NOTES AND DISCUSSIONS

Two highly significant contributions due to Harsanyi (1953, 1955) paved the way for a theory of social welfare under uncertainty. The doctrine of using the von Neumann–Morgenstern (vNM) utility function for the purpose of making interpersonal utility comparison of well-being originated in Harsanyi (1953, 1955, 1977a). This has been upheld by Adler (2012, 2016) in his extended preference approach. According to Harsanyi, utility is an indicator of the extent of satisfaction, more accurately, of perception of satisfaction. Harsanyi (1975) emphatically argued that evaluation of social well-being is no way less sensible than individual decision-making, and, therefore, should be of an expected value type. Harsanyi's work deals with risk. Since everybody in society may experience a loss of utility resulting from risk, and may be willing to forgo income in order to avoid risk, the social counterpart to risk may lead to a social welfare loss as well (see Chapter 8).

In social aggregation theorems, Harsanyi obtained social welfare function as an additive function of individual utility functions, where both individual and social utilities are of the vNM type.

He claimed that this social welfare function is utilitarian. More precisely, Harsanyi's utilitarianism theorem says: a social welfare standard must be a weighted affine combination of individual utilities, where individuals and society have expected utility preferences represented by vNM utility functions. Sen (1969, 1974) and others countered this claim for technical reasons associated with vNM theory. According to Sen, in the Harsanyi theorems utility is used only to represent preferences and possesses no other independent basis. Consequently, Sen's position is that Harsanyi's results are about representation of social preferences and not about utilitarianism. Lively exchanges between Harsanyi and Sen on the ethical significance of Harsanyi's contribution and its relationship to utilitarianism have been the subjects of the articles of Harsanyi (1975, 1977b) and Sen (1976, 1977, 1986). The literature often refers to this as the Harsanyi–Sen debate.[5] In a recent contribution, Fleurbaey and Mongin (2016) argued that Harsanyi's claim concerning support of utilitarianism using the vNM theory was correct, although a full argument in support of the claim was not provided by Harsanyi. These authors noted that Sen's critique (see Sen 1986) indirectly suggested this solution, which they executed axiomatically. Hammond (1992) provided an alternative axiomatic foundation for Harsanyi's utilitarianism theorem. Mandler (2005) provided a linear programming-based proof of the Harsanyi theorem. Fleurbaey (2010) opposed the full application of the Pareto principle in risky frameworks for the reason that individual ex ante preferences rely on ignorance. A new result indicating the conflict between inequality aversion and recognition of individual ex ante preferences in the marrow of the Harsanyi aggregation theorem was proved. Danan, Gajdos, and Tallon (2015) suggested a generalization of Harsanyi's aggregation theorem (Harsanyi 1955) under incompleteness of individual and social preferences. McCarthy, Mikkola, and Thomas (2020) showed that any individual preorder or quasi-order, a reflexive and transitive binary relation, of prospects determines a unique social preorder of lotteries. This result may be regarded as a generalization

---

[5] See Weymark (1991) for a discussion.

of Harsanyi's utilitarian theorem. They have considered both the fixed and variable population sizes.[6]

According to Harsanyi (1953, 1955, 1977a), each individual in a society should consider himself as an "impartial observer" who does not know which person he is going to be. Thus, the impartial observer faces not only the real lottery over the set of social outcomes, but also a hypothetical lottery over which identity he will assume in the set of all individuals. The impartial observer's preferences are defined over all such extended lotteries.[7] When the impartial observer regards himself as person i, his preferences are represented by i's preferences. Each individual is assumed to be an expected utility maximizer and he continues to maintain this in his character as an impartial observer. Harsanyi argued that for all extended lotteries of the type (z, p), in which there is a probability $z_i \times x$ that the impartial observer will pinpoint himself as person i and that the outcome x materializes, the impartial observer's preferences can be represented functionally as $\sum_i z_i U_i(p)$, where $U_i(p)$ is the von Neumann–Morgenstern expected utility of person i from the real lottery p. Thus, implicit under the derivation of the impartial observer theorem is a veil of ignorance. In contrast, the aggregation theorems employ the Pareto principles.[8] For a very recent treatment, see Mongin and Pivato (2016), Dahlby (1987) demonstrated that many well-known economic inequality indices can be interpreted, in the Harsanyi (1953, 1955, 1975) framework, as measures of riskiness of an income distribution from behind a veil of ignorance. One section of Chapter 8 of this monograph presents a discussion on this.

---

[6] See also Adler (2019) for a recent discussion.

[7] Extended preferences have been analyzed extensively in several contributions, including, Harsanyi (1953, 1955, 1977a, 1982); Arrow (1977); Roberts (1980a, 1995, 1997); Kolm (1996); Suzumura (1996); Mongin and d'Aspremont (1998); Mongin (2001); Ooghe and Lauwers (2005); Grant et al. (2010, 2012a, 2012b) and Adler (2012, 2014, 2016).

[8] For earlier treatments related to the impartial observer theorem, see Lerner (1944); Vickrey (1945). For later discussions, see, among others, Pattanaik (1968); Sen (1986); Weymark (1991); Karni and Weymark (1998); Mongin and d'Aspremont (1998); Mongin (2001), Grant et al. (2010, 2012a, 2012b).

REFERENCES

Adler, M. D. 2012. *Well-Being and Fair Distribution: Beyond Cost-Benefit Analysis*. Oxford: Oxford University Press.

———. 2014. "Extended Preferences and Interpersonal Comparisons: A New Account." *Economics and Philosophy* 30 (2): 123–162.

———. 2016. "Extended Preferences." In *The Oxford Handbook of Well-Being and Public Policy: Economics and Finance, Health, Education, and Welfare*, edited by Matthew D. Adler and Marc Fleurbaey, 476–517. New York: Oxford University Press.

———. 2019. *Measuring Social Welfare*. Oxford: Oxford University Press.

Arrow, K. J. 1977. "Extended Sympathy and the Possibility of Social Choice." *American Economic Review* 67 (1): 219–225.

Border, K. 1981. "Notes on von Neumann–Morgenstern Social Welfare Functions." Unpublished, Division of the Humanities and Social Sciences, California Institute of Technology.

———. 1985. "More on Harsanyi's Utilitarian Cardinal Welfare Function." *Social Choice and Welfare* 1 (4): 279–281.

Coulhan, T., and P. Mongin. 1989. "Social Choice Theory in the Case of von Neumann–Morgenstern Utilities." *Social Choice and Welfare* 6 (3): 175–187.

Dahlby, B. G. 1987. "Interpreting Inequality Measures in a Harsanyi Framework." *Theory and Decision* 22 (3): 187–202.

Danan, E., T. Gajdos, and J. M. Tallon. 2015. "Harsanyi's Aggregation Theorem with Incomplete Preferences." *American Economic Journal: Microeconomics* 7 (1): 61–69.

Domotor, Z. 1979. "Ordered Sum and Tensor Product of Linear Utility Structures." *Theory and Decision* 11 (4): 375–399.

Fishburn, P. 1984. "On Harsanyi's Utilitarian Cardinal Welfare Theorem." *Theory and Decision* 17 (1): 21–28.

Fleurbaey, M. 2010. "Assessing Risky Social Situations." *Journal of Political Economy* 118 (4): 649–680.

Fleurbaey, M., and P. Mongin. 2016. "The Utilitarian Relevance of the Aggregation Theorem." *American Economic Journal: Microeconomics* 8 (3): 289–306.

Gale, D. 1960. *The Theory of Linear Economic Models.* New York: McGraw-Hill.

Grant, S., A. Kajii, B. Polak, and Z. Safra. 2010. "Generalized Utilitarianism and Harsanyi's Impartial Observer Theorem." *Econometrica* 78 (6): 1939–1971.

———. 2012a. "Equally-Distributed Equivalent Utility, Ex Post Egalitarianism and Utilitarianism." *Journal of Economic Theory* 147 (4): 1545–1571.

———. 2012b. "A Generalized Representation Theorem for Harsanyi's ('Impartial') Observer." *Social Choice and Welfare* 39 (4): 833–846.

Hammond, P. J. 1992. "Harsanyi's Utilitarian Theorem: A Simpler Proof and Some Ethical Considerations." In *Rational Interaction: Essays in Honor of John C.Harsanyi*, edited by Reinhard Selten, 305–319. Berlin; New York: Springer-Verlag.

Harsanyi, J. C. 1953. "Cardinal Utility in Welfare Economics and in the Theory of Risk-bearing." *Journal of Political Economy* 61 (5): 434–435.

———. 1955. "Cardinal Welfare, Individualistic Ethics, and Interpersonal Comparisons of Utility." *Journal of Political Economy* 63 (4): 309–321.

———. 1975. "Non-linear Social Welfare Functions: Do Welfare Economists Have a Special Exemption from Bayesian Rationality?" *Theory and Decision* 6 (3): 311–332.

———. 1977a. *Rational Behavior and Bargaining Equilibrium in Games and Social Situations.* New York: Cambridge University Press.

———. 1977b. "Nonlinear Social Welfare Functions: A Rejoinder to Professor Sen." In *Foundational Problems in the Special Sciences*, edited by Robert E. Butts and Jaakko Hintikka, 293–296. Vol. 10 of the University of Western Ontario Series in Philosophy of Science. Dordrecht, The Netherlands: D. Reidel Publishing Company.

———. 1982. "Morality and the Theory of Rational Behavior." In *Utilitarianism and Beyond*, edited by Amartya Sen and Bernard Williams, 39–62. Cambridge, UK: Cambridge University Press.

Karni, E., and J. A. Weymark. 1998. "An Informationally Parsimonious Impartial Observer Theorem." *Social Choice and Welfare* 15 (3): 321–332.

Kolm, S. C. 1996. *Modern Theories of Justice.* Cambridge, MA: MIT Press.

Lerner, A. P. 1944. *The Economics of Control.* London: Macmillan.

Mandler, M. 2005. "Harsanyi's Utilitarianism via Linear Programming." *Economics Letters* 88 (1): 85–90.

McCarthy, D., K. Mikkola, and T. Thomas. 2020. "Utilitarianism with and without Expected Utility." *Journal of Mathematical Economics* 87 (March): 77–113.

Mongin, P. 2001. "The Impartial Observer Theorem of Social Ethics." *Economics and Philosophy* 17 (2): 147–179.

Mongin, P., and C. d'Aspremont. 1998. "Utility Theory and Ethics." In *Principles*, edited by Salvador Barbera, Peter Hammond, and Christian Seidl, 371–481. Vol. 1 of *Handbook of Utility Theory*. Dordrecht, The Netherlands: Kluwer Academic Publisher.

Mongin, P., and M. Pivato. 2016. "Social Evaluation under Risk and Uncertainty." In *The Oxford Handbook of Well-Being and Public Policy: Economics and Finance, Health, Education, and Welfare*, edited by Matthew D. Adler and Marc Fleurbaey, 711–745. Oxford, UK: Oxford University Press.

Ooghe, E., and L. Lauwers. 2005. "Non-dictatorial Extensive Social Choice." *Economic Theory* 25 (3): 721–743.

Pattanaik, P. K. 1968. "Risk, Impersonality, and the Social Welfare Function." *Journal of Political Economy* 76 (6): 1152–1169.

Roberts, K. W. S. 1980. "Interpersonal Comparability and Social Choice Theory." *Review of Economic Studies* 47 (2): 421–439.

———. 1995. "Valued Opinions or Opinionated Values: The Double Aggregation Problem." In *Choice, Welfare, and Development: A Festschrift in Honour of Amartya K. Sen*, edited by Kaushik Basu, Prasanta K. Pattanaik, and Kōtarō Suzumura, 1:141–165. Oxford; New York: Clarendon.

———. 1997. "Objective Interpersonal Comparisons of Utility." *Social Choice and Welfare* 14 (1): 79–96.

Sen, A. K. 1969. "Planner's Preferences, Optimality, Distribution and Social Welfare." In *Public Economics*, edited by J. Margolis and H. Guitton, 201–221. London, UK: Macmillan.

———. 1974. "Rawls versus Bentham: An Axiomatic Examination of the Pure Distribution Problem." *Theory and Decision* 4 (3–4): 301–309.

———. 1976. "Welfare Inequalities and Rawlsian Axiomatics." *Theory and Decision* 7 (4): 243–262.

———. 1977. "Non-linear Social Welfare Functions: A Reply to Professor Harsanyi." In *Foundational Problems in the Special Sciences*, edited by R. E. Butts and J. Hintikka, 297–302. Vol. 10 of the University of Western Ontario Series in Philosophy of Science. Dordrecht, The Netherlands: Springer.

———. 1986. "Social Choice Theory." In *Handbook of Mathematical Economics*, edited by Kenneth Arrow and Michael Intriligator, 3:1073–1181. Amsterdam, The Netherlands: Elsevier.

Suzumura, K. 1996. "Interpersonal Comparisons of the Extended Sympathy Type and the Possibility of Social Choice." In *Social Choice Reexamined: Proceedings of the IEA Conference held at Schloss Hernstein, Berndorf, Vienna, Austria*, edited by Kenneth J. Arrow, Amartya Sen, and Kōtarō Suzumura, 2:202–229. London, UK: Palgrave Macmillan.

Tucker, A. W. 1956. "Dual Systems of Homogeneous Linear Equations." In *Linear Inequalities and Related Systems: Annals of Mathematical Studies*, edited by H. W. Kuhn and A. W. Tucker, 3–18. Princeton, USA: Princeton University Press.

Vickrey, W. S. 1945. "Measuring Marginal Utility by Reaction to Risk." *Econometrica* 13 (4): 319–333.

Weymark, J. A. 1991. "A Reconsideration of the Harsanyi–Sen Debate on Utilitarianism." In *Interpersonal Comparisons of Well-Being*, edited by Jon Elster and John E. Roemer, 255–320. Cambridge: Cambridge University Press.

———. 1994. "Harsanyi's Social Aggregation Theorem with Alternative Pareto Principles." In *Models and Measurement of Welfare and Inequality*, edited by Eichhorn W, 869–887. Berlin: Springer.

DISTRIBUTIONAL ETHICS

SINGLE DIMENSIONAL APPROACHES

8

8.1 INTRODUCTION

Often the literature on inequality measurement regards income as the only yardstick of well-being. One plausible reason for this assumption is that an increase in a person's income is likely to increase his level of living. However, in the recent period the literature has observed a shift of emphasis from a single-dimensional structure to a multidimensional framework for the purpose of inequality evaluation. (We analyze this issue in greater detail in the next chapter.) As a starting point, in this chapter we treat income as the only dimension of well-being. This chapter forms the basis of multidimensional approaches to inequality evaluation to be analyzed in Chapter 9.

After presenting the basics and preliminaries in the next section, in Section 8.3 we analyze common features of the inequality evaluators that rely respectively on the direct and inclusive measure of well-being approaches. While in the former outlook a social welfare function is defined directly on the set of income distributions, in the latter individual utilities are aggregated to generate a welfare metric of society. The next two consecutive sections deal explicitly with inequality assessment from these two perspectives. Section 8.6 stipulates how some standard inequality indices can be interpreted within the Harsanyi (1953, 1955) framework (Dahlby 1987).

The current literature on the measurement of inequality at times considers both achievement and shortfall inequalities in some dimension of human well-being and establishes a relation between them. Section 8.7 presents a condensed essay on the related literature. A person often may desire to have access to one or more opportunities available in society from the perspectives of happiness and success. The subject of Section 8.8 is a brief discussion on opportunity equality. In the next two sections we deal with inequality for an ordinal dimension of human well-being and an ordinal approach to inequality evaluation. In the context of network engineering, a fairness indicator determines the extent to which users are receiving fair shares of resources. The concern of Section 8.11 is a brief review of the axiomatic literature developed along this line. As we will argue, the use of conventional equality metrics may not be suitable for the evaluation of fairness.

8.2 BASICS AND PRELIMINARIES

Implicit under the formulation of an index of inequality are some reasonable postulates or axioms that should be verified by the index. We therefore begin by specifying a set of such postulates and provide justifications for them. All the inequality postulates as well those we assume for social evaluation functions in the two chapters on distributional ethics represent some notions of value judgment that may not be verified using factual information. Consequently, some of them may be debatable to some extent (Amiel and Cowell 1992).

Let us denote the set of income distributions in an n person society by $\Re^n_{++}$, the non-negative part $\Re^n_+$, of the n-dimensional Euclidean space $\Re^n$, with the origin deleted. More concretely, $\Re^n_+ = \{v \in \Re^n | v_i \geq 0 \text{ for all } i \in \{1, 2, \ldots, n\}\}$ and $\Re^n_{++} = \Re^n_+/\{0.1^n\}$, where 1^n is the n-coordinated vector each of whose coordinates is one. A typical element of $\Re^n_{++}$ is $v = (v_1, v_2, \ldots, v_n)$, where v_i is person i's income. The set of all positive income distributions in this society is $D^n = \{v \in \Re^n_{++} | v_i > 0 \text{ for all } i \in \{1, 2, \ldots, n\}\}$. The associated sets of all possible income distributions are respectively $\Re_{++} = \bigcup_{n \in N} \Re^n_{++}$ and $D = \bigcup_{n \in N} D^n$, N being the set of positive integers. Unless specified, $\Re_{++}$ will be treated as the set of all possible income distributions.

For any $n \in N$, $v \in \Re^n_{++}$, we denote the mean $\frac{1}{n}\sum_{i=1}^n v_i$ of v by $\mu(v)$ (μ, for brevity). The mean income is taken as the reference income or norm. More precisely, if everybody in society enjoys the mean income, then inequality becomes the minimum. Inequality is, therefore, a consequence of the gaps between the individuals' actual incomes and the reference or benchmark package. In other words, inequality in any distribution v is a scalar representation of the difference between $v = (v_1, v_2, \ldots, v_n)$ and the benchmark package $(\mu, \mu, \ldots, \mu)$, defined in an unambiguous way. We write $\bar{v}$ and v^0 respectively for the illfare and welfare ranked permutations of v, that is, $\bar{v}_1 \leq \bar{v}_2 \leq \ldots \leq \bar{v}_n$ and $v^0_1 \geq v^0_2 \geq \ldots \geq v^0_n$. An inequality indicator is a non-constant real-valued function l that summarizes interpersonal income differences in a society in an unambiguous way. The non-constancy assumption guarantees that the metric l cannot assume the same value over the set of income distributions. Formally, $I : \Re_{++} \rightarrow \Re^1$. Given that l takes into account income discrepancies across individuals, for inequality to be a non-vacuous concept we need the restriction $n > 1$. In consequence, when we use the notation $n \in N$, we assume implicitly that $n > 1$. This will be maintained throughout the chapter.

Generally, inequality indices can be classified into two broad categories: relative and absolute. An inequality quantifier I is a relative index or ratio scale invariant if it remains invariant under equi-proportional variations in all incomes. Formally, for any $n \in N$, $v \in \Re^n_{++}$, $c > 0$, $I(cv) = I(v)$. In contrast, an inequality metric I is an absolute inequality index or translation scale invariant, if it does not change under equal absolute changes in all incomes. That is, for any $n \in N$, $v \in \Re^n_{++}$, $I(v + c.1^n) = I(v)$, where c is a scalar such that $(v + c.1^n) \in \Re^n_{++}$. In view of the non-constancy assumption, an inequality indicator cannot be of both relative and absolute categories simultaneously. Each of these two invariance criteria representing size independence becomes helpful in transforming different-sized distributions into equal-sized distributions without altering inequality. To illustrate this, consider the distributions

$u = (2,4,6)$ and $v = (2,6,10)$ whose sizes are respectively $2 + 4 + 6 = 12$ and $2 + 6 + 10 = 18$. A scaling up of the incomes in u by 1.5 generates the distribution $u' = (3,6,9)$ whose size is 18. Under ratio scale invariance, inequality comparison of the different-sized distributions u and v is the same as that of the equal-sized distributions u' and v. Likewise, translation scale invariance can be used for the said purpose.

Each of these two invariance criteria reflects some particular subjectivity and has its own implications. For instance, an equi-proportionate augmentation in all incomes increases their absolute gaps, whereas an equal absolute reduction in all incomes increases their ratios. Alternatives and variants of these concepts of invariance have been suggested in the literature.[1]

Below, we specify four basic axioms that should be fulfilled by any arbitrary inequality indicator $I : \Re_{++} \to \Re^1$, irrespective of the notion invariance it meets.

8.2.1 *Symmetry*

For all $n \in N$, $v \in \Re_{++}^n$, $I(v) = I(vP)$, where P is any $n \times n$ permutation matrix, a non-negative square matrix of order n, with entries 0 and 1, and each of whose rows and columns sums to 1.

Symmetry is an anonymity postulate. It demands impartiality between rearrangements (permutations) of the income vector. In other words, inequality remains unchanged for any reordering of incomes. This core axiom shapes up an ethical attitude of impartiality. To illustrate this postulate, consider the income distribution $(3,5,6)$ in a three-person economy. If we post-multiply this distribution by the 3×3 permutation matrix $\begin{pmatrix} 0 & 0 & 1 \\ 0 & 1 & 0 \\ 1 & 0 & 0 \end{pmatrix}$, then the resulting distribution turns out to be $(3,5,6)\begin{pmatrix} 0 & 0 & 1 \\ 0 & 1 & 0 \\ 1 & 0 & 0 \end{pmatrix} = (6,5,3)$,

---

[1] See, for example, Besley and Preston (1988); Bossert and Pfingsten (1990); Zoli (1999); and Del Rio and Ruiz-Castillo (2000). For a recent discussion, see Chakravarty (2015). Zheng (2007) introduced a unit consistency axiom which demands that ordinal inequality rankings should remain unaltered when incomes are expressed in different units. Clearly, unit consistency implies ratio scale invariance but the converse is not true.

a reordering of the original profile $(3,5,6)$. Symmetry stipulates that the inequality levels of the distributions $(3,5,6)$ and $(6,5,3)$ are the same. Consequently, under symmetry any attribute other than income becomes immaterial to the measurement of inequality. Given that income is taken as the only determinant of well-being, this axiom is hard to dispute.

If two income distributions have different population sizes, then we can consider income by income replications of the distributions to make their population sizes the same. If the inequality statistic I is population replication invariant, then a comparison of inequality levels of the original populations with differing population sizes is the same as that of their replicated counterparts with the same population size.

The following postulate of I, which demands its neutrality property with respect to the population size, equivalently, population-size neutrality, indicating its invariance under replications of the population, becomes useful for cross-population comparisons of inequality.

8.2.2 *Daltonian population principle*

For all $n \in N$, $v \in \Re_{++}^n$, $I(v) = I(v^{nk})$, where $v^{nk} \in \Re_{++}^{nk}$ is the k-fold replication of $v \in \Re_{++}^n$, that is, $v^{nk} = (v^1, v^2, \ldots, v^k)$, where each $v^i = v$ and $k \geq 2$ is any positive integer.

For instance, given the different population-sized income distributions $(3,5,6)$ and $(2,4)$, we can replicate the former twice and the latter thrice so that the replicated distributions comes to be $(3,3,5,5,6,6)$ and $(2,2,2,4,4,4)$ respectively. If the inequality indicator fulfills the population-size neutrality property, then comparisons of inequalities of $(3,5,6)$ and $(2,4)$ are same as that of the equal population-sized distributions $(3,3,5,5,6,6)$ and $(2,2,2,4,4,4)$.

The next desideratum we analyze deals with responsiveness of the indicator I to redistribution of incomes across individuals. It is quite sensible to claim that an inequality statistic should reduce under a transfer of income from a person to anyone who has a lower income such that in the post-transfer profile the donor of the transfer does not become worse off than its recipient. Formally, for all $n \in N$, $v, v' \in \Re_{++}^n$, v is said to be obtained from v' by a progressive transfer or a Robin Hood operation, if for some i, j and $c > 0$, $v_i = v_i' + c \leq v_j$, $v_j = v_j' - c$, and $v_k = v_k'$ for all $k \neq i, j$. Here c amount of income is transferred from the richer person j, the donor, to person i, the recipient. Equivalently, one can say that v' is obtained from v by a regressive transfer.

8.2.3 Pigou–Dalton transfer principle

For all $n \in N$, for all $v, v' \in \Re_{++}^n$, if v is obtained from v' by a progressive transfer, then $I(v) < I(v')$.

All inequality indicators that verify the Pigou–Dalton transfer principle, also known as the Robin Hood principle, will be referred to as redistribution sensitive. To understand the principle, note that we generate $v = (3, 4, 6)$ from $v' = (3, 2, 8)$ by a progressive transfer of income from person 3 to person 2, and in the post-transfer distribution the beneficiary does not become richer than the donor, although he becomes better off than person 1, who remains unaffected under the transfer. However, under symmetry only rank preserving transfers are allowed. Thus, by including symmetry we transform a progressive transfer into a pure gap-diminishing transfer, leaving everyone else's position unaffected. As we will observe in the next section, such a transfer provides an ethical improvement in distributional judgment.

Continuity of an inequality statistic guarantees that it will not be oversensitive to minor observational errors in incomes. The following, therefore, is a sensible requirement.

Continuity: For all $n \in N$, $I : \Re_{++}^n \to \Re^1$ is continuous in its arguments.

Apart from the four basic properties stated above, inequality assessors are often assumed to be normalized; they should take on the value zero when all the incomes are equal. Analytically,

Normalization: For all, $n \in N$, $c > 0$, $I(c1^n) = 0$.

The well-known Lorenz curve that plots cumulative proportions of the total income of a distribution possessed by the bottom $t(0 \leq t \leq 1)$ proportions of the population becomes helpful in developing an inequality ordering of income distributions. Of two profiles

$u, v \in \Re_{++}$, for all Lorenz consistent; more precisely, relative, symmetric, population-size neutral, and redistribution sensitive; inequality standards $I : \Re_{++} \to \Re^1$, $I(u) < I(u)$ holds if and only if u is Lorenz superior to v; the Lorenz curve of u is nowhere below that of v and strictly inside at least at some places. If, however, the curves cross, it is possible to get two different inequality standards of the type that will rank the profiles differently. Thus, the Lorenz superiority relation is transitive but not complete. The incompleteness of the Lorenz supremacy relation can be overcome by a fuzzy inequality ranking relation, defined in an unambiguous way (Banerjee 2019).

8.3 COMMON FEATURES

In this section we introduce some essential ingredients of normative inequality analysis. These primitives are common constituents of the two approaches to inequality evaluation we adopt here. While inequality measurement looks at only distribution (equity), in welfare evaluation society becomes concerned with both size (efficiency) and distribution. In order to present the common characteristics formally, we assume the existence of a continuous social welfare function W that ranks alternative income distributions of society in terms of its preference. It is a tool for structuring ethical evaluation of income distributions.

Formally, $W : \Re_{++} \to \Re^1$. For all $n \in N$, $v \in \Re_{++}^n$, $W(v)$ specifies the level of welfare indicated by v. In other words, the function W assigns a given distribution of income an overall value, an ethical score. Since W depends only on individual incomes, we may refer to it as an individualistic welfare function. Often we will refer to it as social evaluation function or social standard, since it is used to evaluate the welfare standard of a society.

For all $n \in N$, $v \in \Re_{++}^n$, we say that $u \in \Re_{++}^n$ is obtained from v by a simple increment if $u_j > v_j$ for some j and $u_i = v_i$ for all $i \neq j$. Then W is said to satisfy the strong Pareto principle if $W(u) > W(v)$. Equivalently, we say that W is increasing. Since of the profiles $v' = (3, 5, 6)$ and $v = (2, 5, 6)$, v' obtained from v by increasing person 1's income by 1 unit, strong Pareto demands that $W(v') > W(v)$. The weak Pareto principle that requires W to be increasing when all the incomes increase simultaneously follows from the strong principle.

Apart from continuity and increasingness, we assume that W is strictly S-concave. S-concavity of $W : \Re_{++} \to \Re^1$ demands that for all $n \in N$, $v \in \Re_{++}^n$, $W(vB) \geq W(v)$, where B is any $n \times n$ bistochastic matrix, a non-negative square matrix of order n, each of whose rows and columns sums to 1. W is called strictly S-concave if the weak inequality is replaced by a strict inequality whenever vB is not a permutation of v. If W is strictly S-concave, then $-W$ is strictly S-convex and vice-versa. All S-concave and S-convex functions are symmetric.

To understand the ethical implications of strict S-concavity, we consider a theorem of Dasgupta, Sen, and Starrett (1973), which says that of two income distributions $u, v \in \Re_{++}^n$ of a given total, Lorenz superiority of u over v is equivalent to the condition that we can get u from v by a sequence of rank-preserving progressive transfers. These two conditions are the same as the stipulation that there exists in an $n \times n$ bistochastic matrix B such that $u = vB$. These three statements are equivalent to the specification that $W(u) > W(v)$ for all strictly S-concave social welfare functions $W : \Re_{++} \to \Re^1$. All these four positions are indistinguishable from the proposition that u is regarded as better than v by the symmetric utilitarian rule, that is, $\sum_{i=1}^{n} U(u_i) > \sum_{i=1}^{n} U(v_i)$, where $U : \Re_+^1 \to \Re^1$ is the individual utility function. A utility function U that maps each income onto a number quantifies an individual's well-being level. It is assumed to be continuous, increasing, and strictly concave.[2]

To illustrate the idea numerically, note that the three-person income distribution $(5, 6, 7)$ is obtained from the distribution $(3, 6, 9)$ by a rank progressive transfer of 2 units of income from the richest persons to the poorest person. The ordinates of the Lorenz curve of $(5, 6, 7)$ corresponding to the population proportions $0, \frac{1}{3}, \frac{2}{3}$, and 1 are respectively $0, \frac{5}{18}, \frac{11}{18}$, and 1. (It is assumed that 0 percent of the population enjoys 0 percent of the total income.) The analogous ordinates for the Lorenz curve of $(3, 6, 9)$ are respectively $0, \frac{3}{18}, \frac{9}{18}$, and 1. Evidently, $(5, 6, 7)$ is Lorenz superior to $(3, 6, 9)$. In view of the Dasgupta–Sen–Starrett theorem, the converse is true as well, that

---

[2]   See also Marshall, Olkin, and Arnold (2011, 35).

is, given the Lorenz superiority of $(5, 6, 7)$ over $(3, 6, 9)$, the former can be obtained from the latter by a sequence of rank preserving progressive transfers. The 3×3 bistochastic matrix that establishes the equality $(5, 6, 7) = (3, 6, 9)B$ is defined as follows:

$$(3, 6, 9)B = (3, 6, 9) \begin{pmatrix} \frac{4}{6} & 0 & \frac{2}{6} \\ 0 & 1 & 0 \\ \frac{2}{6} & 0 & \frac{4}{6} \end{pmatrix} = (5, 6, 7).$$

Thus, strict S-concavity of W is a sufficient condition to incorporate equitability leaning into distributional ethics. It provides a judgment about the ethical merits employed in the aggregation rule W by determining whether it satisfies or violates some plausible axioms that have been endorsed. It also bestows an ethical justification for the transformation $v \rightarrow vB$. In fact, the transformation $u = vB$ means that each income in u is a weighted average of incomes in v, where the non-negative weights add up to one. For instance, in our three-person example, $(3, 6, 9) \begin{pmatrix} \frac{4}{6} & 0 & \frac{2}{6} \\ 0 & 1 & 0 \\ \frac{2}{6} & 0 & \frac{2}{6} \end{pmatrix} =$ $(5, 6, 7)$, $5 = \frac{4}{6} \times 3 + 0 \times 6 + \frac{2}{6} \times 9$, and so on. This averaging means that vB can be obtained from v by a sequence of rank preserving progressive transfers so that the Lorenz superiority of vB over v is established.

The key elements we present here rely on the pioneering contributions of Atkinson (1970), Kolm (1969), and Sen (1973). Given a social evaluation function $W : \Re_{++} \rightarrow \Re^1$, for arbitrary $n \in N$, $v \in \Re_{++}^n$, the Atkinson–Kolm–Sen (AKS) representative income v_e corresponding to v is defined as that level of income which, if possessed by everybody, will make the existing distribution ethically indifferent. More concretely,

$$W(v_e 1^n) = W(v). \tag{8.1}$$

The representative-income method claims that the well-being number assigned to a profile of incomes is just a representative income. Given continuity and increasingness of W, we can solve (8.1) uniquely for v_e and express it as $v_e = E(u)$, where E is a particular numerical representation of W that possesses all its properties. Isowelfare contours of E are enumerated so that for any $c > 0$, $E(c1^n) = c$.

Given $W : \Re_{++} \to \Re^1$, for arbitrary $n \in N$, $v \in \Re_{++}^n$, the AKS inequality index is defined as

$$I_{AKS}(v) = 1 - \frac{E(v)}{\mu(v)}. \tag{8.2}$$

It is continuous, strictly S-convex (hence symmetric and redistribution sensitive), and bounded from below by 0, which is achieved if incomes are equally distributed. It is population replication invariant if E is so. The inequality metric I_{AKS} pins down the fraction of the total income $n\mu(v)$ that could be saved if the society distributed incomes equally without any welfare loss. Using the fact that contours of E are numbered, we can write $\mu(v)$ as $E(\mu(v)1^n)$. Hence, I_{AKS} can also be regarded as the fraction of welfare loss arising due to the existence of inequality. Evidently, we can recover the welfare function using the equations (8.2) and (8.1). The welfare standard $E(v) = \mu(v)(1 - I_{AKS}(v))$, which we can rewrite as $V(\mu(v), I_{AKS}(v))$, where $V : D^1 \to \Re^1$ is increasing in its first argument and decreasing in the second argument, can be referred to as an abbreviated or a reduced form welfare function because its arguments abbreviate the entire distribution in terms of the mean income $\mu(v)$ and equality measure $(1 - I_{AKS}(v))$. An increase in the value of the AKS equality standard $(1 - I_{AKS}(v))$, keeping mean income unchanged, say, through an egalitarian redistribution of income, is ethically desirable. Likewise, an increase in the mean income, keeping inequality fixed, say, by increasing all incomes equi-proportionately, indicates an efficiency preference.

Blackorby and Donaldson (1980), and Kolm (1976) suggested the use of the following as an alternative to I_{AKS}:

$$I_K(v) = \mu(v) - E(v), \tag{8.3}$$

where $v \in \Re_{++}^n$ and $n \in N$ are arbitrary. This continuous, strictly S-convex calibrator achieves its lower bound 0 whenever all the incomes are equal. It nails down the per capita income that could be saved if society redistributed incomes equally without any loss of welfare. Consequently, it may be regarded as a per capita index. We can recapture the welfare standard by exploiting the abbreviated welfare standard $E(v) = \mu(v) - I_K(v)$ and (8.1).

8.4 THE DIRECT APPROACH

In this approach an inequality standard is designed from a social welfare function W defined directly on the set of income distributions instead of treating the individual utilities as primitives of the welfare function.

Since I_{AKS} involves $E(v)$ and $\mu(v)$ in ratio form, it is reasonable to interpret it as a relative standard. The inequality metric I_{AKS} is relative if and only if the representative income E is linear homogenous; $E(cv) = cE(v)$ for all $n \in N$, $v \in \Re^n_{++}$, and $c > 0$ (Blackorby and Donaldson 1978).

The first example we choose to illustrate the AKS indicator within the purview of the direct approach is the Donaldson–Weymark (1980) S-Gini index I^ρ_{DW}, which corresponds to the linear homogenous S-Gini welfare function $E^\rho(v) = \frac{1}{n^\rho} \sum_{i=1}^{n} [i^\rho - (i-1)^\rho]v_i^0$, through the relation (8.2), where $v \in \Re^n_{++}$ and $n \in N$ are arbitrary, and $\rho > 1$ is a parameter. The parametric restriction $\rho > 1$ is necessary and sufficient for E^ρ to be strictly S-concave. It assigns more weights to lower incomes in the aggregation as the value of ρ increases. The parameter ρ can, thus, be regarded as a priority parameter, indicating priority for worse off individuals. The well-known Gini welfare standard $\frac{1}{n^2} \sum_{i=1}^{n} [i^2 - (i-1)^2]v_i^0$, also known as the Gini mean, drops out as a polar case of $E^\rho(v)$ for $\rho = 2.$[3] In terms of the illfare ranked permutation $\bar{v}$ of v, it can be written as $\frac{1}{n^2} \sum_{i=1}^{n} [2(n-i)+1]\bar{v}_i$. As $\rho \to \infty$, $E^\rho(v) \to \min_i\{v_i\}$, the Rawlsian maximin welfare function (Rawls 1971). The inequality indicator I^ρ_{DWR} related to E^ρ is then defined as

$$I^\rho_{DWR}(v) = 1 - \frac{1}{\mu(v)n^\rho} \sum_{i=1}^{n} [i^\rho - (i-1)^\rho]v_i^0, \qquad (8.4)$$

The well-known relative Gini index $I_{GR}(v) = \frac{1}{2n^2\mu(u)} \sum_{i=1}^{n} \sum_{j=1}^{n} |v_i - v_j|$, which can be rewritten in terms of welfare ranked permutations of incomes as $1 - \frac{1}{\mu(v)n^2} \sum_{i=1}^{n} [i^2 - (i-1)^2]y_i^0$,

---

[3] See also Sen (1974); Blackorby and Donaldson (1978); and Fleurbaey and Maniquet (2006).

drops out as a special case of I^ρ_{DWR} for $\rho = 2$. In the extreme situation when $\rho \to \infty$, $I^\rho_{DWR}(v)$ approaches the relative maximin inequality rule $1 - \frac{\min_i\{v_i\}}{\mu(v)}$. For the illfare ranked distribution $\bar{v}$,

$$I_{GR}(v) = 1 - \frac{1}{n^2\mu(v)}\sum_{i=1}^{n}(2(n-i)+1)\bar{v}_i = \frac{1}{n^2\mu(v)}\sum_{1\le i\le j\le n}(\bar{v}_j - \bar{v}_i).$$

Since I_K involves $\mu(v)$ and $E(v)$ in difference form, it is sensible to regard it as an absolute indicator. The indicator I_K is an absolute index if and only if E is unit translatable; $E(v + c.1^n) = E(v) + c$, where c is a scalar such that $(v + c.1^n) \in R^n_{++}$ (Blackorby and Donaldson 1980). The Donaldson–Weymark S-Gini social evaluation function E^ρ has a nice compromise property; it is both linear homogenous and unit translatable.[4] The underlying S-Gini absolute inequality standard is given by

$$I^\rho_{DWA}(v) = \mu(v) - \frac{1}{n^\rho}\sum_{i=1}^{n}[i^\rho - (i-1)^\rho]v_i^0. \qquad (8.5)$$

The absolute Gini index $I_{GA}(v) = \mu(v) - \frac{1}{n^2}\sum_{i=1}^{n}[i^2 - (i-1)^2]v_i^0$ emerges as a polar case of the general evaluator I^ρ_{DWA} for $\rho = 2$. As $\rho \to \infty$, $I^\rho_{DWA}(v)$ approaches the absolute maximin inequality criterion $\mu(v) - \min_i\{v_i\}$. With an increase in the value of ρ, the underlying ethics come to be closer to the absolute maximin inequality rule $\mu(v) - \min_i\{v_i\}$.

An alternative inequality standard that fits within the range of the direct approach is the Bonferroni (1930) index, which can be interpreted as an AKS inequality metric using the linear homogenous and unit translatable Bonferroni social evaluation function $E_B(v) = \frac{1}{n}\sum_{i=1}^{n}\frac{1}{i}\sum_{j=1}^{i}\bar{v}_j$, where $v \in \Re^n_{++}$ and $n \in N$

---

[4] A social evaluation function satisfying this compromise property is known as distributionally homogenous (Blackorby and Donaldson 1982). This characteristic of an evaluation standard has been employed by Chakravarty and Dutta (1987) to characterize an ethical distance function between two income distributions, which reflects the well-being of one distribution relative to that of another (see also Shorrocks 1982).

are arbitrary.[5] The Bonferroni inequality indicator I_{BR} defined is as

$$I_{RB}(v) = 1 - \frac{1}{\mu(v)n} \sum_{i=1}^{n} \frac{1}{i} \sum_{j=1}^{i} \bar{v}_j = 1 - \frac{1}{\mu(v)n} \sum_{i=1}^{n} \bar{\mu}_i$$

$$= \frac{1}{\mu(v)n} \sum_{i=1}^{n} (\mu(v) - \bar{\mu}_i), \tag{8.6}$$

where $\bar{\mu}_i$ is the ith partial mean of the illfare ranked distribution $\bar{v}$, that is, $\bar{\mu}_i = \frac{1}{i} \sum_{j=1}^{i} \bar{v}_j$. Clearly, $\bar{\mu}_n = \mu(v)$. While the relative Gini standard I_{GR} is given by twice the area enclosed between the diagonal line of equality of the Lorenz curve and the Lorenz curve itself, the relative Bonferroni aggregator I_{BR} comes to be the area between the Bonferroni curve and the horizontal line at height 1. The Bonferroni curve of an illfare ranked income distribution is defined as the plot of the ratios between cumulative income shares and cumulative population proportions against the cumulative population proportions (Aaberge 2007; Bárcena-Martin and Silber 2013). Whilst the Bonferroni standard looks at inequality in terms of the absolute differences $(\mu - \bar{\mu}_i)$ between the population mean and the partial means, the Gini metric considers inequality with respect to the simple income differences $(\bar{v}_j - \bar{v}_i)$.

Since the evaluation function E_B is a compromise welfare aggregator, the Bonferroni absolute inequality standard can be defined as $I_{BA}(v) = \mu - \frac{1}{n} \sum_{i=1}^{n} \frac{1}{i} \sum_{j=1}^{i} \bar{v}_j$. Although the relative and per capita Bonferroni standards are normalized, symmetric, redistribution sensitive, and continuous, they violate the population-size neutrality postulate, and hence become unsuitable for cross-population comparison of inequality. The S-Gini relative metric and its absolute sister, however, satisfy all four postulates. If individuals in a society earn incomes from more than one source and the rank order of incomes is the same across sources, then the absolute Gini and Bonferroni indices are respectively the sums of source-wise absolute Gini and Bonferroni indices.[6]

---

[5] See Chakravarty (2007) for a detailed discussion.
[6] See Chakravarty (2007), and Chakravarty and Sarkar (2021) for detailed discussions.

8.5 THE INCLUSIVE MEASURE OF WELL-BEING APPROACH

In this approach a real number summarizing the well-being of a person, as a function of his income, is specified at the outset. These individual well-being magnitudes are then aggregated across persons in an unambiguous way to arrive at a societal level of well-being. Equivalently, the inclusive-measure approach goes in for welfarism (Sen 1977). Welfarism is used as a synonym for welfare-consequentialism. In other words, welfarism is a configuration in which only welfare consequences count. Welfarism treats individual utilities, individual well-being measures, as basic ingredients for overall ethical valuations of alternative social states, which may be single or multidimensional. If each person in the society is just as well off in state a as in state b, welfarism regards the two states as ethically equivalent. In consequence, all non-utility aspects are overlooked in the evaluation of social well-being.[7] The aggregated well-being is then employed to figure out the level of inequality in society.

The two well-known indices of inequality that fit within this approach are the Atkinson (1970) and Kolm–Pollak indices (Kolm 1976; Pollak 1971). For arbitrary $n \in N$ and $v \in D^n$, Atkinson employed the symmetric utilitarian social welfare function $\sum_{i=1}^n U(v_i)$ to evaluate the well-being of a society, where the individual utility function U that quantifies individual well-being levels is continuous, increasing, and strictly concave. The representative income v_e associated with an arbitrary profile $v = (v_1, v_2, \ldots, v_n)$ is defined by the equation $\sum_{i=1}^n U(v_e) = \sum_{i=1}^n U(v_i)$. We solve this equation uniquely to determine $v_e = E_U(v) = U^{-1}\left(\frac{1}{n}\sum_{i=1}^n U(v_i)\right)$, where U^{-1} is the inverse of the function U. As Atkinson demonstrated, the only continuous utility function U for

---

[7] See, among others, Hammond (1979); Blackorby, Donaldson, and Weymark (1984); d'Aspremont and Gevers (2002); Bossert and Weymark (2004); Kaplow (2008); and Adler (2012). For recent discussions, see Maniquet (2016); Weymark (2016); and Adler (2019). Boadway (2016) analyzes the role of welfarism in the evaluation of benefits and costs of a project undertaken by an organization.

which E_U becomes linear homogenous is

$$U(v_i) = \begin{cases} e_1 + e_2 \frac{v_i^\theta}{\theta}, & \theta \neq 0, \\ e_1 + e_2 \log v_i, & \theta = 0, \end{cases} \tag{8.7}$$

where e_1 and e_2 are constants. Increasingness and strict concavity of U demand that $e_2 > 0$ and $\theta < 1$. The form of $E_U(v)$, calculated using U given by (8.7), which when substituted into (8.2), generates the following explicit form of the Atkinson index:

$$I_{AKS}^\theta(v) = \begin{cases} 1 - \frac{\left(\frac{1}{n}\sum_{i=1}^n v_i^\theta\right)^{\frac{1}{\theta}}}{\mu(v)}, & \theta < 1,\ \theta \neq 0, \\ 1 - \frac{\prod_{i=1}^n (v_i)^{\frac{1}{n}}}{\mu(v)}, & \theta = 0. \end{cases} \tag{8.8}$$

The parameter θ in the inequality evaluator I_{AKS}^θ is an indicator of the relative sensitivity of the evaluator to income transfers at different income locations. For any $\theta < 1$, for a given income of the donor, the higher the extent of reduction in I_{AKS}^θ is, the lower is the income of the progressive transfer recipient. The level of reduction in I_{AKS}^θ under a progressive transfer increases as the value of θ decreases. As $\theta \to -\infty$, I_{AKS}^θ approaches the relative maximin inequality rule. Thus, θ, like the S-Gini parameter ρ, can as well be treated as a priority parameter.

Pollak (1971) considered the continuous, increasing, and strictly concave exponential additive welfare function $W_P^\alpha(v) = -\sum_{i=1}^n \exp(-\alpha v_i)$, where 'exp' stands for the exponential function, $v \in \Re_+^n$ and $n \in N$ are arbitrary, $\alpha > 0$ is a priority parameter. This is a symmetric utilitarian social welfare function, where the identical individual utility function is given by $U(v_i) = -\exp(-\alpha v_i)$. The associated unit translatable representative income is $-\frac{1}{\alpha} \log \left(\frac{1}{n}\sum_{i=1}^n \exp(-\alpha v_i)\right)$, which, when substituted into (8.3), brings about the following form of the absolute index, which we refer to as the Kolm–Pollak index:

$$I_{KP}^\alpha(v) = \frac{1}{\alpha} \log \left(\frac{1}{n}\sum_{i=1}^n e^{\alpha(\mu(v)-v_i)}\right). \tag{8.9}$$

The positive priority parameter α attaches higher weight to a progressive income transfer as the income of the transfer recipient decreases, given the income of the donor. In the extreme case, as α approaches ∞, $I^{\alpha}_{KP}(v)$ approaches absolute maximin inequality criterion.

Often, for deeper analysis, it becomes necessary to disaggregate the overall inequality of a society in a well-defined manner. A concrete approach is subgroup decomposability, which for any portioning of the population into subgroups using some homogenous attribute, say, age, sex, region, ethnicity, health status, and so on, allows a particular quantifier of inequality to be decomposed into components that represent between-group and within-group inequalities. For example, given an inequality indicator, how much of the total inequality of a country is due to inequality between its rural and urban sectors, and how much is due to inequality in the urban sector and that in the rural sector?

To understand this in greater detail, we partition the population indexed by the set $\{1, 2, \dots, n\}$ into $k \geq 2$ subgroups $S^1, S^2, \dots, S^k$, where $S^i \cap S^j = \phi$ for all $i \neq j = 1, 2, \dots, k$ and $\bigcup_{i=1}^{k} S^i = \{i, 2, \dots, n\}$. We can write any n-person income distribution v in terms of the partitioned population as $v = (v^1, v^2, \dots, v^k)$, where v^i denotes the distribution of incomes in the subgroup S^i whose population size, mean income, and representative income are respectively n_i, μ_i, and v_e^i.

An ethical approach to the inequality decomposition by population subgroups was developed by Blackorby, Donaldson, and Auersperg (1981), which was later refined by Blewett (1982).[8] Ethical decomposition of inequality requires that the representative income of any subgroup should be independent of the incomes in other subgroups. This proposal defines the AKS between-group inequality index I^{BI}_{AKS} as the proportion of total income that could be saved, without any welfare loss, by moving from the subgroup-wise ethically supreme distribution $(v_e^1 I^{n_i}, \dots, v_e^k I^{n_k})$ that allocates the representative income of a subgroup to everybody in the subgroup to the population-wise ethically supreme distribution $(v_e 1^n)$, in which everybody enjoys the society representative income. Formally, $I^{BI}_{AKS}(v) = \dfrac{\sum_{i=1}^{k} n_i v_e^i - n v_e}{n \mu(v)}$, where $\sum_{i=1}^{k} n_i = n$.

---

[8] See also Blackorby, Bossert, and Donaldson (1999).

The within-group AKS index I_{AKS}^{WI} is defined as the proportion of the total income that could be saved in the transition from the actual distribution $v = (v^1, v^2, \ldots, v^k)$ to the subgroup-wise supreme distribution by maintaining social indifference. Formally,

$$I_{AKS}^{WI}(v) = \frac{n\mu(v) - \sum_{j=1}^{k} n_i v_e^j}{n\mu(v)} = \sum_{j=1}^{k} \frac{n_j \mu_j}{n\mu(v)} \left[1 - \frac{v_e^i}{\mu_i} \right] = \sum_{j=1}^{k} \frac{n_j \mu_j}{n\mu(v)}$$

$I_{AKS}(v^j)$, which is the weighted average of subgroup AKS indices, where the weights are the income shares of the different subgroups. Evidently, $I_{AKS}(v) = I_{AKS}^{WI}(v) + I_{AKS}^{BI}(v)$. The only relative index for which the representative income of a subgroup becomes independent of the incomes of other subgroups is the Atkinson index.

For inequality indices of the absolute variety, the Blackorby–Donaldson–Auersperg criterion defines the within-group inequality metric I_K^{WI} as the per capita income that could be saved, without any loss of welfare, in movement from the actual distribution $v = (v^1, \ldots, v^k) \in R_+^n$ to the subgroup-wise ethically supreme distribution. Formally, $I_K^{WI}(v) = \mu(v) - \sum_{i=1}^{k} \frac{n_i v_e^i}{n} = \sum_{i=1}^{k} \frac{n_i}{n} (\mu_i - v_e^i)$, which is the population share weighted average of Blackorby–Donaldson–Kolm subgroup inequality indices. The saving in per capita income for the transition from subgroup-wise ethically supreme distribution to the population-wise ethically supreme distribution, under ethical indifference, is the between-group inequality index I_K^{BI}, that is, $I_K^{BI}(v) = \sum_{i=1}^{k} \frac{n_i v_e^i}{n} - v_e$. The sum of these two sub-indices comes to be the overall per capita index. The only absolute inequality metric that fulfills this aggregation is the Kolm–Pollak index.

8.6 DIRECT DESCRIPTIVE INEQUALITY INDICES AND REDUCED FORM WELFARE FUNCTIONS

The inequality literature contains several indices that have been suggested without using any notion of welfare. These are direct descriptive measures in the sense that they are defined directly on income distributions without taking into account any normative feature. In this sense they are different from the ones analyzed in Section 8.4. Each of them has been introduced with a specific objective in mind. A concrete purpose is subgroup decomposability. Generally, for the between-group component, this sort of decomposition of descriptive indices uses subgroup means as primitives.[9] Consequently, the inequality between subgroups is determined by examining the mean incomes of the subgroups.

Shorrocks (1980, 1983) characterized the entire family of relative subgroup decomposable inequality indices, which is given by

$$
I_S^c(v) = \begin{cases} \frac{1}{nc(c-1)} \sum_{i=1}^n \left[\left(\frac{v_i}{\mu(v)} \right)^c - 1 \right], & c \neq 0, 1, \\ \frac{1}{n} \sum_{i=1}^n \left[\log \left(\frac{\mu(v)}{v_i} \right) \right], & c = 0, \\ \frac{1}{n} \sum_{i=1}^n \left[\left(\frac{v_i}{\mu(v)} \right) \log \left(\frac{v_i}{\mu(v)} \right) \right], & c = 1, \end{cases} \tag{8.10}
$$

where $n \in N$ and $v \in D^n$ are arbitrary. This family is popularly known as the generalized entropy family. The parameter c represents different extents of awareness about inequality. The particular cases of $I_S^c(v)$ that correspond to $c = 0$ and $c = 1$ are respectively the Theil (1972) mean logarithmic deviation index and the Theil (1967) entropy index of inequality.[10] Half the squared coefficient of variation drops out as a special case of I_S^c for $c = 2$. For all real values of c, I_S^c is strictly S-convex, population-size neutral, continuous, and normalized. For any $c < 1$, it assigns greater weights to transfers at the lower end of the income profile.

We can relate I_S^c with the reduced form welfare standard V^c : $D^1 \times \Re^1 \to \Re^1$ as follows:

$$
V^c(\mu(v), I_S^c(v)) = \mu(v) \exp(-I_S^c(v)), \tag{8.11}
$$

where $v \in D^n$ and $n \in N$ are arbitrary. When efficiency considerations are absent (μ is fixed), a reduction in inequality is equivalent to an increase in welfare and vice versa. The evaluation function V^c indicates that the fraction of the maximum welfare $\mu(v)$ that the society enjoys due to the existence of inequality is given by $\exp(-I_S^c(v))$. To understand this, note that for a given $v \in D^n$,

---

[9] See, among others, Cowell (1980); Shorrocks (1980); Foster and Shneyerov (1999); Kanbur (2006); Ebert (1987); and Bárcena-Martin and Silber (2013).
[10] They were characterized independently by Bourguignon (1979) and Foster (1983), respectively. A generalization of the former was developed by Chattopadhyay and Tyagarupananda (2019).

V^c achieves its maximum value $\mu(v)$ if and only if the equality component $\exp(-I_S^c(v))$ is 1, that is, inequality is 0. Since inequality is related to V^c in a decreasing way, any value of welfare less than $\mu(v)$ arises due to the positivity of inequality. The fraction of the maximum welfare lost because of the existence of inequality is given by $\frac{\mu(v)-V^c(\mu(v),I_S^c(v))}{\mu(v)} = (1 - \exp(-I_S^c(v)))$, and hence the fraction of the maximum welfare enjoyed by society is $\exp(-I_S^c(v))$.

Although the linear homogenous social evaluation function W_S^c is continuous, strictly S-concave and population-size neutral, it may not satisfy strong Pareto. The reason behind this is that an increase in the income of a person certainly increases the mean income but may increase the inequality as well. The resulting change in welfare will be determined by the trade-off between efficiency μ and equality $\exp(-I_S^c)$. However, it satisfies a weaker monotonicity principle, the scale improvement principle: for all, $v \in D^n$ and $n \in N$, $V^c(\mu(qv), I_S^c(qv)) > V^c(\mu(v), I_S^c(v))$, where $q > 1$ is any scalar (see Shorrocks 1983).[11]

We can also suggest other forms of reduced form welfare functions to relate them with relative inequality evaluators in a negative monotonic way. For instance, for the relative Gini metric itself the following variants of reduced form welfare functions are available: $n^2(1 - 1_G)\mu$ (Sheshinski 1972); $\log \mu - I_G$ (Kats 1972); $\frac{1-I_G}{1+I_G}$ (Chipman 1974); and $\frac{\mu}{1+I_G}$ (Kakwani 1986) The Sheshinski formulation can be written more explicitly as $\sum_{i=1}^{n}[i^2 - (i - 1)^2]v_i^0$, the gross counterpart to the Gini mean. This increasing, symmetric, redistribution sensitive, social evaluation standard is a violator of the population-size neutrality principle. While the Kats and Kakwani recommendations respect the scale improvement condition, Chipman's form assumes that efficiency considerations are absent. In order to justify the choice of a particular form of welfare standard, it will be worthwhile to characterize the function axiomatically so that its pickup will enable us to understand the properties of the welfare standard that are being guided by its selection.

---

[11] An axiomatic characterization of this welfare standard using any arbitrary relative inequality metric was developed in Chakravarty (2009). See also Amiel and Cowell (2003) for a detailed discussion on reduced form welfare functions.

The class of subgroup decomposable absolute inequality indices contains increasing transformations of the variance ($\frac{1}{n}\sum_{i=1}^{n} v_i^2 - \mu^2$) and the Kolm–Pollak index as its members (Chakravarty and Tyagarupananda 2009; Bosmans and Cowell 2010; and Chakravarty 2015). For all absolute descriptive indices, including the variance, a reduced form social evaluation function that has been suggested in the literature is $V(\mu, I_A) = \mu - qI_A$, where $q > 0$ is a constant and I_A is any arbitrary absolute inequality metric.[12] This evaluation function, although may not satisfy strong Pareto, satisfies the absolute incremental principle; an equal absolute increase in all incomes increases welfare (Shorrocks 1983).

In a recent contribution, Jayadeb and Reddy (2019) analyzed inequality between groups from a different perspective. They introduced and examined analytically the concepts of "representational inequality," "sequence inequality," and "group inequality comparison." Representational inequality indicates how an attribute is shared by individuals in different subgroups. Sequence inequality is concerned with the hierarchical ordering of the subgroups with respect to the attribute under consideration. The subject of group inequality comparison is the extent to which between-group inequalities influence the overall inequality. An innovative feature of their article is that the concepts become helpful in explaining segregation, separation of subgroups by some univocal criterion, and polarization that looks at the division of the society into subgroups as a possible evaluative factor for social conflicts. An increased between-group inequality, under ceteris paribus assumptions, increases the distance between the subgroups making the society more polarized.[13]

8.7 MEASURING INEQUALITY WITHIN THE HARSANYI FRAMEWORK

In the Harsanyi framework, inequality is measured in terms of riskiness, as anticipated by an individual, under a veil of ignorance.

---

[12] See Chakravarty (2009) for an axiomatic characterization of this social evaluation function.
[13] See Chakravarty (2015) for a detailed discussion.

This framework is a particular form of utilitarianism in which social evaluation judgments are done under a veil of ignorance using von Neumann–Morgenstern utility functions and equi-probability assumption. Within this structure, a distribution $v \in \Re_{++}^n$ of n incomes can be regarded as incomes from n states of a risky or uncertain prospect, where $n \in N$ is arbitrary. Thus, each v_i is a state-contingent income or return from a risky prospect, where the set of states is $\{i, 2, \ldots, n\}$.

Dahlby (1987) interpreted different inequality indicators in terms of measures of risk. Of two uncertain prospects A and B with respective state-contingent income distributions $v \in \Re_{++}^n$ and $v' \in \Re_{++}^n$, A is regarded as riskier than B if and only if $v \in \Re_{++}^n$ is more unequal than $v' \in \Re^n$.

Any individual evaluates a state-controlled income distribution $v \in \Re_{++}^n$ using his expected utility under equi-probability of states. Formally, if U stands for (increasing, strictly concave) von Neumann–Morgenstern utility function of the individual, then expected utility under equi-probability assumption is given by $\Xi U = \frac{1}{n} \sum_{i=1}^n U(v_i)$, where the operator Ξ denotes expectation. The certainty equivalent v_c associated with the state-contingent income distribution $v \in \Re_{++}^n$ is that level of income, which, if received from each state, will generate the same level of expected utility as that produced by the prospect. Formally, $U(v_e) = \frac{1}{n} \sum_{i=1}^n U(v_i)$. Hence, $v_e = U^{-1}(\frac{1}{n} \sum_{i=1}^n U(v_i))$, where U^{-1} is the inverse of U.

The measure $\frac{\mu - v_e}{\mu}$ indicates the relative cost of risk, the amount of relative risk premium that the individual would like to pay to avoid the prospect. In other words, it is the proportion of the total $\sum_{i=1}^n v_i$ that can be paid as premium so that the resulting state-dependent income distribution could be received with certainty and the expected utilities of this profile and the prospect coincide. Since v_e is formally equivalent to the AKS representative income, $\frac{\mu - v_e}{\mu}$ is the Atkinson inequality metric given by (8.8), corresponding to the state-contingent return vector $v \in \Re_{++}^n$. (Note that the utility function given by [8.7] is the only utility function for which the measure $\frac{\mu - v_e}{\mu}$ remains invariant under equi-proportionate changes in state-contingent returns.)

The per-state risk premium $(\mu - v_e)$ is the amount of risk premium which, if taken away from each state's income, would generate a profile of state-dependent incomes that becomes available without any risk and whose expected utility coincides with that of the prospect. The only utility function for which this risk premium measure survives invariance under equal absolute changes in all state-dependent incomes is $U(v_i) = -\sum_{i=1}^{n} \exp(-\alpha v_i)$, where, as before, "exp" symbolizes the exponential function; $v \in \Re_+^n$ and $n \in N$ are arbitrary, and $\alpha > 0$ is a parameter. The explicit form of the underlying per-state risk premium coefficient comes to be the Kolm–Pollak standard given by (8.9).

Since $\frac{\mu - v_e}{\mu}$ can be approximated by $\frac{U(\mu) - \Xi U}{\mu U'(\mu)}$, the generalized entropy family $I_S^c = \frac{U(\mu) - \Xi U}{\mu U'(\mu)(1-c)}$, defined in (8.10), can be interpreted in the Harsanyi structure as an approximation to the relative risk premium $\frac{\mu - v_e}{\mu}$ divided by the coefficient of relative risk aversion $-\frac{v_i U'(v_i)}{U''(v_i)} = (1 - c) > 0$, where U' and U'' stand respectively for the first and second derivatives of U. The underlying utility function here is of the form (8.7), assuming that $\theta(< 1)$ in (8.7) equals c.

We now explore the possibility of accommodating the Donaldson–Weymark S-Gini standard (8.4) within the Harsanyi system. One way to proceed is to assume that the expected utility is of the form $\Xi U = \sum_{i=1}^{n} \frac{1}{n^\rho}[i^\rho - (i - 1)^\rho]v_i^0$, where v^0 is the welfare ranked permutation of state-restricted incomes and $\rho > 1$ is a parameter. This expected utility function portrays risk neutrality. If we regard $\frac{[i^\rho - (i-1)^\rho]}{n^\rho}$ as probability p_i of appearing state i, then $0 \le p_i \le 1$ and $\sum_{i=1}^{n} p_i = \frac{1}{n^\rho}\sum_{i=1}^{n}[i^\rho - (i - 1)^\rho]$. But this leads to a violation of the equi-probability assumption. Alternatively, define $\Xi U = \frac{1}{n}\sum_{i=1}^{n}\frac{1}{n^{\rho-1}}[i^\rho - (i - 1)^\rho]v_i^0$ so that the equi-probability assumption holds. However, in such a case, the utility $\frac{1}{n^{\rho-1}}[i^\rho - (i - 1)^\rho]v_i^0$ from income in any arbitrary state i is dependent on its rank in the entire profile v^0. This is a clear violation of the axiom of independence maintained in the expected utility framework.

The build-up considered in this section employs the theory of risk in single-dimensional inequality assessment to reduce the problem of inequality evaluation under the veil of ignorance to a single decision maker's choice in the presence of risk, say, to choose among distributions on the basis of inequality. However, the Donaldson–Weymark S-Gini (hence the Gini which corresponds to the particular case $\rho = 2$) inequality quantifier cannot be interpreted as an indicator of inequality in this structure.

8.8 COMPARABILITY BETWEEN ACHIEVEMENT AND SHORTFALL INEQUALITY: AN EXPOSITORY ANALYSIS

Given that the earlier section deals with interpretations of inequality metrics when information on incomes is characterized by risk, in this section we look at inequality from a different perspective, namely showing the relationship between achievement and shortfall inequalities in some dimension of human well-being. While achievement inequality deals with differences between the attainments of the individuals in the dimension, the concerns of shortfall inequality are the shortages of the individual attainments from the maximum possible attainment level. This in turn will enable us to investigate the interrelation between the underlying social evaluation standards. For instance, if we regard daily energy consumption in calories as an indicator of health status, while achievement inequality is a demonstration of inequality in good health, shortfall inequality looks at the shortages of the calorie intakes from the required level of calories across individuals. The latter is a representation of differences in bad health. If we regard land ownership as a dimension of wealth, then achievement inequality is evidence of inequality in the distribution of amounts of land owned by different individuals. However, shortfall inequality is a summary statistic of the gaps between the maximum amount of land that can be owned by a person, as fixed by the land ceiling regulation, and the actual amount of land possessed by different individuals.[14]

One line of investigation in this context has been to identify the metrics that satisfy the "perfect complementarity" property (Erreygers 2009). An inequality indicator is said to fulfill the perfect complementarity property if it takes on the same value

---

[14] For reducing inequality in the distribution of agriculture land in India, state governments made a lot of endeavors and executed several land reforms laws including Land Ceiling Acts.

for an attainment distribution and the corresponding shortfall distribution. In other words, achievement and shortfall inequalities are evaluated identically by a perfectly complementary inequality standard. Erreygers (2009) characterized two well-known absolute inequality standards, namely the absolute Gini index and the variance as perfectly complementary indicators of inequality.[15] Lambert and Zheng (2007) demonstrated that the only subgroup decomposable absolute inequality index that possesses the capability of evaluating attainment and shortfall inequalities identically is the variance. Lasso de la Vega and Aristondo (2012) designed a method for transforming any inequality metric into an inequality metric that evaluates achievement and shortfall inequalities equally.

In order to present the discussion analytically, assume that for any person i the level of attainment u_i indicating achievement in the dimension takes on values in the non-degenerate interval $[0, b]$, and for any $n \in N$ the achievement distribution is denoted by $u = (u_1, u_2, \ldots, u_n) \in [0, b]^n$, where the upper bound $b > 0$ of the attainment quantities is finite and $[0, b]^n$ is the n-fold Cartesian product of $[0, b]$. Assume at the outset that for any $n \in N, u \in [0, b]^n$, the mean attainment level $\mu(u)$ is positive. Denote the set of all achievement distributions by $\Re_{++}(b)$, that is, $\Re_{++}(b) = \bigcup_{n \in N} [0, b]^n$.

We say that an inequality index $I : \Re_{++}(b) \to \Re^1$ satisfies the perfect complementarity property if for all $n \in N$ and for all $v \in [0, b]^n$, $I(u) = I(b1^n - u)$. Lambert and Zheng (2007) proposed a "strong consistency" postulate, which may be regarded as a generalization of the complementarity rule. It demands that the rankings are preserved irrespective of whether we measure two distributions in terms of achievement or by shortfall. Formally, an inequality index $I : \Re_{++}(b) \to \Re^1$ satisfies the strong consistency

---

[15] For the socioeconomic inequality of health, which primarily focuses on extensions and variations of the concentration index, Erreygers (2009) replaced the complementarity property by the "mirror axiom," which says that for a given distribution of health situations of individuals, the health indicator and the ill-health indicator should have equal absolute value but opposite signs. The ill-health status of a person is defined as the gap between the maximum value that the health status can take and actual health status of the person. See also Erreygers and Van Ourti (2011); Wagstaff (2011); and O'Donnell, Doorslaer, and Ourti (2015).

property if for all $n \in N$ and all $u, v \in [0, b]^n$, we have:

$$I(u) \leq I(v) \text{ if and only if } I(b1^n - u) \leq I(b1^n - v). \tag{8.12}$$

Chakravarty, Chattopadhyay, and D'Ambrosio (2016) characterized the following linear homogenous family of symmetric mean of order $r(\geq 1)$ of attainment gaps $|u_i - u_j|$ as a family of strongly consistent inequality standards:

$$I^r(u) = \left(\frac{1}{n^2} \sum_{i=1}^{n} \sum_{j=1}^{n} |u_i - u_j|^r \right)^{1/r}, \tag{8.13}$$

where $n \in N$ and $u \in [0, b]^n$ are arbitrary. For a given $u \in [0, b]^n$, as the value of r increases $I^r(u)$ assigns higher weights to lower gaps. For $r = 1$, $I^r(u)$ turns out to be twice the absolute Gini index of inequality, whereas for $r = 2$, it coincides with $\sqrt{2}$ times the standard deviation. As $r \to \infty$, $I^r(u) \to \max_{i,j}\{|u_i - u_j|\}$, the maximax attainment gap. Ebert (1988) showed that positive multiples of the absolute Gini index and the variance respect a weak decomposability postulate, which demands that for any two-subgroup partitioning of the population, overall inequality can be decomposed into a within-group component and a between-group component. More generally, the ordinal transformation $(I^r(u))^r$ of the absolute inequality metric $I^r(u)$ fulfills this postulate.

One common feature of all the above approaches is that the shortfalls are defined in terms of differences of attainments from the highest level of attainment. These proposals, as a whole, reduce the allowable class of strongly consistent inequality standards substantially (Allanson and Petrie 2014; Kjellsson and Gerdtham 2013; and Bosmans 2016). As Bosmans noted, no relative inequality index can be strongly consistent.

Bosmans argued that the set of inequality indicators can be expanded greatly if a weaker version of the strong consistency postulate is considered. To discuss this weak postulate, let us denote attainment and shortfall inequality metrics, defined on $[0, b]^n$, by I_a and I_s, respectively. Then a pair of inequality metrics (I_a, I_s) is said to fulfill the weak consistency property if for all $n \in N$, and all

$u, v \in [0, b]^n$, we have:

$$I_a(u) \leq I_a(v) \text{ if and only if } I_s(b1^n - u) \leq I_s(b1^n - v). \qquad (8.14)$$

Weak consistency ensures that inequality evaluation does not rely on whether data are represented in terms of attainments or shortfalls. He established rigorously that a pair of inequality metrics (I_a, I_s) satisfies the weak consistency property if and only if there exists an increasing transformation $f : \Re^1 \to \Re^1$ such that for all $n \in N$ and $u \in [0, b]^n$,

$$I_a(u) = f(I_s(b1^n - u)). \qquad (8.15)$$

This stipulation means that given an attainment metric I_a, if the shortfall metric I_s is defined via the relation (8.15), then the pair (I_a, I_s) is weakly consistent. Conversely, weak consistency permits an inequality metric to be the shortfall indicator I_s if its attainment twin is defined using the relation (8.15). Note that if f is the identity mapping, that is, $f(t) = t$, then (8.15) means that $I_a(u) = I_s(b1^n - u)$.

By increasingness of f, $f^{-1} : \Re^1 \to \Re^1$ is also increasing, where f^{-1} is the inverse of f. Consequently, we can rewrite condition (8.15) as

$$(I_s(b1^n - u)^n) = f^{-1}(I_a(u)), \qquad (8.16)$$

where $n \in N$ and $u \in [0, b]^n$ are arbitrary, and $f^{-1} : \Re^1 \to \Re^1$ is increasing.

To understand this more explicitly, let us consider the following achievement inequality indicator

$$I_{Ra}^r(u) = \left(\frac{1}{n^2 (\mu(u))^r} \sum_{i=1}^{n} \sum_{j=1}^{n} |u_i - u_j|^r \right)^{1/r}, \qquad (8.17)$$

the relative sister of I^r, defined in (8.13). The particular cases $I_{Ra}^1(u)$ and $I_{Ra}^2(u)$, which correspond respectively to $r = 1$ and 2, become positive multiples of the relative Gini index and the coefficient of variation of achievement inequality. Now, by (8.15), the associated shortfall indicator must be equal to (an increasing transformation of)

$$I_{Rs}^r(b-u) = \left(\frac{1}{n^2(b-\mu(u))^r} \sum_{i=1}^n \sum_{j=1}^n |u_i - u_j|^r \right)^{1/r}, \qquad (8.18)$$

Thus, while both the metrics I_{Ra}^r and I_{Rs}^r are violators of the strong consistency criterion, the pair (I_{Ra}^r, I_{Rs}^r) is weakly consistent. This, in particular, shows that each of the coefficients of variation and the relative Gini indicators of achievement inequality, when combined with the respective shortfall partner via the relation (8.15), forms a weakly consistent inequality pair. However, none of the relative Gini index and the coefficient of variation is strongly consistent. Evidently, the strongly consistent achievement inequality index I^r, when combined with its associated shortfall index using the relation (8.15), also constitutes a weakly consistent inequality pair. This clearly establishes that fulfillment of the weak consistency criterion is not dependent on the notion of inequality invariance; both relative and absolute inequality standards can conquer the objective.

It will now be worthwhile to give an example to illustrate how the weak consistency property can be related to a welfare consistency postulate. For simplicity of exposition, we consider the reduced form social evaluation function $V(\mu(u), I(u)) = \mu(u) \exp(-I(u))$, where $n \in N$ and $u \in [0,b]^n$ are arbitrary. The inequality indicators we choose for our illustration are I_{Ra}^r and I_{Rs}^r. Now for arbitrary $u, v \in [0,b]^n$, where $\mu(u) = \mu(v) = \bar{\mu}$, say, the welfare consistency property, defined as $\bar{\mu} \exp(-I_{Ra}^r(u)) \geq \bar{\mu} \exp(-I_{Ra}^r(v))$ if and only if $(b - \bar{\mu}) \exp(-I_{Rs}^r(u)) \geq (b - \bar{\mu}) \exp(-I_{Rs}^r(v))$, is the same as the consistency rule defined in (8.14) under the assumptions that efficiency considerations are absent and the achievement and shortfall inequality standards are given respectively by I_{Ra}^r and I_{Rs}^r. In fact, a general statement concerning equivalence between the weak consistency criterion and welfare consistency property can be made using reduced form achievement and shortfall social evaluation standards defined over achievement profiles with a fixed mean and the inequality pair (I_a, I_s), provided that the pair (I_a, I_s) obeys the condition (8.14).

8.9 EQUALITY OF OPPORTUNITY: AN ILLUSTRATIVE DISCUSSION

Desirability of an opportunity in a person's life is a quite rational assumption. This is because as the set of opportunities available to a person expands, the person's quality of life is likely to increase. For instance, an improvement in the financial position of a person may enable him to pay higher rent for better accommodation, spend more for better health care, purchase a car for personal use, invest in a specialized training program that will facilitate him to earn more in the future, and so on. Embodying egalitarian bias in the distribution of opportunities across persons in a society is a concern of distributive justice.

Opportunity is a many-faceted phenomenon. Opportunities can be classified broadly into two categories: circumstantial and non-circumstantial or effort based. All opportunities that come under the former category are exogenously given advantages. One cannot expand this set or improve the position in a particular advantage of this set using personal endeavor. Examples of such conveniences include inherited wealth, parental education, social connections arising from parents' social status, ethnicity, gender, religion, and so on. Since individuals do not have any command over them, they cannot be a source of opportunity inequality. Consequently, in the assessment of opportunity inequality we regard the circumstantial opportunities as irrelevant alternatives. However positions in effort-based opportunities may be improved by personal endeavors. Such opportunities are non-rival, which means the simultaneous possible availability of a given opportunity to all individuals of the society. They are excludable as well. This characteristic means that administering an opportunity to some individuals does not ensure that it will be accessible to everyone in society. Examples are education, earning, health care facilities, housing, participation in job markets, social communing, and so on. The set of such advantages constitute the source of opportunity inequality.[16]

---

[16] See, among others, Kranich (1996); Ok (1997); Weymark (2003); Hild and Voorhoeve (2004); Gaston et al. (2012); Roemer and Trannoy (2015); and Ferreira and Peragine (2016).

In order to present some analytical forms of opportunity equality evaluators, let $O_i \in L$ be the opportunity set of person i in an n-person society, where L stands for the set of all opportunity sets. A profile of opportunity sets in this community is $O = (O_1, O_2, \ldots, O_n)$. For instance, let the population size n be 3, the number of opportunities be 5, say, health (o_1), education (o_2), income (o_3), housing (o_4), and cable TV connection (o_5), so that $O_1 = \{o_2, o_3, o_4, o_5\}$, $O_2 = \{o_1, o_4\}$, and $O_3 = \{o_1, o_2, o_3, o_4, o_5\}$. This example clearly shows that the non-rival characteristic of opportunities does not necessarily imply that each person has all opportunities.

Given the population size n, we write L^n for the set of all opportunity profiles. For any $O \in L^n$, let $|O|$ stand for the vector $(|O_1|, |O_2|, \ldots, |O_n|)$, where for any set S, $|S|$ stands for the cardinality of S; the number of elements in S. Thus, for our three-person example, $|O| = (4, 2, 5)$. For any $O_i \in L$, we call $|O_i|$ the opportunity score of person $i \in \{1, 2, \ldots, n\}$. For any $O \in L^n$, denote the illfare ranked permutation of the vector $(|O_1|, |O_2|, \ldots |O_n|)$ by $O_{\uparrow} = (|O_1|_{(1)}, |O_2|_{(2)}, \ldots, |O_n|_{(n)})$.

For a vector $\underline{a} = (a_1, a_2, \ldots, a_n) \in \Re^n$, where $\sum_{i=1}^{n} a_i = 0$, let $T^{\underline{a}} : L^n \to \Re^1$ be the function defined by

$$T^{\underline{a}}(O) = \sum_{i=1}^{n} a_i |O_i|_{(i)}, \tag{8.19}$$

where $O \in L^n$ is arbitrary (Weymark 2003). Non-decreasingly ordered scores associated with the individual opportunity sets are aggregated using the weights defined by $(a_1, a_2, \ldots, a_n)$ to arrive at the summary metric $T^{\underline{a}}$. Given that the opportunity scores are non-decreasingly permutated, we may refer to $T^{\underline{a}}$ as a generalized Gini opportunity equality standard if $a_i s$ are non-increasingly ordered, that is, $a_1 \geq a_2 \geq \ldots \geq a_n$ (Weymark 1981).

$T^{\underline{a}}$ is the Kranich evaluator of opportunity equality if $a_i > 0$ for all $i < \frac{(n+1)}{2}$ and $a_i < 0$ for all $i > \frac{(n+1)}{2}$. Thus, the Kranich opportunity equality evaluation rule assigns a positive (negative) weight if the score of an opportunity set is less (more) than the median opportunity score. For our three-person example with the opportunity score vector $= (4, 2, 5)$, the components in its illfare ranked permutation $|O|_{\uparrow} = (|O_1|_{(1)}, |O_2|_{(2)}, |O_3|_{(3)}) = (2, 4, 5)$ can be assigned the weights $a_1 = 1$, $a_2 = 0$ and $a_3 = -1$, so that the value of the Kranich opportunity equality index becomes -3. We say that an opportunity equality ordering on L^n is a Kranich equality ordering if it can be represented by a Kranich equality opportunity standard. Kranich (1996) developed two characterizations of the class of the Kranich opportunity equality orderings.

Following an idea put forward by Weymark (2003), for a vector $\underline{a} = (a_1, a_2, \ldots, a_n) \in D^n$, we define the function $W^{\underline{a}} : L^n \to \Re^1$ specified by

$$ W^{\underline{a}}(O) = \frac{1}{\sum_{i=1}^{n} a_i} \sum_{i=1}^{n} a_i |O_i|_{(i)}, \qquad (8.20) $$

as a social evaluation standard for profiles of opportunity sets. If the weight sequence $\{a_i\}$ obeys the constraint $a_1 > a_2 > \cdots > a_n$, $W^{\underline{a}}$ is called a generalized Gini social opportunity evaluation function.[17]

To get deeper insight into the evaluation metric (8.20), we now study some of its important properties in detail. The first maxim is anonymity or symmetry. This saying, which stipulates invariance of opportunity welfare evaluation under any reordering of opportunity scores, ensures that the only relevant features of the persons in opportunity evaluation are their opportunity scores. Since we make the assumption that the opportunity welfare of any score profile is the same as the opportunity welfare in its any reordered counterpart, $W^{\underline{a}}$ verifies anonymity.

The next adage we consider, following Adler (2019), is the opportunity Pigou–Dalton principle. While Adler considers "gap diminishing transfer of opportunity value" (254), our formulation relies simply on the gap-reducing transfer of opportunity score. This is because in the present set-up "opportunity value" is represented by opportunity score.[18] We formulate the postulate

---

[17] Strictly speaking, Weymark refers to an ordering on i as a generalized Gini social preference ordering for opportunity profiles if it can be represented by a social evaluation function $W^{\underline{a}}$ when the underlying non-increasingly arranged weight vector $\underline{a}$ obeys the condition $\underline{a} \in \Re^n$ and $\sum_{i=1}^{n} a_i = 1$. To ensure non-negativity of the evaluation function, we assume that the weights are positive.
[18] For alternative suggestions, see, among others, Ok and Kranich (1998); and Weymark (2003).

rigorously as follows. Given $O = (O_1, O_2, \ldots, O_n) \in L^n$, suppose there exist persons i and j such that in the ordered score profile $(|O_1|_{(1)}, |O_2|_{(2)}, \ldots, |O_n|_{(n)})$, $|O_i|_{(i1)} < |O_j|_{(j)}$, that is, person i is less privileged than person j in terms of opportunity score. Then we say that $\hat{O} = (\hat{O}_1, \hat{O}_2, \ldots, \hat{O}_n) \in L^n$ is obtained from O by transferring one or more opportunities that the more privileged person j has but the less privileged person i does not have if $\hat{O}_i = O_i \cup A$, $\hat{O}_j = O_j / A$, and $\hat{O}_k = O_k$ for all $k \in \{1, 2, \ldots, n\}/\{i, j\}$ such that $|\hat{O}_i|_{(i1)} \leq |\hat{O}_j|_{(j)}$, where $A \subseteq O_j/O_i$. Thus, we transfer some opportunities of the set A, none of which are in O_i but all of them are in O_j. Evidently, the transfer does not require that O_i be a subset of O_j. Note also that the transfer is opportunity-score rank preserving, that is, it does not alter the opportunity score ranks of the individuals. For the three-person example we have considered, although $O_3/O_2 = \{o_2, o_3, o_5\}$, we can transfer at most one opportunity, say o_2, from O_3 to O_2 to keep ranks of the individuals in the original score profile $|O|_\uparrow = (|O_1|_{(1)}, |O_2|_{(2)}, |O_3|_{(3)})$ unchanged, so that $\hat{O}_2 = O_2 \cup \{o_2\}$, $\hat{O}_3 = O_3/\{o_2\}$ and $\hat{O}_1 = O_1$.

We say that an opportunity social evaluation standard $W : L^n \rightarrow \Re^1$ satisfies the opportunity Pigou–Dalton principle if for any $O \in L^n$, $W(O) < W(\hat{O})$, where $\hat{O} \in L^n$ is obtained from O by a transfer of one or more opportunities from a more privileged person to a less privileged person, as defined above.

To demonstrate that $W^{\underline{a}}$ fulfills the opportunity transfer postulate, note that $\sum_{i=1}^{n} |O_i|_{(i)} = \sum_{i=1}^{n} |\hat{O}_i|_{(i)}$ and $\sum_{i=1}^{k} |O_i|_{(i)} \leq \sum_{i=1}^{k} |\hat{O}_i|_{(i)}$ for all $1 \leq k < n$, with $<$ for some $k < n$. This is essentially the condition that of two distributions $|O|_\uparrow$ and $|\hat{O}|_\uparrow$ of opportunity scores of a given total, the latter integer Lorenz dominates the former (Savaglio and Vannucci 2007; Chakravarty and Zoli 2012). As Chakravarty and Zoli established, this is the same as the condition that the value of the generalized Gini opportunity welfare social metric $W^{\underline{a}}$ increases if $|\hat{O}|_\uparrow$ is arrived from $|O|_\uparrow$ by a sequence of opportunity transfers from more privileged persons to less privileged persons, where at each stage of the sequence exactly one opportunity is transferred. Thus, $W^{\underline{a}}$ satisfies the opportunity transfer postulate unambiguously.

An increase in opportunities in some circumstances is likely to indicate social improvement. For instance, if we consider a common expansion of everyone's opportunity set from any initial distribution by a new set of opportunities, then opportunity social evaluation should go up. Evidently, the generalized Gini social evaluation metric respects this stipulation. This maxim parallels the absolute incremental principle we considered for income social welfare functions.

Formally, an opportunity social evaluation function $W : L^n \to \Re^1$ is said to satisfy the opportunity absolute incremental principle if for any $O \in L^n$, and for a non-empty set of available opportunities S, where $O_i \bigcap S = \phi$ for all $i \in \{1, 2, \ldots, n\}$, $W(O) < W(O_1 \bigcup S, O_2 \bigcup S, \ldots, O_n \bigcup S)$. The set S may consist of newly available opportunities or some existing opportunities to which nobody had access.

One limitation of $W^{\underline{a}}$ is its unsuitability for cross-population comparison of opportunity social evaluation. It is a violator of the population-size neutrality property, which requires opportunity social welfare to remain unchanged under any replication of the population, assuming that the opportunity set is fixed. If we choose $a_i = (2(n - i) + 1)$ in (8.20), then the underlying metric, the Gini opportunity social welfare function $\frac{1}{n^2} \sum_{i=1}^{n} (2(n - i) + 1)|O_i|_{(i)}$, passes the property unambiguously.

Our analysis did not consider opportunities that are circumstantial. In a general framework, an individual's well-being is determined by a combination of his efforts and circumstances. Consequently, in this framework wellbeing is associated both with attributes for which individuals are not liable (circumstances) and with attributes for which they can be held liable (efforts). Adler (2019) provides a discussion on how these individual wellbeing levels can be aggregated in an axiomatic structure to arrive at an opportunity social evaluation metric. For further discussions on opportunity equality, the readers are referred to two recent survey articles by Roemer and Trannoy (2015) and Ferreira and Peragine (2016)[19]

---

[19] Highly valuable contributions also came from Pattanaik and Xu (1990); Gravel (1994, 1998); Herrero, Iturbe-Ormaetxe, and Nieto (1998); Ok and Kranich (1998);

8.10 INEQUALITY AND WELFARE WITH AN ORDINAL DIMENSION OF WELL-BEING

Several dimensions of human well-being are ordinally significant in contrast to income which is measurable on a ratio scale and hence possesses cardinal significance. Examples of ordinal dimensions are self-reported health status, educational attainment, and happiness. Each of them can be ordered by two or more exclusive and ranked categories. For instance, individuals in a society can be partitioned with respect to their self-reported health statuses into the following six categories, arranged in increasing order of importance: very bad, bad, fair, good, very good, and excellent. These categories can be assigned real numbers arbitrarily by maintaining the restriction that a higher number should be assigned to a better category. For instance, they can be accredited the numbers 1, 2, 3, 4, 5, and 6, respectively. One can also assign the numbers 2, 8, 10, 11, 12, and 15 respectively to them.

In the current context, we will be concerned with health inequality only. However, the methodology analyzed in the section is quite general and applies to other such dimensions such as educational attainments and happiness. The standard theory of inequality in which the mean is taken as the reference point cannot be applied since mean is not a well-defined concept here. Consequently, the Pigou–Dalton transfer principle becomes inappropriate as a redistributive criterion. Some studies argued that the median can be used as an equality notion corresponding to the case of the mean in the standard inequality investigation (Allison and Foster 2004; Abul Naga and Yalcin 2008). "But median is not well defined for ordinal data, in particular when there is a small number of categories" (Cowell and Flachaire 2017, 319).

Cowell and Flachaire suggested a satisfactory approach to inequality measurement in an ordinal framework. In a more recent

---

Roemer (1998, 2012); Arlegi and Nieto (2001); Ooghe, Schokkaert, and Van de Gear (2007); Alcalde-Unzu, Arlegi, and Nieto (2007); Savaglio and Vannucci (2007); Foster (2010); Almas et al. (2011); Fleurbaey and Maniquet (2012); Pignataro (2012); Fajrado-Gonzalez (2016); Kanbur and Stiglitz (2016); and others.

contribution, Gravel, Macdalou, and Moyes (2021) identified a normative dominance principle and a statistically implementable criterion for a categorical variable, where each of these conditions is equivalent to the notion of equalization underlying the Hammond (1976) equity principle, which is concerned with the distribution of a variable possessing ordinal significance.[20]

Here we briefly discuss the Cowell–Flachaire approach. They argued that a person's location in the underlying distribution is related to his "status" in society. In order to formally present the concept of status, let ϑ_i denote person i's endowment of utility, P be the distribution function of utility for a population of size n, and K be the number of categories. Then the status s_i of person i is defined uniquely as a function of ϑ_i, P, and n such that the status becomes independent of the cardinalization of ϑ_i. One simple specification of s_i is the standard definition of position, the cumulative proportion of population not better than person i. Formally, $S_i = P(\vartheta_i)$. As Cowell and Flachaire (2017) argued, for categorical data where only the ordered categories and number of individuals in each category are available, it is quite plausible to take the status measure as $s_i = \frac{1}{n} \sum_{j=1}^{k(i)} n_j$, where n_j is the number of individuals in category j; $j = 1, 2, \ldots, K$; $n = \sum_{j=1}^{K} n_j$, and $k(i)$ is the category to which person i belongs.

The reference point e may be given exogenously or it may be assumed to depend on the vector $s \in S^n \subseteq \Re^n$ of individual statuses. Let S_e^n denote the subset of S^n that consists of status distributions with the same value of e. That is, for the population under consideration S_e^n is the set of all status distributions that are conditional on the reference point.

Cowell and Flachaire (2017) axiomatized a general class of inequality indices on S_e^n. While the Pigou–Dalton condition does not have any relevance here, these authors suggested a postulate that indicates sensitivity to the distance of an individual's status

---

[20] See Chapter 7 for a discussion on Hammond equity. In an earlier contribution, Gravel, Macdalou, and Moyes (2018) derived the analogue of the Lorenz superiority relation using the Hammond equity principle for a continuous ordinal variable. They also provided social choice interpretations of some of their characterizations.

from the reference point. More precisely, their "monotonicity in distance" axiom stipulates that given two status distributions that differ only with respect to one person's status, the distribution under which the person's status is closer to the reference point designates lower inequality. Consequently, perfect equality arises if the distance from the reference point is zero for everyone. The postulate, thus, embodies equity biasness into distributional judgments. A natural extension of the single dimensional ratio scale invariance axiom to the current framework says that an equi-proportional change in all individual status values and the reference point keeps inequality unvarying. Given a reference point, the index is assumed to satisfy symmetry in individual statuses.

For illustrative purposes, we choose the following special case of the Cowell–Flachaire general class:

$$I_{CF}(s,e) = -\frac{1}{n} \sum_{j=1}^{n} \log \left(\frac{s_j}{e} \right). \tag{8.21}$$

Given problems with the mean and the median as the reference point, an alternative option is to choose the reference point independent of the distribution s. If we define status as an individual position in the distribution, then the situation of perfect equality arises only when $e = 1$, the maximum possible value of s_j for all $j = 1, 2, \ldots, n$. Evidently, in the case of perfect equality, the inequality evaluator I_{CF} becomes zero, otherwise it takes on a positive value since for any $j = 1, 2, \ldots, n, 0 < s_j \leq 1$.

We conclude this section by suggesting a direct approach to welfare and inequality evaluation for the dimension health. As before, assume that individuals can be partitioned into K categories, organized in increasing order of importance. For simplicity of exposition, let h_i be the positive integer weight accredited to category i, where $h_1 < h_2 < \cdots < h_K$. The status s_j of person j is the weight assigned to the category of the dimension to which he belongs, where $j = 1, 2, \ldots, n$. The illfare ranked permutation of the status vector s is denoted by $\bar{s}$. Clearly, more than one individual may have the same status. If more than one person possesses the same status, then in $\bar{s}$ the tie should be broken arbitrarily. A health social evaluation function W_H is a real-valued function defined on S_e^n. Formally, $W_H : S_e^n \to \Re^1$.

Following Chakravarty and Zoli (2012), we consider a form of the Pigou–Dalton transfer principle that bears a similarity with the Hammond equity principle. Suppose the status of a person, say person i, increases by 1 and that of person j, who has a higher status than person i, reduces by 1, and statuses of all other persons remain unaffected. Since this compound change indicates an egalitarian bias in the health standing distribution, we refer to it as a favorable composite change.[21] Then the postulate demands that welfare does not reduce under a favorable composite change. A health social evaluation function is said to satisfy the health monotonicity principle if its value does not reduce under a minimal increment, that is, the health status of only one person goes up by 1, and the health statuses of all other persons remain unaffected.[22] We refer to this as minimal increment since the categories are assigned positive integral weights in increasing order.

To understand these two elementary transformations, assume that in a ten-person society with three categories, the category-wise distribution of individuals is $(5, 3, 2)$. Now, consider a person in category 1 and suppose because of a minimal increment he moves to the adjacent higher category, category 2. The consequential splitting of the population with respect to categories becomes $(4, 4, 2)$. Next, given $(5, 3, 2)$, suppose under a favorable composite change one person in category 3 moves down to category 2 and one person in category 1 moves up to category 2. The resulting categorical partition of the population comes to be $(4, 5, 1)$. Evidently, upward and downward movements of the individuals across categories explicitly depend on the positive integral weights assigned to the categories. Since there is more than one person in a category, in the rank-ordered status vector we break the ties arbitrarily. For instance, since in $(5, 3, 2)$ there are two persons in category 3, in the ordered status profile $\bar{s}$ one of them should be assigned the rank 10 and the other gets the rank 9. There is no loss of generality here.

---

[21] See also Fishburn and Lavalle (1995); and Chakravarty and D'Ambrosio (2006).
[22] See also Gravel, Magdalou, and Moyes (2020).

It is easy to verify that the Gini health social welfare function $W_{GH} : S_e^H \to \Re^1$, defined as,

$$W_{GH}(s) = \frac{1}{n^2} \sum_{i=1}^{n} (2(n-i)+1)\bar{s}_i, \qquad (8.22)$$

verifies these two postulates. Satisfaction of the monotonicity postulate follows from positivity of the sequence $\{(2(n-i)+1)\}$. Non-decreasingness of W_{GH} under a favorable composite change is ensured by decreasingness of the sequence $\{(2(n-i)+1)\}$. This symmetric population replication invariant social evaluation standard is bounded between h_1 and h_K, where the lower and upper bounds are attained respectively in the extreme cases when all the individuals possess the worst possible and the best possible health conditions.

8.11 INEQUALITY AS AN ORDINAL NOTION

In the inequality evaluation methods we have presented until now, the inequality and equality numbers have cardinal significance. In case we regard inequality as an ordinal conception, then an increasing (ordinal) transformation of the inequality standard may generate different social evaluation ranking by any procedure discussed in Sections 8.3–8.5. To understand this more explicitly, consider a non-identity increasing transformation $g : \Re_+^1 \to [0,1)$ of the Atkinson–Kolm–Sen index I_{AKS}. For instance, we may choose $g(z) = z^2$. Then $1 - \mu(u)(1 - g(I_{AKS}(u)))$ cannot be expressed as increasing transformations of the Atkinson–Kolm–Sen social evaluation function $\mu(u)(1 - I_{AKS}(u))$.

The issue of ethical inequality measurement with ordinal significance have been addressed, among others, by Blackorby and Donaldson (1984), Ebert (1987), and Dutta and Esteban (1992). We briefly summarize here the Ebert approach.

We assume the existence of a continuous, relative inequality ordering $\geq_I$ on $\Re_{++}^n$, where $n \geq 2$ is arbitrary. These two assumptions about $\geq_I$ ensure, respectively, the existence of a continuous inequality index I on $\Re_{++}^n$ and scale invariance of

I. Because of the ordinal characteristic of I, any increasing transformation of I conveys the same information as I itself.

Trade-offs between equality and efficiency can be represented by a continuous ordering $\geq_{EE}$ defined on $\Re^n_{++} \times \Gamma_I$, where Γ_I stands for the set of indifference classes of $\geq_I$. For any $u \in \Re^n_{++}$, we write u_I for the indifference class of $\geq_I$ to which u belongs. Consistency between the trade-off ordering $\geq_{EE}$ and the inequality ordering $\geq_I$ demands that for a given efficiency level $\bar{\mu}$, two arbitrary profiles $u, v \in \Re^n_{++}$ are ordered by $\geq_I$ in the same way as the associated indifference classes are ranked by $\geq_{EE}$. Formally, the consistency requirement demands that $u \geq_I v \leftrightarrow [(\bar{\mu}, u_I) \geq_{EE} (\bar{\mu}, v_I)]$ for all $u, v \in \Re^n_{++}$ and for all arbitrarily given $\bar{\mu} > 0$.

Given the orderings $\geq_I$ and $\geq_{EE}$, we can now define a social welfare ordering $\geq_W$ as follows: For all $u, v \in \Re^n_{++}$,

$$u \geq_W v \leftrightarrow [(\mu(u), u_I) \geq_{EE} (\mu(v), v_I)]. \qquad (8.23)$$

Continuity of $\geq_W$ follows from continuity of $\geq_I$ and $\geq_{EE}$. Consistency between $\geq_I$ and $\geq_{EE}$, combined with the relativity of $\geq_I$, guarantees that welfare ordering $\geq_W$ has the following characteristic: For all $u, v \in \Re^n_{++}$ and for all scalars $c > 0$,

$$\left[\frac{u}{\mu(u)} \geq_W \frac{v}{\mu(v)} \right] \leftrightarrow \left[\left[\frac{cu}{\mu(u)} \geq_W \frac{cv}{\mu(v)} \right] \right]. \qquad (8.24)$$

This stipulation, which we refer to as scaling consistency, is weaker than homotheticity. It is possible to reverse the procedure. For any $\geq_W$ obeying scaling consistency, it is possible to get continuous orderings $\geq_I$ and $\geq_{EE}$ that maintain consistency between them and $\geq_I$ is also relative. Scaling consistency describes the properties that a social evaluation ordering should possess for deriving ordinally significant ethical inequality indices.[23]

---

[23] See also Blackorby and Donaldson (1984).

8.12 FAIRNESS IN NETWORK RESOURCE ALLOCATION: AN ANALYTICAL EXPOSITION

Fairness of a system looks at its rightness by taking into account the distinctiveness of each person's perspective. In the theory of distribution it demonstrates impartial treatment of claimants without favoritism. In social welfare evaluation, fairness as impartiality is formalized via symmetry.

In wireless networks each user is assigned a share of the resource by resource allocation algorithms.[24] A fairness measure of a wireless network algorithm determines to what extent the resource has been distributed among the users without any discrimination. In this section we briefly analyze some of the fairness metrics that have been suggested in the newly emerging computer science literature on fairness in discrete division models.

Given that there are $n \in N$ wireless network users, $x = (x_1, x_2, \ldots, x_n) \in \Re_{++}^n$ represents a typical resource allocation vector, where for all $i \in \{1, 2, \ldots, n\}$, x_i stands for the resource allocated to user i. In other words, $(x_1, x_2, \ldots, x_n)$ is a representative allotment of the throughput $\sum_{j=1}^{n} x_j$ across the users. The set of all possible resource allocation vectors is given by R_{++}. This formulation allows the existence of zero-resource users. A fairness standard F in network resource allocation is a non-negative real-valued function defined on $\Re_{++}$. Formally, $F : \Re_{++} \to \Re_+^1$. For any $n \in N$, $x \in \Re_{++}^n$, $F(x)$ is a (non-negative) quantification of how justly the resource x has been apportioned among the users.

Several intuitively reasonable axioms for a fairness evaluator have been proposed in the literature. Our presentation in this section relies on Lan et al. (2010), who assumed single-user normalization at the outset. According to this condition, for any $x_i \in \Re_{++}^1$, $F(x_1) = 1$. Apart from continuity and scale invariance, the authors have suggested three more axioms. Of these, the "axiom of asymptotic saturation" demands that fairness arising from sharing of 1 unit of the resource by each user becomes independent of the

---

[24] See the recent survey by Ahmad, Beg, and Ahmad (2016) and references cited therein for discussion on this issue.

number of users as this number increases substantially. Formally, $\frac{F(1^n)}{F(1^{n+1})} \to 1$ as $n \to \infty$. The second postulate, "axiom of irrelevance of partition," is a separability condition. It says that for any partitioning of the set of users into two non-empty subgroups with respect to some attribute, say, regions of residences, overall fairness can be calculated using subgroup fairness levels. The third maxim, "axiom of monotonicity," claims that if the number of users is two, then the value of the fairness metric $F(c, 1 - c)$ increases as the absolute difference $|(1 - 2c)|$ between the shares of the total resource of the users decreases. In words, a more equitable distribution of resources between two users increases fairness.

Lan et al. (2010) demonstrated that a fairness metric satisfying these five postulates is strictly S-concave and hence symmetric, manifesting indifference between rearrangements of a given pattern of resource allocation. This pinpoints impartial treatments of the resource users. Symmetry enables us to restrict attention on the illfare ranked permutation $\bar{x} = (\bar{x}_1, \bar{x}_2, \ldots, \bar{x}_n)$ of $x = (x_1, x_2, \ldots, x_n)$. The authors have rigorously established that the following functional form can be regarded as a unified representation of their fairness measures derived by employing the five axioms considered above

$$F^\beta_{LKCS}(x) = \left(\left(\frac{\bar{x}_i}{\sum_{j=1}^n \bar{x}_j} \right)^{(1-\beta)} \right)^{\frac{1}{\beta}}, \qquad (8.25)$$

where $n \in N$ and $x \in \Re^n_{++}$ are arbitrary, $\beta < 1$ is any real number.[25]

We refer to F^β_{LKCS} as the La–Ka–Chiang–Sabharwal (LKCS) fairness metric. At $\beta = 1$, the continuity axiom is violated. For any $n \in N$ and $x \in \Re^n_{++}$, $\beta \in (-\infty, 1)$, F^β_{LKCS} is bounded between 1 and n, where the lower bound is achieved when only one user is allotted the entire resource $\sum_{j=1}^n x_j$, the situation of imperfect fairness, and the upper bound is attained when absolute or perfect fairness materializes, that is, when the total resource is equally

---

[25] As Lan et al. (2010, Theorem 5) demonstrated, if the range of the fairness metric is the entire real line, then $\beta > 1$ is allowable. Since we have assumed at the outset that the fairness metric is non-negative, the case $\beta > 1$ is excluded.

shared by the users. For any given $n \in N$ and $x \in \Re_{++}^n$, F_{LKCS}^β is non-decreasing in $\beta \in (-\infty, 1)$. For a given resource allocation $(c, 1 - c)$, an increase in the value of β over $(-\infty, 1)$ pushes the fairness contour toward the low fairness region. Consequently, the parameter β describes the shape of the fairness metric; an increase in the value of β forces the fairness contours to be concentrated in the low-fairness region.

A Robin Hood operation increases the value of F_{LKCs}^β univocally, signifying egalitarian inclination of fairness. (By strict S-concavity of F_{LKCS}^β, only rank-preserving Robin Hood operations are permitted.) If the resource allotted to user i under the scheme $\bar{x}$ is increased by a small amount ε such that the rank orders of the users remain unchanged in $\bar{x}$, then F_{LKCS}^β increases if and only if

$$\bar{x}_i < \left(\frac{\sum_{j=1}^n \bar{x}_j}{\sum_{i=1}^n \bar{x}_i^{(1-\beta)}} \right)^{\frac{1}{\beta}} \text{ and } 0 < \varepsilon < \left(\frac{\sum_{j=1}^n \bar{x}_j}{\sum_{j=1}^n \bar{x}_i^{(1-\beta)}} \right)^{\frac{1}{\beta}} - \bar{x}_i. \text{ This property}$$

of F_{LKCS}^β, which buttons down efficiency bias of fairness may be termed "axiom of bounded monotonicity."

The next property of F_{LKCs}^β, the axiom of inactive user independence, stipulates that the addition of users with zero resources does not change fairness. Formally:

Axiom of inactive user independence: For any $n \in N$ and $x \in \Re_{++}^n$, $F_{LKCS}^\beta(x) = F_{LKCS}^\beta(y)$ where $y \in \Re_{++}^{n+m}$ is given by $y = (01^m, x)$.

Likewise, the deletion of inactive users does not alter the level of fairness. The attainable upper bound of the number of inactive users is $(n - F_{LKCS}^\beta)$, and the attainable lower bound of the maximum resource to a user is $\frac{\sum_{i=1}^n x_i}{F_{LKCS}^\beta}$ (Lan et al. 2010).

This inactive user independence postulate makes the fairness metric F_{IKCS}^β different from usual equality standards. In contrast to the insensitivity of F_{IKCS}^β to zero users, an equality standard decreases if one or more individuals enter the society with zero income. This can be verified easily using the Bonferroni and Gini equality standards $\frac{1}{\mu(v)n} \sum_{i=1}^n \bar{\mu}_i$ and $\frac{1}{n^2\mu(v)} \sum_{i=1}^n [(2(n - i) + 1)]\bar{v}_i$, respectively. To understand this clearly, rewrite the Gini equality metric explicitly in terms of the size $\sum_{i=1}^n v_i$ and the Gini social evaluation standard $\frac{1}{n^2} \sum_{i=1}^n [(2(n - i) + 1)]\bar{v}_i$ as

$\frac{1}{n}\frac{\sum_{i=1}^{n}[((2n-i))+1]\bar{v}_i}{\sum_{i=1}^{n}v_i}$. Now, with the inclusion of zero incomes, the size remains unaffected. However, the numerator $\frac{1}{n}\sum_{i=1}^{n}[((2n-i))+1]\bar{v}_i$, the social evaluation standard multiplied by the population size n, decreases when one or more zero incomes are included. This explicitly demonstrates the reduction of the Gini equality metric under the addition of zero incomes to the distribution.

We now analyze some important special cases of F_{LKCS}^{β} to understand it in greater detail. For $\beta = -1$, F_{LKCS}^{β} becomes $\frac{(\sum_{i=1}^{n}x_i)^2}{\sum_{i=1}^{n}x_i^2} = nJ(x)$, where J is Jain's fairness measure (Jain, Chiu, and Hawe 1984). Although a Robin Hood operation increases the value of J unambiguously, the increment becomes independent of how high or low x_j is, given that the difference $(x_j-x_i) > 0$ between the resources of the donor j and the recipient i is fixed. However, J is a violator of the inactive user independence principle. As $\beta \to 0$, F_{LKCS}^{β} becomes $\exp(K(x))$, where "exp" is the exponential transformation and $K(x) = -\sum_{j=1}^{n}\left(\frac{x_j}{(\sum_{i=1}^{n}x_i)}\log\frac{x_j}{(\sum_{i=1}^{n}x_i)}\right)$ is the Shannon entropy function. Continuity of the entropy function on $\Re_{++}^{n}$ is ensured under the conventional assumption that $0\log 0 = 0$. The value of the fairness metric $\exp(K(x))$ associated with the entropy function increases under a Robin Hood operation by a higher amount with a lower resource of the recipient. In fact, this is true for all members of F_{LKCS}^{β} when $0 \le \beta < 1$ holds. As $\beta \to -\infty$, F_{LKCS}^{β} approaches $\min_i \frac{(\sum_{i=1}^{n}x_i)}{x_i}$, the min ratio.

Since F_{LKCS}^{β} is bounded above by n, the shortfall $(n - F_{LKCS}^{\beta})$, if it is positive, arises due to the unfair distribution of the throughput $(\sum_{i=1}^{n}x_i)$ among the users. Hence the gap $(1 - F_{LKCS}^{\beta})$ may be marked as a measure of discrimination. It indicates how unjustly the throughput is allotted among the users. For a fixed level of throughput $(\sum_{i=1}^{n}x_i)$, a reduction in discrimination is equivalent to an increase in fairness and vice versa.

Often from an ethical perspective it may be necessary to compare two or more networks in terms of fairness. Such a comparison may involve a different number of users across networks. To understand this explicitly, suppose that of the two networks I and II, the former provides service to m users and the latter is utilized by n customers, where $m < n$, say. To compare the two networks with respect to fairness, we expand I by adding $(n - m)$ inactive users so that the common user size of the networks III, the expanded form of I, and II becomes n. By the inactive user independence principle, $F(y) = F(z)$, where $y = (y_1, y_2, \ldots, y_m) \in \Re^m_{++}$ and $z = (01^{(n-m)}, y) \in \Re^n_{++}$ are respectively the resource allocation vectors associated with the network I and III. This enables us to compare the fairness levels of the networks II and I, using an intermediate network III, which is fairness equivalent to I.

We conclude the section with the remark that the following simple transformation of the Gini equality metric enables us to consider it as a fairness measure:

$$F_G(x) = \frac{\sum_{i=1}^{n}[((2n - i)) + 1]\bar{x}_i}{\sum_{i=1}^{n} x_i}. \tag{8.26}$$

Since it employs Gini-type aggregation, we call it the Gini fairness index. The value of this continuous, symmetric and inactive user insensitive fairness indicator does not decrease under a rank preserving increment in the resource of any user. Higher weights assigned to lower resource quantities ensure that F_G obeys the Robin Hood principle. Like F^β_{LKCS}, the Gini fairness metric is also bounded between 1 and n.

8.13 EXERCISES

(E-8.1) Show that if the rank order of individuals across different sources of income are the same, then the overall absolute Gini index is the simple sum of the absolute Gini indices for different types of incomes.

(E-8.2) Give a numerical example to demonstrate that the Bonferroni inequality index is a violator of the Daltonian population principle.

(E-8.3) Consider the social evaluation function $\sum_{i=1}^{n} a_i v_i^0$, where v^0 is the non-increasingly ordered permutation of the income distribution $v = (v_1, v_2, \ldots, v_n) \in \Re^n_{++}$, with $\Re^n_{++}$ being the non-negative orthant of the

n-dimensional Euclidean space excluding the origin and the sequence $\{a_i\}$ is positive. Show that increasingness of the sequence $\{a_i\}$ is necessary and sufficient for the evaluation function to be strictly S-concave.

(E-8.4) Clearly argue why for the Atkinson inequality index to be well defined, all incomes should be positive.

(E-8.5) Consider an arbitrary income distribution $v = (v_1, v_2, \ldots, v_n) \in \Re^n_{++}$, where $\Re^n_{++}$ is the non-negative orthant of the n-dimensional Euclidean space with the origin deleted. Let $\mu(v)$ stand for the mean of v, and $\bar{v}$ and v^0 stand respectively for the non-decreasingly and non-increasingly ordered permutations of v. Suppose $I_{GR}(v)$ denotes the relative Gini index of v. Show that the following formulations of the Gini social evaluation function $\mu(v)(1 - I_{GR}(v)) = \mu(v) - \frac{1}{2n^2} \sum_{i=1}^n \sum_{j=1}^n |v_i - v_j|$ are equivalent:

(a) $\mu(v) - \frac{1}{n^2} \sum_{1 \leq i \leq j \leq n} (\bar{v}_j - \bar{v}_i)$,

(b) $\mu(v) - \frac{1}{n^2} \sum_{i=1}^n \sum_{j=1}^n \min(v_i, v_j)$,

(c) $\mu(v) - \frac{1}{2n^2} \sum_{i=1}^n \sum_{j=1}^n (\max(v_i, v_j) - \min(v_i, v_j))$,

(d) $\frac{1}{n^2} \sum_{i=1}^n [2i - 1]v_i^0$,

(e) $\frac{1}{n^2} \sum_{i=1}^n [2(n - i) + 1]\bar{v}_i$.

(E-8.6) Show that a social evaluation function satisfying the strong Pareto principle satisfies the weak Pareto principle as well.

(E-8.7) Check if the standard deviation and the coefficient of variation can be interpreted in terms of measures of risk within the Harsanyi framework.

(E-8.8) Show that if the rank order of individuals across different sources of income are the same, then the overall relative Gini index is a weighted average of the relative Gini indices for different income sources and types of income, where the weights sum to unity.

(E-8.9) Consider an arbitrary resource allocation vector $x = (x_1, x_2, \ldots, x_n) \in \Re^n_{++}$ of the throughput $\sum_{j=1}^n x_j$ across users, where $\Re_{++}^n$ is the non-negative orthant of the n-dimensional Euclidean space excluding the origin. Examine the suitability of the function $\sum_{j=1}^n \left(\frac{x_j}{\sum_{i=1}^n x_i} \right)^r$ as a fairness metric in terms of its satisfaction of the postulates (a) non-negativity, (b) single-user normalization, (c) symmetry, (d) increasingness under a Robin Hood operation, and (e) inactive user independence principle.

(E-8.10) Argue rigorously how a real-valued linear homogenous function of attainment gaps can be regarded as a strongly consistent inequality metric.

(E-8.11) Show that the illfare-ranked S-Gini opportunity welfare metric $\frac{1}{n^\beta} \sum_{i=1}^n \left(i^\beta - (i-1)^\beta \right) |O_i|_{(i)}$ satisfies the following postulates: (a) opportunity absolute incremental principle, (b) opportunity Pigou–Dalton principle, (c) anonymity, and (d) population-size neutrality property, where $(|O_1|_{(1)}, |O_2|_{(2)}, \ldots, |O_n|_{(n)})$ is the non-decreasingly ordered permutation of the opportunity-score profile $(|O_1|, |O_2|, \ldots, |O_n|)$ and $0 < \beta < 1$ is a parameter.

(E-8.12) Consider the mean logarithmic deviation index of inequality. Give a numerical example to illustrate its subgroup decomposability property by determining its within-group and between-group components.

(E-8.13) Demonstrate rigorously that the Atkinson index is increasingly related to the generalized entropy family.

8.14 BIBLIOGRAPHICAL NOTES

Ebert (1988) and Cowell (2016) provide in-depth presentations of axioms of single-dimensional inequality. For deeper discussions on ethical approaches to single-dimensional inequality evaluation, see Blackorby, Bossert, and Donaldson (1999) and chapter 1 of Chakravarty (2015). A nice treatment of the measurement of inequality under uncertainty using von Neumann–Morgenstern utility functions is available in Dahlby (1987). An excellent discussion on the relationship between attainment and shortfall inequality indices in a descriptive framework can be found in Bosmans (2016). Two highly informative recent surveys on equality of opportunity are Roemer and Trannoy (2015) and Ferreira and Peragine (2016). An axiomatic analysis of inequality measurement with ordinal data is available in Cowell and Flachaire (2017). Ebert (1987) made a rigorous discussion on inequality as an ordinal concept. A good reference for an axiomatic treatment of fairness in network resource allocation is Lan et al. (2010).

REFERENCES

Aaberge, R. 2007. "Characterizations of Lorenz Curves and Income Distributions." *Social Choice and Welfare* 17 (4): 639–653.

Abul Naga, R. H., and T. Yalcin. 2008. "Inequality Measurement for Ordered Response Health Data." *Journal of Health Economics* 27 (6): 1614–25.

Adler, M. D. 2012. *Well-Being and Fair Distribution: Beyond Cost-Benefit Analysis.* Oxford: Oxford University Press.

———. 2019. *Measuring Social Welfare.* Oxford: Oxford University Press.

Ahmad, A., M. T. Beg, and S. N. Ahmad. 2016. "Fairness Issues and Measures in Wireless Networks: A Survey." *IOSR Journal of Electronics and Communication Engineering* 11 (6): 20–24.

Alcalde-Unzu, J., R. Arlegi, and J. Nieto. 2007. "Cardinality-Based Equality of Opportunities." *Review of Economic Design* 10 (4): 285–304.

Allanson, P., and D. Petrie. 2014. "Understanding the Vertical Equity Judgments Underpinning Health Inequality Measures." *Health Economics* 23 (11): 1390–1396.

Allison, R. A., and J. E. Foster. 2004. "Measuring Health Inequality Using Qualitative Data." *Journal of Health Economics* 23 (3): 505–552.

Almas, I., A. W. Cappelen, J. T.Lind, E. Sorensen, and B. Tungodden. 2011. "Measuring Unfair (in) Equality." *Journal of Public Economics* 95 (1–8): 488–499.

Amiel, Y., and F. A. Cowell. 1992. "Measurement of Income Inequality: Experimental Test by Questionnaire." *Journal of Public Economics* 47 (1): 3–26.

———. 2003. "Inequality, Welfare and Monotonicity." *Research on Economic Inequality* 9 (1): 35–46.

Arlegi, R., and J. Nieto. 2001. "Ranking Opportunity Sets: An Approach Based on the Preference for Flexibility." *Social Choice and Welfare* 18 (1): 23–36.

Atkinson, A. B. 1970. "On the Measurement of Inequality." *Journal of Economic Theory* 2 (3): 244–263.

Banerjee, A. K. 2019. "Fuzzy Inequality Ranking Relations and Their Crisp Approximations." In *Deprivation, Inequality and Polarization: Essays in Honor of S. R. Chakravarty*, edited by I. Dasgupta and M. Mitra, 67–81. New York: Springer.

Bárcena-Martin, E., and J. Silber. 2013. "On the Generalization and Decomposition of the Bonferroni Index." *Social Choice and Welfare* 41 (4): 763–787.

Besley, T., and I. Preston. 1988. "Invariance and the Axiomatics of Income Tax Progressivity: A Comment." *Bulletin of Economic Research* 40 (2): 159–163.

Blackorby C., W. Bossert, and D. Donaldson. 1999. "Income Inequality Measurement: The Normative Approach." In *Handbook of Income Inequality Measurement*, edited by J. Silber, 133–157. Boston: Kluwer.

Blackorby, C., and D. Donaldson. 1978. "Measures of Relative Equality and Their Meaning in Terms of Social Welfare." *Journal of Economic Theory* 18 (1): 59–80.

———. 1980. "A Theoretical Treatment of Indices of Absolute Inequality." *International Economic Review* 21 (1): 107–136.

———. 1982. "Ratio-Scale and Translation-Scale Full Interpersonal Comparability without Domain Restrictions: Admissible Social Evaluation Functions." *International Economic Review* 23 (2): 249–268.

———. 1984. "Ethically Significant Ordinal Indexes Relative Inequality." In *Advances in Econometrics*, edited by R. Basmann and G. Rhodes, 3:131–147. Greenwich: JAI Press.

Blackorby C., D. Donaldson, and M. Auersperg. 1981. "A New Procedure for the Measurement of Inequality within and among Population Subgroups." *Canadian Journal of Economics* 14 (4): 665–685.

Blackorby C., D. Donaldson, and J. A. Weymark. 1984. "Social Choice with Interpersonal Utility Comparisons: A Diagrammatic Introduction." *International Economic Review* 25 (2): 327–356.

Blewett, E. 1982. "Measuring Lifecycle Inequality." PhD diss., University of British Columbia, Vancouver.

Boadway, R. 2016. "Cost–Benefit Analysis." In *Oxford Handbook of Well-Being and Public Policy*, edited by M. D. Adler and M. Fleurbaey, 47–81. New York: Oxford University Press.

Bonferroni, C. E. 1930. *Elementi di statistica generate*. Firenze: Libreria Seber.

Bosmans, K. 2016. "Consistent Comparisons of Attainment and Shortfall Inequality: A Critical Examination." *Health Economics* 25 (11): 1425–1432.

Bosmans, K., and F. A. Cowell. 2010. "The Class of Absolute Decomposable Inequality Measures." *Economics Letters* 109 (3): 154–156.

Bossert, W., and A. Pfingsten. 1990. "Intermediate Inequality, Concepts, Indices and Implications." *Mathematical Social Sciences* 19 (2): 117–134.

Bossert, W., and J. A. Weymark. 2004. "Utility Theory in Social Choice." In *Extensions*, edited by S. Barbera, P. J. Hammond, and C. Seidl, 1099–1177. Vol. 2 of *Handbook of Utility Theory*. Boston: Kluwer Academic.

Bourguignon, F. 1979. "Decomposable Income Inequality Measures." *Econometrica* 47 (4): 901–920.

Chakravarty, S. R. 2007. "A Deprivation-Based Axiomatic Characterization of the Absolute Bonferroni Index of Inequality." *Journal of Economic Inequality* 5 (3): 339–351. Reprinted in *The Economic Theory of Income Inequality*, edited by R. A. Becker. Cheltenham: Edward Elgar, 2013.

———. 2009. "Equity and Efficiency as Components of a Social Welfare Function." *International Journal of Economic Theory* 5 (2): 181–199.

———. 2015. *Inequality, Polarization and Conflict: An Analytical Study*. New York: Springer.

Chakravarty, S. R., N. Chattopadhyay, and C. D'Ambrosio. 2016. "On a Family of Achievement and Shortfall Inequality Indices." *Health Economics* 25 (12): 1503–1513.

Chakravarty, S. R., and C. D'Ambrosio. 2006. "The Measurement of Social Exclusion." *Review of Income and Wealth* 52 (2): 377–398. Reprinted in *Measuring Poverty*, edited by S. Klasen, 619–640. Cheltenham: Edward Elgar, 2018. Also reprinted in *Poverty, Social Exclusion and Stochastic Dominance*, edited by S. R. Chakravarty, 83–107. Singapore: Springer, 2019.

Chakravarty, S. R., and B. Dutta. 1987. "A Note on Measures of Distance between Income Distributions." *Journal of Economic Theory* 41 (1): 185–188.

Chakravarty, S. R., and P. Sarkar. 2021. "New Perspectives on the Gini and Bonferroni Indices of Inequality." *Social Choice and Welfare* (forthcoming). https://doi.org/10.1007/s00355-021-01311-4.

Chakravarty, S. R., and S. Tyagarupananda. 2009. "The Subgroup Decomposable Intermediate Indices of Inequality." *Spanish Economic Review* 11 (2): 83–97.

Chakravarty, S. R., and C. Zoli. 2012. "Stochastic Dominance Relations for Integer Variables." *Journal of Economic Theory* 147 (4): 1331–1134. Reprinted in *Poverty, Social Exclusion and Stochastic Dominance*, edited by S. R. Chakravarty, 211–222. Themes in Economics (Theory, Empirics, and Policy). Singapore: Springer, 2019. https://doi.org/10.1007/978-981-13-3432-0_13.

Chattopadhyay, N., and S. Tyagarupananda. 2019. "A Generalization of the Theil Measure of Inequality." In *Deprivation, Inequality and Polarization: Essays in Honor of S. R. Chakravarty*, edited by I. Dasgupta and M. Mitra, 147–160. New York: Springer.

Chipman, J. S. 1974. "The Welfare Ranking of Pareto Distributions." *Journal of Economic Theory* 9 (3): 275–282.

Cowell, F. A. 1980. "On the Structure of Additive Inequality Measures." *Review of Economic Studies* 47 (3): 521–531.

———. 2016. "Inequality and Poverty Measures." In *Oxford Handbook of Well-Being and Public Policy*, edited by M. D. Adler and M. Fleurbaey, 82–125. New York: Oxford University Press.

Cowell, F. A., and E. Flachaire. 2017. "Inequality with Ordinal Data." *Economica* 84 (334): 290–321.

Dahlby, B. G. 1987. "Interpreting Inequality Measures in a Harsanyi Framework." *Theory and Decision* 22 (3): 187–202.

Dasgupta, P., A. K. Sen, and D. Starrett. 1973. "Notes on the Measurement of Inequality." *Journal of Economic Theory* 6 (2): 180–187.

D'Aspremont, C., and L. Gevers. 2002. "Social Welfare Functionals and Interpersonal Comparability." In *Handbook of Social Choice and Welfare*, edited by K. J. Arrow, A. K. Sen, and K. Suzumura, 1:459–541. Amsterdam: North Holland.

Del Rio, C., and J. Ruiz-Castillo. 2000. "Intermediate Inequality and Welfare." *Social Choice and Welfare* 17 (2): 223–239.

Donaldson D., and J. A. Weymark. 1980. "A Single Parameter Generalization of the Gini Indices of Inequality." *Journal of Economic Theory* 22 (1): 67–86.

Dutta, B., and J. Esteban. 1992. "Social Welfare and Equality." *Social Choice and Welfare* 9 (4): 267–276.

Ebert, U. 1987. "Size and Distribution of Incomes as Determinants of Social Welfare." *Journal of Economic Theory* 41 (1): 23–33.

———. 1988. "Measurement of Inequality: An Attempt at Unification and Generalization." *Social Choice and Welfare* 5 (2–3): 147–169.

———. 2010. "The Decomposition of Inequality Reconsidered: Weakly Decomposable Measures." *Mathematical Social Sciences* 60 (2): 94–103.

Erreygers, G. 2009. "Can a Single Indicator Measure Both Attainment and Shortfall Inequality?" *Journal of Health Economics* 28 (4): 885–893.

Erreygers, G., and T. Van Ourti. 2011. "Measuring Socioeconomic Inequality in Health, Health Care and Health Financing by Means of Rank-Dependent Indices: A Recipe for Good Practice." *Journal of Health Economics* 30 (4): 685–694.

Fajrado-Gonzalez, J. 2016. "Inequality of Opportunity in Adult Health in Colombia." *Journal of Economic Inequality* 14 (4): 395–416.

Ferreira, F. H. G., and V. Peragine. 2016. "Individual Responsibility and Equality of Opportunity." In *Oxford Handbook of Well-Being and Public Policy*, edited by M. D. Adler and M. Fleurbaey, 746–784. New York: Oxford University Press.

Fishburn, P. C., and I. H. Lavalle. 1995. "Stochastic Dominance on Unidimensional Grids." *Mathematics of Operations Research* 20 (2): 513–525.

Fleurbaey, M., and F. Maniquet. 2011. *A Theory of Fairness and Social Welfare.* New York: Cambridge University Press.

———. 2012. *Equality of Opportunity: The Economics of Responsibility.* New Jersey: World Scientific.

Foster, J. E. 1983. "An Axiomatic Characterization of the Theil Measure of Inequality." *Journal of Economic Theory* 31 (1): 105–121.

———. 2010. "Freedom, Opportunity and Wellbeing." In *Handbook of Social Choice and Welfare,* edited by K. J. Arrow, A. K. Sen, and K. Suzumura, 2:687–728. Amsterdam: North Holland.

Foster, J. E., and A. Shneyerov. 1999. "A General Class of Additively Decomposable Inequality Measures." *Economic Theory* 14 (1): 89–111.

Gaston, Kevin J., Thomas W. Davies, Jonathan Bennie, and John Hopkins. 2012. "Reducing the Ecological Consequences of Night-Time Light Pollution: Options and Developments." *Journal of Applied Ecology* 49 (6): 1256–1266.

Gravel, N. 1994. "Can a Ranking of Opportunity Sets Attach an Intrinsic Importance to Freedom of Choice?" *American Economic Review* 84 (2): 454–458.

———. 1998. "Ranking Opportunity Sets on the Basis of Their Freedom of Choice and Their Ability to Satisfy Preferences: A Difficulty." *Social Choice and Welfare* 15 (3): 371–382.

Gravel, N., B. Magdalou, and P. Moyes. 2018. "Inequality Measurement with an Ordinal and Continuous Variable." *Social Choice and Welfare* 52 (3): 453–475.

———. 2021. "Ranking Distributions of an Ordinal Variable." *Economic Theory* 71 (1): 33–80. https://doi.org/10.1007/s00199-019-01241-4.

Hammond, P. J. 1976. "Equity, Arrow's Conditions and Rawls's Difference Principle." *Econometrica* 44 (4): 793–803.

———. 1979. "Equity in Two Person Situations: Some Consequences." *Econometrica* 47 (5): 1127–35.

Harsanyi, J. C. 1953. "Cardinal Utility in Welfare Economics and in the Theory of Risk-Taking." *Journal of Political Economy* 61 (5): 434–435.

———. 1955. "Cardinal Welfare, Individualistic Ethics, and Interpersonal Comparisons of Utility." *Journal of Political Economy* 63 (4): 309–321.

Herrero, C., I. Iturbe-Ormaetxe, and J. Nieto. 1998. "Ranking Opportunity Profiles on the Basis of Common Opportunities." *Mathematical Social Sciences* 35 (3): 273–289.

Hild, M., and A. Voorhoeve. 2004. "Equality of Opportunity and Opportunity Dominance." *Economics and Philosophy* 20 (1): 117–145.

Jain, R., D. Chiu, and W. Hawe. 1984. "A Quantitative Measure of Fairness and Discrimination for Resource Allocation in Shared Computer System." *DEC Technical Report*, no. 301.

Jayadeb, A., and S. Reddy. 2019. "Inequalities and Identities." In *Deprivation, Inequality and Polarization: Essays in Honor of S. R. Chakravarty*, edited by I. Dasgupta and M. Mitra, 109–145. New York: Springer.

Kakwani, N. C. 1986. *Analyzing Redistribution Policies*. Cambridge: Cambridge University Press.

Kanbur, R. 2006. "The Policy Significance of Inequality Decompositions." *Journal of Economic Inequality* 4 (3): 367–374.

Kanbur, R., and J. E. Stiglitz. 2016. "Dynamic Inequality, Mobility and Equality of Opportunity." *Journal of Economic Inequality* 14 (4): 419–434.

Kaplow, L. 2008. *The Theory of Taxation and Public Economics*. Princeton, New Jersey: Princeton University Press.

Kats, A. 1972. "On the Social Welfare Function and the Parameters of Income Distribution." *Journal of Economic Theory* 5 (3): 377–382.

Kjellsson, G., and U. Gerdtham. 2013. "Lost in Translation: Rethinking the Inequality Equivalence Criteria for Bounded Health Variables." *Research on Economic Inequality: Health and Inequality* 21 (December): 3–32.

Kolm, S. C. 1969. "The Optimal Production of Social Justice." In *Public Economics*, edited by J. Margolis and H. Guitton, 145–200. London: Macmillan.

———. 1976. "Unequal Inequalities I." *Journal of Economic Theory* 12 (3): 416–442.

Kranich, L. 1996. "Equitable Opportunities: An Axiomatic Approach." *Journal of Economic Theory* 71 (1): 131–147.

Lambert, P., and B. Zheng. 2011. "On the Consistent Measurement of Attainment and Shortfall Inequality." *Journal of Health Economics* 30 (1): 214–219.

Lan, T., D. Kao, M. Chiang, and A. Sabharwal. 2010. "An Axiomatic Theory of Fairness in Network Resource Allocation." IEEE INFOCOM Proceedings, IEE, San Diego, USA, 1–9.

Lasso de la Vega, C., and C. Aristondo. 2012. "Proposing Indicators to Measure Achievement and Shortfall Inequality Consistently." *Journal of Health Economics* 31 (4): 578–583.

Maniquet, F. 2016. "Social Ordering Functions." In *Oxford Handbook of Well-Being and Public Policy*, edited by M. D. Adler and M. Fleurbaey, 227–245. New York: Oxford University Press.

Marshall, A.W., I. Olkin, and B. Arnold. 2011. *Inequalities: Theory of Majorization and Its Applications*. 2nd edition. New York: Springer.

O'Donnell, O., E. V. Doorslaer, and T. V. Ourti. 2015. "Health and Inequality." In *Handbook of Income Distribution*, edited by A. B. Atkinson and F. Bourguignon, 2B:1419–1533. Amsterdam: North-Holland.

Ok, E. 1997. "On Opportunity Inequality Measurement." *Journal of Economic Theory* 77 (2): 300–329.

Ok, E., and L. Kranich. 1998. "The Measurement of Opportunity Inequality: A Cardinality-Based Approach." *Social Choice and Welfare* 15 (2): 263–287.

Ooghe, E., E. Schokkaert, and D. Van de Gear. 2007. "Equality of Opportunity versus Equality of Opportunity Sets." *Social Choice and Welfare* 28 (7): 209–230.

Pattanaik, P. K., and Y. Xu. 1990. "On Ranking Opportunity Sets in Terms of Freedom of Choice." Special issue, *Recherches Economiques de Louvain* 56 (3): 383–390.

Pignataro, G. 2012. "Equality of Opportunity: Policy and Measurement Paradigms." *Journal of Economic Surveys* 26 (5): 800–834.

Pollak, R. A. 1971. "Additive Utility Functions and Linear Engel Curves." *Review of Economic Studies* 38 (4): 401–413.

Rawls, J. 1971. *A Theory of Justice*. Cambridge: Harvard University Press.

Roemer, J. E. 1998. *Equality of Opportunity*. Cambridge, MA: Harvard University Press.

———. 2012. "On Several Approaches to Equality of Opportunity." Special issue, *Economics and Philosophy* 28 (2): 165–200.

Roemer, J. E., and A. Trannoy. 2015. "Equality of Opportunity." In *Handbook of Income Distribution*, edited by A. B. Atkinson and F. Bourguignon, 2A:217 –300. Amsterdam, The Netherlands: Elsevier B. V.

Savaglio, E., and S. Vannucci. 2007. "Filtral Preorders and Opportunity Inequality." *Journal of Economic Theory* 132 (1): 474–492.

Sen, A. K. 1973. *On Economic Inequality*. Clarendon: Oxford University Press.

———. 1974. "Informational Bases of Alternative Welfare Approaches: Aggregation and Income Distribution." *Journal of Public Economics* 3 (4): 387–403.

———. 1977. "On Weights and Measures: Informational Constraints in Social Welfare Analysis." *Econometrica* 45 (7): 1539–1572.

Sheshinski, E. 1972. "Relation between a Social Welfare and the Gini Index of Inequality." *Journal of Economic Theory* 4 (1): 98–100.

Shorrocks, A. F. 1980. "The Class of Additively Decomposable Inequality Measures." *Econometrica* 48 (3): 613–625.

———. 1982. "On the Distance between Income Distributions." *Econometrica* 50 (5): 1337–1339.

———. 1983. "Ranking Income Distributions." *Economica* 50 (1): 3–17.

Theil, H. 1967. *Economics and Information Theory*. Amsterdam: North Holland.

———. 1972. *Statistical Decomposition Analysis*. Amsterdam: North Holland.

Wagstaff, A. 2011. "The Concentration Index of a Binary Outcome Revisited." *Health Economics* 20 (10): 1155–1160.

Weymark, J. A. 1981. "Generalized Gini Inequality Indices." *Mathematical Social Sciences* 1 (4): 409–430.

————. 2003. "Generalized Gini Indices of Equality of Opportunity." *Journal of Economic Inequality* 1 (1): 5–24.

————. 2016. "Social Welfare Functions." In *Oxford Handbook of Well-Being and Public Policy*, edited by M. D. Adler and M. Fleurbaey, 126–159. New York: Oxford University Press.

Yalonetzky, G. 2012. "A Dissimilarity Index of Multidimensional Index of Opportunity." *Journal of Economic Inequality* 10 (3): 343–373.

Zheng, B. 2007. "Unit-Consistent Decomposable Inequality Measures." *Economica* 74 (293): 97–111.

Zoli, C. 1999. "A Generalized Version of the Inequality Invariance Criterion: A Surplus Sharing Characterization, Complete and Partial Orderings." In *Logic, Game Theory and Social Choice*, edited by H. de Swart, 427–441. Tilburg: Tilburg University Press.

DISTRIBUTIONAL ETHICS

MULTIDIMENSIONAL APPROACHES

9.1 MOTIVATIONS

Often income as the sole dimension of the well-being of a population does not give us an appropriate picture of the living condition of the population since there are non-income dimensions that affect human welfare, for example, habitation, longevity, availability of opportunities from the point of view of contentment, and so on. So, by concentrating on income only, it is implicitly assumed that persons enjoying the same income are considered equally well off regardless of their attainments in the non-income dimensions. However, a non-monetary dimension of well-being need not be perfectly correlated with income. For instance, an income-rich person may not be able to improve the level of sub-optimal supply of a local public good, say, the irregularities of a TV signal that can be received within a specified distance of the signaling station. Thus, apart from the distribution of income, a policy maker might be concerned with the distributions of various non-income goods or dimensions. Examples of such non-income dimensions are health, literacy, housing, and environment. Therefore, to get a complete picture of human well-being it is quite sensible to supplement income with non-income dimensions that influence the contentment of the population. In other words the well-being of a population is a multidimensional phenomenon. This is, in fact, a concretization of our assumption made in the earlier chapters that an individual's (and hence society's) utility depends on several states of nature.

In the words of Stiglitz, Sen, and Fitoussi (2009, 14):

> To define what wellbeing means, a multidimensional definition has to be used.... At least in principle, these dimensions should be considered simultaneously: (i) Material living standards (income, consumption and wealth); (ii) Health; (iii) Education; (iv) Personal activities including work; (v) Political voice and governance; (vi) Social connections and relationships; (vii) Environment (present and future conditions); (viii) Insecurity, of an economic as well as a physical nature. All these dimensions shape people's wellbeing, and yet many of them are missed by conventional income measures.

Intrinsic to the notion of the capability-functioning approach to the evaluation of human well-being is multidimensionality, where functionings refer to the various things such as income, literacy, housing, life expectancy, communing with others, and so on about which a person cares. The capability set of an individual provides information on the functionings that a person could achieve (Sen 1985, 1992).

Various multidimensional well-being evaluators exist in practice. A well-known example of a multidimensional well-being standard is the human development index suggested by the United Nations Development Programme, or UNDP (1990). It aggregates the countrylevel achievements in the dimensions of life expectancy, per capita real gross domestic product (GDP), and educational attainment rate in an unambiguous way. Other examples include better life index suggested by the Organization of Economic Cooperation and Development (Durand 2015), active citizenship composite index that summarizes valuebased involvement of citizens, developed within a European context (Hoskins et al. 2006), index of economic freedom (Holmes et al. 2008), environmental performance index (Esty et al. 2008) the green economy progress index (Acosta et al. 2019), and the progress towards achievements in Millennium Development Goals (Bourguignon et al. 2008, 2010; Permanyer 2013; Chakravarty 2018). Examples of multidimensional inequality and deprivation metrics incorporate the human poverty index that looks at development from a deprivation perspective in the same dimensions as the human development index (UNDP 1997), the gender inequality index, which looks at inequality between male and female achievements in the dimensions of reproductive health, empowerment, and labor market participation (UNDP 2019), the human opportunity index (Paes de Barros et al. 2009; Ferreira and Peragine 2016; Roemer and Trannoy 2015) and the air quality index (Plaia and Ruggieri 2011; US Environmental Protection Agency 2013; Chakravarty 2021).[1]

The basics and preliminaries required for our purpose are presented in the next section. The common features of the two approaches, the direct and inclusive measure of well-being, which define welfare respectively straightaway on the set of distributions of multidimensional achievements and in terms of aggregations of individual utilities, are described analytically in Section 9.3. The two outlooks of inequality evaluation are scrutinized in Sections 9.4 and 9.5. The subject of Section 9.6 is a clear exposition of how direct multidimensional descriptive inequality indices can be related to reduced-form welfare functions. Finally, Section 9.7 is concerned with the evaluation of inequality under uncertainty where both ex ante and ex post inequality considerations are taken into account (see Ben-Porath, Gilboa, and Schmeidler 1997).

9.2 BASICS AND PRELIMINARIES

With a population of $n \in N$ individuals, let there be d dimensions of well-being. We write Q for the set dimensions $\{1, 2, \ldots, d\}$ of well-being. We assume at the outset that the number of dimensions

---

[1] The necessity for regarding well-being as a multidimensional aspect has also been advocated, among others, by Rawls (1971); Kolm (1977); Townsend (1979); Streeten (1981); Sen (1985); Dutta, Pattanaik, and Xu (2003); Savaglio (2006a, 2006b); Weymark (2006); Lugo (2005); Muller and Trannoy (2012); Pattanaik, Reddy, and Xu (2012); Alkire et al. (2015); Decancq, Fleurbaey, and Schokkaert (2015); Duclos and Tiberti (2016); Chakravarty and Lugo (2016); Bellani and Fusco (2018); Chakravarty (2018); Chakravarty and Chattopadhyay (2018); Guio (2018); Seth and Villar (2018); and Banerjee (2020). In a recent contribution, Hussain, Siersbæk, and Østerdal (2020) compared multidimensional welfare in European Union member states, using first-order dominance, before, during, and after the financial crisis, both spatially and temporally.

d is exogenously given. Let $x_{ij.} \geq 0$ denote person $i's$ achievement or attainment in dimension j. For instance, if dimension j represents the literacy rate, then $x_{ij.}$ stands for person $i's$ literacy attainment rate. These are the basic ingredients of our analysis.

The distribution of dimension-wise achievements of individuals in the population is represented by an $n \times d$ distribution matrix $X_{n \times d}$ (X, for short) whose (i,j)th entry is $x_{ij.}$, where $i \in \{1, 2, \ldots, n\}$ and $j \in Q$ are arbitrary. Often we refer to X as a social distribution matrix (social matrix, for short), or an achievement matrix. The distribution of the total attainment $\sum_{i=1}^{n} x_{ij.}$ in dimension j among n individuals, which we denote by $x_{.j}$, is given by the jth column of X. Let $\mu(x_{.j})$ stand for the mean of the distribution $x_{.j}$. Person $i's$ achievements in different dimensions are represented by $x_{i.}$, the ith row of X.

Let M_1^n be the set of all $n \times d$ distribution matrices with non-negative entries so that $M_1^n = \{X | x_{ij} \geq 0$ for all $i \in \{1, 2, \ldots, n\}$ and $j \in Q\}$. Let M_2^n be that subset of M_1^n such that the mean of the distribution of attainments in each $j \in Q$ is positive. Thus, $M_2^n = \{X \in M_1^n | \mu(x_{.j}) > 0$ for all $j \in Q\}$. Finally, we denote the set of all $n \times d$ social matrices with positive entries by M_3^n. Analytically, $M_3^n = \{X \in M_1^n | x_{ij} > 0$ for all $i \in \{1, 2, \ldots, n\}$ and $j \in Q\}$. We write M_1 for the set of all possible social matrices associated with M_1^n, that is, $M_1 = \bigcup_{n \in N} M_1^n$.

Likewise, the respective sets associated with M_2^n and M_3^n are denoted by M_2 and M_3. Unless explicitly specified, our analytical formulations of the axioms for an arbitrary multidimensional inequality standard will be presented using an arbitrary $M \in \{M_1, M_2, M_3\}$.

For all $n \in N$, $X, Y \in M^n$, $X \geq Y$ means that $x_{ij} \geq y_{ij}$ for all $(i,j) \in \{1, 2, \ldots, n\} \times \{1, 2, \ldots, d\}$ and if, furthermore, there exists a pair $(h, q) \in \{1, 2, \ldots, n\} \times \{1, 2, \ldots, d\}$ such that $x_{hq} > y_{hq}$, then the inequality $X \geq Y$ is to be replaced by $X > Y$.

A multidimensional inequality index I is a non-constant real-valued function defined on M. Formally, $I : M \rightarrow \Re^1$. For any $n \in N$, $X \in M^n$, the real number $I(X)$ signifies the extent of inequality that exists in the distribution matrix $X \in M^n$. As in the single-dimensional case, a multidimensional inequality indicator can be of relative or absolute variety.

To make these notions explicit, we begin by specifying two properties, namely, strong ratio scale invariance and strong absolute or translation scale invariance axioms. The first axiom demands that post-multiplication of the distribution matrix by a $d \times d$ positive diagonal matrix does not change the level of multidimensional inequality, where by a positive diagonal matrix we mean a matrix whose diagonal entries are positive but off-diagonal entries are zero. Formally:

Strong ratio scale invariance: For all $n \in N$, $X \in M^n$, $I(X\Omega) = I(X)$, where Ω is any $d \times d$ positive diagonal matrix, denoted by $\Omega = \text{diag}(\omega_1, \omega_2, \ldots, \omega_d)$, $\omega_j > 0$ for all $j \in Q$.

Hence, any alteration in the units of measurements of attainments in different dimensions keeps inequality invariant (Tsui 1995).To illustrate the axiom, consider the following distribution matrix X_1 with four individuals and three dimensions of well-being:

$$X_1 = \begin{bmatrix} 706 & 61 & 74 \\ 808 & 58 & 69 \\ 511 & 59 & 66 \\ 608 & 67 & 65 \end{bmatrix}.$$

The entry in the ith row and jth column of the matrix represents person $i's$ achievement in dimension j, where $i = 1, 2, 3, 4$ and $j = 1, 2, 3$. Let the three dimensions of well-being be wage income, interest income, and life expectancy, respectively.

Now, suppose wage income increases by 10 per cent, interest income reduces by 5 per cent, and life expectancy remains unchanged. Then strong ratio scale invariance demands that $I(X_1\Omega_1) = I(X_1)$, where Ω_1 is the 3×3 positive diagonal matrix given by $\Omega_1 = \text{diag}(1.1, 0.95, 1)$.

A weaker form of this postulate, ratio scale invariance, does not change inequality when the dimension-wise multiplicative factors ω_js are assumed to be the same. Evidently, while for the strong form of the axiom variability of proportionality factors across dimensions is allowed, for the weak form it is not so.[2]

---

[2] See Weymark (2006) for a detailed discussion.

Strong translation scale invariance: For all $n \in N$, $X \in M^n$, $I(X + A) = I(X)$, where A is any $n \times d$ dimensional matrix with common rows such that $X + A \in M^n$.

This axiom demands invariance of inequality under equal absolute changes in achievements of different individuals in the dimensions. We may refer to the matrix A as a translation matrix. For the illustrative example we considered above, the particular 4×3 translation matrix A is the one whose identical row is given by $(0.1, -0.05, 0)$.

While in strong translation scale invariance the translation matrix A possesses identical rows, it is not assumed that the entries in the identical rows are the same. Under the additional assumption of equality of entries in the identical rows, the postulate is known as translation scale invariance. A multidimensional inequality index $I : M \to \Re^1$ is called a relative or an absolute index according as it satisfies the ratio scale invariance or the translation scale invariance axiom.

A multidimensional inequality indicator $I : M \to \Re^1$, whether of relative or absolute variety, should satisfy the following two postulates, which are multidimensional sisters of the respective single dimensional versions.

(a) Symmetry: For all $n \in N$, $X \in M^n$, $I(\Pi X) = I(X)$, where Π is any permutation matrix of order n.

This axiom demands that when individuals trade their positions, inequality remains uninterrupted. Thus, in the social matrix X_1, if individuals 1 and 3 interchange their positions and 2 and 4 maintain their original positions, then symmetry demands that $I(\Omega_1 X_1) = I(X_1)$, where Ω_1 is the 4×4 permutation matrix

$$\Omega_1 = \begin{bmatrix} 0 & 0 & 1 & 0 \\ 0 & 1 & 0 & 0 \\ 1 & 0 & 0 & 0 \\ 0 & 0 & 0 & 1 \end{bmatrix}.$$

(b) Daltonian population principle: For all $n \in N$, $X \in M^n$, $I(X) = I(X^{(l)})$, where $X^{(l)}$ is the l-fold replication X, that is,

$$X^{(l)} = \begin{pmatrix} X^1 \\ X^2 \\ \vdots \\ X^l \end{pmatrix} \text{ with each } X^i = X, i \in \{1, 2, \ldots, l\} \text{ and } l \geq 2 \text{ is any}$$

integer.

To understand the need for this postulate, let us consider two societies with population sizes 2 and 3, respectively, and a common set of dimensions $\{wage\ income,\ interest\ income,\ life\ expectancy\}$. Let the corresponding achievement matrices be $X_2 = \begin{bmatrix} 500 & 50 & 66 \\ 600 & 40 & 67 \end{bmatrix}$

and $X_3 = \begin{bmatrix} 550 & 49 & 64 \\ 610 & 58 & 60 \\ 580 & 40 & 61 \end{bmatrix}$, respectively. Given that the societies have

differing population sizes, we are unable to compare them in terms of inequality. One way to resolve the problem is to replicate X_2 three times and X_3 two times so that the corresponding replicated social matrices become

$$X_2^{(3)} = \begin{bmatrix} 500 & 50 & 66 \\ 600 & 40 & 67 \\ 500 & 50 & 66 \\ 600 & 40 & 67 \\ 500 & 50 & 66 \\ 600 & 40 & 67 \end{bmatrix} \text{ and } X_3^{(2)} = \begin{bmatrix} 550 & 49 & 64 \\ 610 & 58 & 60 \\ 580 & 40 & 61 \\ 550 & 49 & 64 \\ 610 & 58 & 60 \\ 580 & 40 & 61 \end{bmatrix}.$$

Under the Daltonian population principle, $I(X_2) = I(X_2^{(3)})$ and $I(X_3) = I(X_3^{(2)})$, since $X_2^{(3)}$ and $X_3^{(2)}$ have a common population size of 6, we can compare their inequality levels. But when the population principle is satisfied, a comparison of inequalities of $X_2^{(3)}$ and $X_3^{(2)}$ is same as that of X_2 and X_3, whose population sizes are different.

The two major forms of multidimensional counterparts of the Pigou–Dalton transfer principle that have been suggested in the literature are the uniform majorization principle and the uniform Pigou–Dalton majorization principle (see Kolm 1977; Savaglio 2002; Weymark 2006; and Marshall, Olkin, and Arnold 2011). While the former requires that multiplication of a distribution matrix by a non-permutation bistochastic matrix of appropriate order should reduce inequality, the latter demands inequality reduction under multiplication of the distribution matrix by a product of a finite number of Pigou–Dalton matrices of appropriate order. An $n \times n$ Pigou–Dalton matrix, also known as a strict T-transformation, a linear transformation defined by an $n \times n$ matrix T, is a weighted average of the identity matrix of order n and a permutation matrix of the same order that just interchanges two coordinates, where the positive weights sum up to 1. Barring some exceptional circumstances, the latter is more general than the former (see Weymark 2006; Marshall, Olkin, and Arnold 2011, 53–54).

Each of these two egalitarian principles involves transfers across persons in the same proportion in each dimension. A transfer between two persons becomes well defined when one is unambiguously richer than the other in all the dimensions. But none of the two postulates takes this issue into consideration. Further, not all dimensions in the distribution matrix may be redistributable, that is, the achievements in some dimensions may not be transferable between two persons.[3]

Fleurbaey and Trannoy (2003) proposed the Pigou–Dalton bundle transfer principle, an intuitive multidimensional generalization of the single dimensional Pigou–Dalton transfer principle that evades this problem.[4] Assume that achievements in all the dimensions of the social matrices $X, Y \in M^n$ are redistributable, where $n \in N$ is arbitrary. We then say that X is deduced from Y by a Pigou–Dalton bundle of progressive transfers if there exist two persons $i, h \in \{1, 2, \ldots, n\}$ such that the following conditions hold: (i) $y_{ij} < y_{hj}$ for all $j \in Q$, (ii) there exists $\delta = (\delta_1, \delta_j, \ldots, \delta_d) \in \Re_{++}^d$ such that $x_{ij} = y_{ij} + \delta_j, x_{hj} = y_{hj} - \delta_j$ for all $j \in Q$, (iii) $x_{ij} \leq x_{hj}$ for all $j \in Q$, and (iv) $y_{lj} = x_{lj}$ for all $l \neq i, h \in \{1, 2, \ldots, n\}$, and for all $j \in Q$.

Condition (i) of the postulate demands that in the achievement matrix Y, person h has higher achievements than person i in all the dimensions. According to condition (ii), dimension-wise transfers from the achievement profile of person h, represented by $y_{h.}$, in Y to respective dimensional achievements of person i give rise to the

---

[3] For further discussion, see Savaglio (2006a); Trannoy (2006); Lasso de la Vega, Urrutia, and Sarachu (2010); Banerjee (2014); and Pattanaik and Xu (2019).
[4] See also Fleurbaey (2006); and Fleurbaey and Maniquet (2011).

achievement profiles of the two persons h and i, in X, represented respectively by $x_h.$ and $x_i.$. The d dimensional row vector δ indicates the sizes of progressive transfers across dimensions. Given that $\delta \in \Re^d_{++}$, there is at least one dimension for which the size of transfer is positive. Condition (iii) guarantees that in the post-transfer situation, achievement of the recipient (person i) in any dimension is not higher than that of the donor (person h). Finally, condition (iv) stipulates that the achievements of all other persons in all the dimensions are not affected by the transfer operations performed between the two persons h and i.

The following axiom may be regarded as a multidimensional sister of the univariate Pigou–Dalton transfer principle:

Multidimensional transfer principle: For all $n \in N$, $X, Y \in M^n$, if X is deduced from Y by Pigou–Dalton bundle of progressive transfers, then $I(X) < I(\bar{Y})$.

To understand this principle, let us consider a four-person society with three redistributable dimensions of well-being so that it is possible to transfer achievements in different dimensions across individuals. For concreteness, assume that the dimensions are wage income, interest income, and land, and the distribution matrix of the society is given by

$$\bar{Y} = \begin{bmatrix} 707 & 60 & 410 \\ 758 & 65 & 863 \\ 261 & 59 & 489 \\ 108 & 67 & 603 \end{bmatrix}.$$

Note that person 2 has higher achievements than person 1 in all three dimensions. Let $\delta = (10, 2, 5)$ be the vector of sizes of dimension-wise transfers from person 2 to person 1 so that 10 units of wage income is transferred from person 2 to person 1, and so on. Consequently, the vectors of the achievements of persons 1 and 2 in the post-transfer achievement matrix $\bar{X}$ are given respectively by $\bar{x}_1 = (717, 62, 415)$ and $\bar{x}_2 = (748, 63, 858)$. Thus, in the post-transfer situation the donor does not come to be poorer than the recipient in any dimension. Assume further that for $i = 3, 4$, $\bar{x}_{i3} = \bar{y}_{i3}$, and $\bar{x}_{i4} = \bar{y}_{i4}$. Then the multidimensional transfer principle demands that $I(\bar{X}) < I(\bar{Y})$.

The three axioms we have proposed so far are multidimensional extensions of their single-dimensional counterparts. However, none of them takes into account the dependence between dimensions, a notion innate to the analysis of multidimensional inequality. Consequently, we need a separate axiom that incorporates inter-dimensional association (see Epstein and Tanny 1980; Tchen 1980; Atkinson and Bourguignon 1982; Bourguignon and Chakravarty 2003; Banerjee 2010; Alkire et al. 2015; and Chakravarty 2018).

To understand this in greater detail, let us consider a two-person society in which there are two dimensions of well-being. Given the achievement distributions (x_{11}, x_{12}) and (x_{21}, x_{22}) of the two individuals, assume additionally that $x_{11} > x_{21}$ and $x_{12} < x_{22}$, indicating that while person 1 is richer than person 2 in dimension 1, the opposite situation arises in dimension 2. If an exchange takes place between attainments of the two persons in dimension 2, then the new distributions of the attainments turn out to be (x_{11}, x_{22}) and (x_{21}, x_{12}). After the swap, person 1, who was richer in dimension 1 only, has become richer in dimension 2 as well. This swap increases the correlation between the dimensional achievements without changing the total of achievements in each dimension. This correlation is an indicator of inter-dimensional association.

If the two dimensions underlying a switch are substitutes, then achievement in one of them can compensate for the lack of that in the other. In other words, two substitutable dimensions represent a similar phenomenon of well-being. Hence, the switch makes a rich person better off and a poor person worse off. This enables us to argue that the switch should increase inequality when the dimensions are substitutes. Analogously, inequality should reduce when the dimensions involved in the switch are complements. For a switch involving independent dimensions, inequality remains unaltered.

In the general case of n individuals and d dimensions, a correlation increasing switch can formally be defined as follows:

Definition 9.1 For all $n \in N$, $X, Y \in M^n$, Y is said to be obtained from X by a correlation increasing switch between two persons if the following conditions hold: let there be two persons $i, h \in \{1, 2, \cdots, n\}$ and dimensions $j, q \in Q$, where (a) $x_{ij} < x_{hj}$,

(b) $\quad x_{hq} < x_{iq}$, and (c) $\quad x_{ik} \leq x_{hk}$ for all $k \neq j, q \in Q$, (d) $\quad y_{hj} = x_{hj}, y_{ij} = x_{ij}$, (e) $\quad y_{hq} = x_{iq}, y_{iq} = x_{hq}$, and (f) $y_{hk} = x_{hk}, y_{ik} = x_{ik}$ for all $k \neq j, q \in Q$, and (g) $y_{l\chi} = x_{l\chi}$ for all $l \neq i, h \in \{1, 2, \cdots, n\}$ and $\chi \in Q$.

Conditions (a) and (b) of the above definition stipulate that in the distribution matrix X, person i is worse off in dimension j but better off in dimension q than person h. Condition (c) claims that person h is not worse off than person i in the remaining dimensions. Condition (d) formally states that achievements of persons i and h in dimension q are swapped. Conditions (e) and (f) ensure that in the post-swap situation, person h is better off than person i in both the dimensions j and q. In other words, after the swap, person h, who was originally richer in dimension j but poorer in dimension q than person i, has become richer and person i has become poorer in both the dimensions j and q. The achievements of all the other individuals in all the dimensions remain unchanged. Evidently, the switch operation does not amend the dimension-wise totals. To explain this definition, let us reconsider the matrix $\vec{Y}$. Between persons 3 and 4, although the former has higher achievement than the latter in dimension 1, the opposite is the case in dimension 2. Further, person 4's achievement in dimension 3 is higher than that of person 3. Thus, a switch between the achievements of persons 3 and 4 in dimension 1, keeping all other achievements in $\vec{Y}$ unchanged, is a correlation increasing switch.

We are now in a position to state the following axiom.

Increasing inequality under correlation increasing switch: For all $n \in N$, $X, Y \in M^n$, if Y is deduced from X by a correlation increasing switch, then $I(X) < I(Y)$ if the dimensions involved in the switch are substitutes.

A parallel axiom claiming that a reverse directional change in inequality occurs if the dimensions underlying the switch are complements can as well be stated.

Next, we assume that the inequality indicator varies continuously with respect to changes in dimensional achievements.

Continuity: For all $n \in N$, I is continuous on M^n.

Often inequality standards are assumed to be normalized. Formally,

Normalization: For all $n \in N$, $X_\mu \in M^n$, $I(X_\mu) = 0$, where $X_\mu \in M^n$ is that achievement matrix whose entries in column j, for all $j \in Q$, are $\mu(x_{.j})$. That is, the extent of inequality is zero if achievements in each dimension are equally distributed across individuals.

9.3 COMMON FEATURES

We begin by assuming the existence of a social welfare function $W : M \to \Re^1$. As stated in Chapter 9, we assume that the framework is welfarist. For any $n \in N$, $X \in M^n$, $W(X)$ represents the extent of well-being inherent in the social matrix X that indicates the distributions of achievements in different dimensions among the individuals. Such a function can be applied to determine the ranking of the social alternatives in terms of society's preference. We assume at the outset that $W : M \to \Re^1$ is continuous and symmetric. It should satisfy the Daltonian population principle as well. As in the single-dimensional case, given other things, multidimensional inequality should be related to multidimensional welfare in a negative monotonic way. Consequently, W should increase under a Pigou–Dalton bundle of progressive transfers. Likewise, its value should decrease or increase under a correlation increasing switch depending on whether the dimensions involved in the switch are substitutes or complements.

It should also fulfill a monotonicity postulate. We say that W satisfies the strong Pareto principle if for $X > Y$, $W(X) > W(Y)$ holds, where $n \in N$ and $X, Y \in M^n$ are arbitrary. For instance, the distribution matrix X_2 is obtained from the matrix $Y_2 = \begin{bmatrix} 496 & 50 & 66 \\ 600 & 40 & 67 \end{bmatrix}$ by increasing the achievement of person 1 in dimension 1 by 4. The strong Pareto principle demands that $W(X_2) > W(Y_2)$. The weak Pareto principle requires welfare to increase when attainments of all individuals in all the dimensions get augmented.

The formal definition of the Kolm (1977) multidimensional inequality index relies on the multidimensional variant of the Atkinson–Kolm–Sen (AKS) representative income. Assume that $M \in \{M_2, M_3\}$ so that the mean of achievements in each dimension is positive. Now, define $\Psi(X)$ implicitly by the equation $W(X_\mu \Psi(X)) = W(X)$. As per the definition, for all $i \in \{1, 2, \ldots, n\}$, the ith row of the matrix X_μ is given by $(\mu(x_{.1}), \mu(x_{.2}), \ldots, \mu(x_{.d}))$. Thus, $\Psi(X)$ is a positive scalar, which, when multiplied with the egalitarian distribution matrix X_μ, makes the existing distribution matrix X ethically indifferent. Under continuity and fulfillment of the strong Pareto principle, $\Psi(X)$ is well defined. It is a multidimensional twin of the AKS representative income (see the earlier chapter). It is a particular numerical representation of W. When $X = X_\mu$, that is, attainments in each dimension are equally distributed across individuals, $\Psi(X)$ attains its upper bound 1.

The multidimensional inequality indicator $I_{KM} : M \to \Re^1$, suggested by Kolm (1977), can be defined as

$$I_{KM}(X) = 1 - \Psi(X), \tag{9.1}$$

where $n \in N$ and $X \in M^n$ is arbitrary. The indicator I_{KM} determines the fraction of total achievements in each dimension that could be saved if the society distributed the dimensional totals equally across individuals without any loss of welfare. It also indicates the proportion of welfare lost because of unequal distribution of dimension-by-dimension achievement totals across individuals. It coincides with the univariate AKS inequality index if there is only one dimension of well-being. This continuous, symmetric inequality evaluator satisfying population-size neutrality decreases under a Pigou–Dalton bundle of progressive transfers. It is bounded between 0 and 1, where the lower bound is achieved if $X = X_\mu$. It comes to be a relative index if W is linear homogeneous. Linear homogeneity claims that when all the entries of the distribution matrix are multiplied by a positive scalar, welfare level gets multiplied by the scalar itself. Under linear homogeneity of W, $\Psi(X) = \frac{W(X)}{W(X_\mu)}$.

To understand the construction of the indicator Ψ, let us consider the matrix X_2, whose underlying Ψ is defined implicitly by
$W\left(\Psi(X_2) \begin{bmatrix} 550 & 45 & 66.5 \\ 550 & 45 & 66.5 \end{bmatrix}\right) = W\left(\begin{bmatrix} 500 & 50 & 66 \\ 600 & 40 & 67 \end{bmatrix}\right)$. The rows in the left-hand side of the matrix in this equation are identical. That is, each individual enjoys the same level of achievement in each dimension. The explicit value of Ψ depends on the form of the welfare evaluation function W.

In order to analyze the Tsui (1995) multidimensional absolute inequality indicator formally, define the scalar $\Lambda(X)$ implicitly by the equation $W(X_\mu - \Lambda(X) 1_{n \times d}) = W(X)$, where $n \in N$ and $X \in M_1^n$ are arbitrary, and $1_{n \times d}$ is the $n \times d$ dimensional social matrix, each of whose entries equals one. Under continuity of W and its satisfaction of the strong Pareto principle, Λ is well defined. Note that the (i, j)th entry of the matrix $X_\mu - \Lambda(X) 1_{n \times d}$ is $\mu(x_{\cdot j}) - \Lambda(X)$, where $(i, j) \in \{1, 2, \dots, n\} \times \{1, 2, \dots, d\}$ is arbitrary. Thus, $\Lambda(X)$ is the per capita achievement level, which, when taken away from the dimension-wise individual achievement levels in the ideal social distribution X_μ, makes the existing social distribution, as represented by X, ethically indifferent.

The Tsui (1995) per capita multidimensional inequality index $I_{TM} : M_1 \to \Re^1$ is defined as

$$I_{TM}(X) = \Lambda(X), \tag{9.2}$$

where $n \in N$ and $X \in M_1^n$ are arbitrary. It is bounded from below by 0, where this bound is achieved if dimension-wise totals are equally distributed across individuals in the society, that is, if $X = X_\mu$. When well-being is determined by only one dimension, that is, if $d = 1$, I_{TM} coincides with I_{KP}. It remains invariant under the equal absolute translation of all achievement quantities if W is unit translatable. Unit translatability means that when each achievement of a distribution matrix increases by some constant amount, welfare increases by the constant amount itself. Given unit translatability of W, it follows that $\Lambda(X) = W(X_\mu) - W(X)$.

The indicator Λ associated with X_2 is defined by the following equation:

$$W\left(\begin{bmatrix} 550 & 45 & 66.5 \\ 550 & 45 & 66.5 \end{bmatrix} - \begin{bmatrix} \Lambda(X_2) & \Lambda(X_2) & \Lambda(X_2) \\ \Lambda(X_2) & \Lambda(X_2) & \Lambda(X_2) \end{bmatrix}\right)$$
$$= W\left(\begin{bmatrix} 500 & 50 & 66 \\ 600 & 40 & 67 \end{bmatrix}\right).$$

The definitive value of Ψ will be determined by the form of the welfare evaluation function W.

9.4 THE DIRECT APPROACH

The Gajdos–Weymark (2005) multidimensional generalized Gini indices have an explicit normative foundation. However, they cannot be accommodated within the welfarism framework. They can be interpreted as direct normative indicators of inequality.

Assuming that $M = M_2$ and $d \geq 3$, the class of welfare functions $W_{GWM} : M_2 \to \Re^1$ characterized by Gajdos-Weymark can be formally defined as:

$$W_{GWM}(X) = \left[\sum_{j=1}^{d} \eta_j \left(\sum_{i=1}^{n} a_{ij} x_{ij}^0 \right)^k \right]^{\frac{1}{k}}, \qquad (9.3)$$

If $k \neq 0$ is any scalar

$$W_{GWM}(X) = \prod_{j=1}^{d} \left(\sum_{i=1}^{n} a_{ij} x_{ij}^0 \right)^{\eta_j}, \qquad (9.4)$$

if $k = 0$, where the multiplicative factors a_{ij}s are positive for all pairs $(i, j) \in \{1, 2, \ldots, n\} \times \{1, 2, \ldots, d\}$; the sequence $\{a_{ij}\}$ is increasing in i, $\sum_{i=1}^{n} a_{ij} = 1$ for all $j \in Q$; $\eta \in D^d$ is a (positive) vector with $\sum_{j=1}^{d} \eta_j = 1$; $x_{.j}^0$ is the welfare ranked permutation of $x_{.j}$, that is, $x_{1j}^0 \geq x_{2j}^0 \geq \ldots \geq x_{nj}^0$; and $n \in N$ and $X \in M_2^n$ are arbitrary. This continuous, symmetric, linear homogenous family increases under a Pigou–Dalton bundle of progressive transfers. In fact, given that $x_{.j}^0$ is welfare ranked, increasingness of the sequence $\{a_{ij}\}$ turns out to be necessary and sufficient for the satisfaction of the multidimensional transfer principle. The two equations (9.3) and (9.4) constitute the family of Gajdos–Weymark multidimensional generalized Gini welfare functions since a single-dimensional generalized Gini type aggregation is employed to combine the dimensional achievements of individuals (see Weymark 1981). The second member of the family is an asymmetric Cobb–Douglas function of dimensional well-being.

It will now be worthwhile to analyze the two-stage aggregation taken up in the Gajdos–Weymark welfare function from a different perspective. At the first stage, for a given dimension, the individual achievements are combined to arrive at a dimensional well-being standard. This generates a dashboard or portfolio of dimension-wise well-being evaluators. Then these individual evaluators are amassed to figure out an overall level of well-being. Thus, the Gajdos–Weymark welfare standard applies a dashboard-dependent aggregation. As a single indicator of welfare, a dashboard-based assessor of welfare avoids the problem of heterogeneity among dimensional metrics (Stiglitz, Sen, and Fitoussi 2009). However, in the process of aggregation it ignores inter-dimensional association and hence is insensitive to a correlation increasing switch.

The explicit forms of the Kolm multidimensional relative inequality indicators associated with the family of Gajdos–Weymark generalized Gini welfare functions are given respectively by

$$I_{GWR}(X) = 1 - \frac{\left[\sum_{j=1}^{d} \eta_j \left(\sum_{i=1}^{n} a_{ij} x_{ij}^{0} \right)^{k} \right]^{\frac{1}{k}}}{\left| \sum_{j=1}^{d} \eta_j \mu \left(x_{\cdot j} \right)^{k} \right|^{\frac{1}{k}}}, \qquad (9.5)$$

where $k \in \Re^{1}$, $k \neq 0$, and

$$I_{GWR}(X) = 1 - \frac{\prod_{j=1}^{d} \left(\sum_{i=1}^{n} a_{ij} x_{ij}^{0} \right)^{\eta_j}}{\prod_{j=1}^{d} \mu \left(x_{\cdot j} \right)^{\eta_j}}, \qquad (9.6)$$

where $k = 0$. We refer to each of (9.5) and (9.6) as a Gajdos–Weymark multidimensional relative Gini index.

For $k = 1$ and for all $j \in Q$ if $\eta_j s$ are the same across dimensions, that is, if $\eta_j = \frac{1}{d}$ for all $j \in Q$, then (9.5) comes to be

$$I_{GWR}(X) = \frac{\sum_{j=1}^{d} \mu \left(x_{\cdot j} \right) I_G \left(x_{\cdot j} \right)}{\sum_{j=1}^{d} \mu \left(x_{\cdot j} \right)}, \qquad (9.7)$$

where $I_G \left(x_{\cdot j} \right) = 1 - \left(\sum_{i=1}^{n} \frac{a_{ij} x_{ij}^{0}}{\mu(x_{\cdot j})} \right)$ is the relative generalized Gini index of the distribution $x_{\cdot j}$ of attainments in dimension j. Thus, in this particular case, I_{GWR} is a weighted average of dimension-wise relative Gini indices, where the positive weights given by $\left(\frac{\mu(x_{\cdot j})}{\sum_{j=1}^{d} \mu(x_{\cdot j})} \right)$, $j \in Q$, add up to 1. This is clearly a dashboard-positioned aggregation. Alternatively, we can say that the multidimensional relative Gini index fulfills source or factor decomposability; it is a weighted average of relative Gini indices of different sources of well-being (see Shorrocks 1982; Koshevoy and Mosler 1997; Chakravarty and Lugo 2016). The particular case $k = 0$ and $\eta_j = \frac{1}{d}$, where $j \in Q$ is arbitrary, also employs a dashboard-dependent aggregation, since in this case $I_{GWR}(X) = 1 - \prod_{j=1}^{d}(1 - I_G(x_{\cdot j}))^{\frac{1}{d}}$.

The Decancq–Lugo (2012) dashboard-relying inequality aggregator drops out as a particular case of (9.5) if a_{ij} in (9.5) is replaced by $\left[\left(\frac{r_j^i}{n}\right)^{\rho} - \left(\frac{r_j^i-1}{n}\right)^{\rho}\right]$, where r_j^i is the rank of person i in $x_{\cdot j}^0$ and $\rho > 1$ is the same as in the Donaldson–Weymark (1980) S-Gini welfare function. Given $\rho > 1$, $k < 1$ is necessitated by the fulfillment of the multidimensional transfer principle.

Gajdos and Weymark (2005) also characterized a unit translatable family of welfare functions. Given $d \geq 3$, this family $W_{GWA} : M_1 \to \Re^1$ is defined as

$$W_{GWA}(X) = \frac{1}{k} \log \left[\sum_{j=1}^{d} \bar{\eta}_j \exp\left(k \sum_{i=1}^{n} a_{ij} x_{ij}^0\right)\right], \qquad (9.8)$$

where k is a non-zero scalar, and

$$W_{GWA}(X) = \left[\sum_{j=1}^{d} \bar{\eta}_j \left(\sum_{i=1}^{n} a_{ij} x_{ij}^0\right)\right], \qquad (9.9)$$

if $k = 0$, where $\bar{\eta} \in D^d$ is a (positive) vector, a_{ij}s and x_{ij}^0 are the same as in (9.3), $n \in N$ and $X \in M_1^n$ are arbitrary. The two-stage aggregation indicates that this family also applies a dashboard-stationed aggregation. Consequently, it treats all the dimensions of well-being as independents. More generally, except linear homogeneity, it shares all other properties of the family constituted by (9.3) and (9.4).

The associated class of Tsui absolute multidimensional inequality indices happens to be

$$I_{GWA}(X) = \frac{1}{k} \log \left[\frac{\sum_{j=1}^{d} \bar{\eta}_j \exp\left(k\mu\left(x_{.j}\right)\right)}{\sum_{j=1}^{d} \bar{\eta}_j \exp\left(k \sum_{i=1}^{n} a_{ij} x_{ij}^{0}\right)} \right], \qquad (9.10)$$

where $k \in \Re^1$, $k \neq 0$ is any scalar, and

$$I_{GWA}(X) = \left[\sum_{j=1}^{d} \bar{\eta}_j \left(\mu\left(x_{.j}\right) - \sum_{i=1}^{n} a_{ij} x_{ij}^{0} \right) \right], \qquad (9.11)$$

where $k = 0$; $n \in N$ and $X \in M_1^n$ are arbitrary, and $d \geq 3$. This absolute sister of the Gajdos–Weymark relative Gini standard shares all properties of the latter except homogeneity of degree 0. Each of the equations (9.10) and (9.11) may be called a Gajdos–Weymark multidimensional absolute Gini index.

To observe its dashboard-based aggregation explicitly, assume that $\bar{\eta}_j = \frac{1}{d}$ for all $j \in Q$. Then (9.11) reduces to

$$I_{GWA}(X) = \sum_{j=1}^{d} \frac{1}{d} A_G\left(x_{.j}\right), \qquad (9.12)$$

where $A_G\left(x_{.j}\right) = \mu\left(x_{.j}\right) - \sum_{i=1}^{n} a_{ij} x_{ij}^{0}$ is the absolute generalized Gini index of $x_{.j}$, the distribution of achievements in dimension j, $n \in N$ and $X \in M_1^n$ being arbitrary. Implicit under the aggregation of the dimension-by-dimension metrics in (9.12) is the value judgment that all the dimensions are assigned equal importance. Thus, in the special case when $k = 0$ and $\bar{\eta}_j = \frac{1}{d}$, I_{GWA} satisfies a simple form of factor decomposability.

9.5 THE INCLUSIVE MEASURE OF WELL-BEING APPROACH

We begin by discussing the multidimensional extensions of the Atkinson (1970) and Kolm (1976) indicators of inequality characterized by Tsui (1995). They both rely on the symmetric utilitarian social welfare function.

The first form of the symmetric utilitarian social evaluation standard $W(X) = \sum_{i=1}^{n} U(x_{i.})$ characterized by Tsui (1995) possesses the following identical individual utility function

$$U(x_{i.}) = a + q \prod_{j=1}^{d} x_{ij}^{\lambda_j}, \qquad (9.13)$$

or,

$$U(x_{i.}) = a + \sum_{j=1}^{d} h_j \log x_{ij}, \qquad (9.14)$$

where $n \geq 3$ and $X \in M_3$ are arbitrary, $U : D^d \to \Re^1$, $h_j > 0$ for all $j \in Q$, a is any arbitrary real number, and the choice of the $(d+1)$ real numbers q and λ_j, $j \in Q$, are guided by the requirement that U is increasing and strictly concave in achievement levels of person i.

The associated Kolm (1977) inequality quantifier turns out to be:

$$I_{AM}(X) = 1 - \left[\frac{1}{n} \sum_{i=1}^{n} \prod_{j=1}^{d} \left(\frac{x_{ij}}{\mu(x_{.j})} \right)^{\lambda_j} \right]^{\frac{1}{\sum_{j=1}^{d} \lambda_j}}, \qquad (9.15)$$

and,

$$I_{AM}(X) = 1 - \left[\frac{1}{n} \prod_{i=1}^{n} \prod_{j=1}^{d} \left(\frac{x_{ij}}{\mu(x_{.j})} \right)^{\frac{h_j}{\sum_{j=1}^{d} h_j}} \right]^{\frac{1}{n}}, \qquad (9.16)$$

where $n \geq 3$ and $X \in M_3^n$ are arbitrary. This parametric multidimensional extension of the single-dimensional Atkinson (1970) index is symmetric, normalized, and population replication invariant. The choices of λ_j are guided by the restrictions that inequality increases under a correlation increasing rearrangement and the uniform majorization principle is verified. If we choose $d = 2$ for illustrative purposes, then the required restrictions become $0 < \lambda_1 < 1$ and $\lambda_2 < (1 - \lambda_1)$.

Tsui (1995) also characterized a second form of the social evaluation standard $W(X) = \sum_{i=1}^{n} U(x_{i.})$ whose underlying identical utility function is given by:

$$U(x_{i.}) = a + q \prod_{j=1}^{d} \exp(\tau_j x_{ij}), \qquad (9.17)$$

where $n \geq 3$ and $X \in M_1$ are arbitrary $U : \Re_+^d \to \Re^1$, a is an arbitrary real number, and $(d+1)$ real numbers q and $\tau_j, j \in Q$, are chosen such that U is increasing and strictly concave in achievement levels of person i.

The corresponding Tsui (1995) indicator of absolute inequality emerges as:

$$I_{KM}(X) = \frac{1}{\sum_{j=1}^{d} \tau_j} \log \left[\frac{1}{n} \sum_{i=1}^{n} \exp \left(\sum_{j=1}^{d} \tau_j \left(\mu(x_{.j}) - x_{ij} \right) \right) \right].$$

$$(9.18)$$

This symmetric, normalized, and population-size neutral multidimensional sister of the Kolm (1976) calibrator too requires restrictions on the parameters τ_js for the satisfaction of the uniform majorization principle and increasingness with respect to a correlation increasing swap.

Earlier, Maasoumi (1986) suggested an indicator that fits into this structure. He first defined the utility function $U : D^d \to D^1$ for person i as $U(x_{i.}) = \left(\sum_{j=1}^{d} w_j x_{ij}^{\theta} \right)^{\frac{1}{\theta}}$ that employs an Atkinson-type aggregation, where $i \in \{1, 2, \cdots, n\}$, $n \in N$ and $X \in M_3^n$ are arbitrary; w_js are positive dimensional weights summing up to 1, and, as in the Atkinson case, $\theta < 1$ is a parameter.

The constant elasticity of substitution between any two dimensions is given by $\frac{1}{1-\theta}$. For $\theta = 0$, we get a Cobb–Douglas utility function, for which the constant elasticity of substitution between any two dimensions happens to be 1. Consequently, the possibility of the choice of other elasticity values in this case is ruled out. (We, therefore, do not analyze this case further.) In the extreme cases where $\theta = 1$ and $\theta \to -\infty$, the scopes of substitutability are respectively the maximum (perfect substitution) and nil (elasticity is 0).[5]

The Maasoumi multidimensional inequality index I_{MM} is then obtained by employing a Shorrocks-type subgroup decomposable aggregation on the space of utility values (Shorrocks 1980). More formally, $I_{MM} : D^n \to \Re^1$

$$
I_{MM}(X) = \begin{cases} \dfrac{1}{nc(c-1)} \displaystyle\sum_{i=1}^{n} \left[\left(\dfrac{u_i}{\mu(u)} \right)^c - 1 \right], & c \neq 0,1, \\[3ex] \dfrac{1}{n} \displaystyle\sum_{i=1}^{n} \left[\log \left(\dfrac{\mu(u)}{u_i} \right) \right], & c = 0, \\[3ex] \dfrac{1}{n} \displaystyle\sum_{i=1}^{n} \left[\left(\dfrac{u_i}{\mu(u)} \right) \log \left(\dfrac{u_i}{\mu(u)} \right) \right], & c = 1, \end{cases} \tag{9.19}
$$

where $U(x_{i.}) = u_i > 0$ is the extent of utility enjoyed by person i, $\mu(u)$ denotes the mean of the utility profile $u = (u_1, u_2, \ldots, u_n)$, and the parameter c is the same as in Shorrocks (1980) (see equation 8.10). Dardanoni (1996) demonstrated that this relative, symmetric, population replication invariant multidimensional inequality quantifier may not verify the uniform majorization principle.

Bosmans, Decancq, and Ooghe (2015) also chose the Maasoumi-type individual well-being standard $U(x_{i.}) = \left(\sum_{j=1}^{d} w_j x_{ij}^\theta \right)^{\frac{1}{\theta}}$ (Maasoumi 1986) by maintaining all the assumptions made in the definition of U. A second Atkinson-type aggregation was then applied over the (positive) individual well-being standards to arrive at the following form of the social evaluation function:

$$
W(X) = \begin{cases} \left(\dfrac{1}{n} \displaystyle\sum_{i=1}^{n} U(x_{i.})^\beta \right)^{\frac{1}{\beta}}, & \beta < 1, \beta \neq 0, \\[3ex] \displaystyle\prod_{i=1}^{n} U(x_{i.}), & \beta = 0. \end{cases} \tag{9.20}
$$

---

[5] See Bourguignon and Chakravarty (2003), who argued in favor of dependence of substitutability on dimensional achievements.

The consequential Kolm multidimensional relative inequality evaluator, which we refer to as the Bosmans–Decancq–Ooghe multidimensional inequality index, emerges as:

$$I_{BDOM}(X) = 1 - \left(\frac{1}{n} \sum_{i=1}^{n} \left(\frac{\sum_{j=1}^{d} w_j x_{ij}^{\theta}}{\sum_{j=1}^{d} w_j \mu (x_{.j})^{\theta}} \right)^{\frac{\beta}{\theta}} \right)^{\frac{1}{\beta}}. \qquad (9.21)$$

This continuous symmetric, population-size neutral, multidimensional inequality assessor satisfies the uniform majorization principle and increases under a correlation increasing switch if and only if $\beta < \theta < 1$.

None of the indices discussed so far can make a distinction between dimensions, needful in a correlation increasing switch, in terms of substitutability and complementarity. An excellent theoretical construct by Bourguignon (1999), which we analyze below, does this highly satisfactorily. For simplicity of exposition, let us assume that $d = 2$. He assumed the symmetric utilitarian type of welfare function $W(X) = \sum_{i=1}^{n} U(x_{i.})$ at the outset, whose identical utility function is of the form

$$U(x_{i.}) = \left(w_1 x_{i1}^{-\delta} + w_2 x_{i2}^{-\delta} \right)^{-\frac{(1+b)}{\delta}}, \qquad (9.22)$$

where $n \in N$ and $X_{n \times 2} \in M_3^n$ are arbitrary, w_js are positive dimensional weights, $b \in (-1, 0)$ is a parameter indicating inequality delicacy, and $\delta > -1$ is related to the extent of substitutability between the two dimensions under consideration. (The elasticity of substitution between the two dimensions is $\frac{1}{1+\delta}$.) The restrictions $b < 0$ and $\delta > -1$ make the utility function strictly quasi-concave. The Bourguignon multidimensional inequality index I_{BM} is defined as the fraction of welfare loss resulting from unequal distribution. Formally,

$$I_{BM}(X) = 1 - \frac{\sum_{i=1}^{n} \left(w_1 x_{i1}^{-\delta} + w_2 x_{i2}^{-\delta} \right)^{\frac{-(1+b)}{\delta}}}{n \left(w_1 (\mu (x_{.1}))^{-\delta} + w_2 (\mu (x_{.2}))^{-\delta} \right)^{\frac{-(1+b)}{\delta}}}. \qquad (9.23)$$

This continuous, normalized, inequality evaluator fulfills the population-size neutrality property and the multidimensional transfer principle. This family may be regarded as a two-dimensional extension of the single-dimensional Dalton (1920) inequality index. Its value decreases or increases under a correlation increasing exchange according as $\delta + 1 + b > 0$ or $\delta + 1 + b < 0$.

9.6 DIRECT DESCRIPTIVE MULTIDIMENSIONAL INEQUALITY INDICES AND REDUCED FORM WELFARE FUNCTIONS

In this subsection we relate two direct descriptive multidimensional inequality calibrators that were suggested without using any normative concern. Tsui (1995) characterized the class of relative aggregative multidimensional inequality evaluators, where the aggregative principle requires that for any partitioning of the population into two subgroups, the overall inequality can be expressed as a real-valued function of inequality levels of subgroups, their mean vectors and population sizes, along with the additional requirement that if inequality of any subgroup increases, the overall inequality increases. This class, known as the multidimensional generalized entropy family, can formally be defined as follows:

$$I_{TME}(X) = \frac{h}{n} \sum_{i=1}^{n} \left(\prod_{j=1}^{d} \left(\frac{x_{ij}}{\mu(x_{.j})} \right)^{b_j} - 1 \right), \qquad (9.24)$$

where $n \geq 4$ and $X \in M_3^n$ are arbitrary and $h, b_1, b_2, \ldots, b_d$ are parameters which need to obey some restrictions for the indicator to satisfy the uniform majorization principle and increase with respect to a correlation increasing switch. As an illustrative example, let $d = 2$. Then the required restrictions turn out to be $(b_1, b_2) \neq (0,0) \neq (1,0) \neq (0,1)$, $h b_1 (b_1 - 1) > 0$, $b_1 b_2 (1 - b_1 - b_2) > 0$, and $h b_1 b_2 > 0$. All members of this multidimensional generalized entropy family are continuous, normalized, and symmetric; and remain unaltered under replications of the population.

The Tsui (1999) family has been investigated further from a different perspective by Lasso de la Vega, Urrutia, and Sarachu (2010). These authors demonstrated that the only family of multidimensional aggregative relative inequality calibrators that satisfies the multidimensional transfer principle and increasingness under a correlation increasing swap is given by:

$$I_{LUS}(X) = \frac{1}{n} \sum_{i=1}^{n} \left(\prod_{j=1}^{d} \left(\frac{x_{ij}}{\mu(x_{.j})} \right)^{b_j} - 1 \right),\qquad (9.25)$$

where all $n \in N$, $n \geq 4$, $X \in M_3^n$ are arbitrary; either $b_j > 1$ for all $j \in Q$ or $b_j < 0$ for all $j \in Q$. In (9.24), for $d = 2$ we can choose $h = 1$ and $b_1, b_2 < 0$. Then in this particular case, the two families coincide, and consequently, the Tsui family verifies the multidimensional transfer postulate.

We may now relate the two families with the following general welfare function in a negative monotonic way:

$$W_{(h,b_1,\ldots,b_d)}(X) = (\mu_1 + \mu_2 + \cdots + \mu_d)\exp(-I_M),\qquad (9.26)$$

where $n \in N$, $n \geq 4$, $X \in M_3^n$ are arbitrary, and $I_M \in \{I_{TME}, I_{LUS}\}$. For appropriate choices of the $(d+1)$ parameters, $(h, b_1, b_2, \ldots, b_d)$, the social evaluation function has a one-to-one correspondence with the inequality indicator in the sense that for a given vector of dimension-wise means, inequality decreases if and only if welfare increases. Since the transfer principles and a correlation increasing swap do not modify the means of the dimensions, welfare increases under a Pigou–Dalton bundle of progressive transfers and decreases under a correlation increasing rearrangement if the parameters are suitably chosen. The value of this continuous, symmetric, population-size neutral welfare function increases if all dimensional achievements are increased equi-proportionately. That is, it satisfies a scale improvement principle. Formally, $W_{(h,b_1,b_2,\ldots,b_d)}(cX) > W_{(h,b_1,b_2,\ldots,b_d)}(X)$, where $c > 1$ is a scalar. Likewise, other functional forms that have been suggested for measuring multidimensional inequality without any explicit normative foundations can be related with appropriate welfare functions in a negative monotonic way.

9.7 INEQUALITY UNDER UNCERTAINTY: A BRIEF DISCUSSION

In the Harsanyi framework considered in the earlier chapter, different inequality indices are interpreted in terms of measures of risk. This structure uses the theory of inequality measurement that does not involve uncertainty to reduce the inequality problem in an uncertain environment to a single decision maker's choice under uncertainty. But as Ben-Porath, Gilboa, and Schmeidler (1997) argued for measuring inequality under uncertainty, both ex ante inequality and ex post inequality should be taken into account.[6] Ex ante welfare evaluation relies on the assessment of prospects on individual valuations. In contrast, ex post welfare evaluation bases assessment on the situation after the uncertainty problem has been resolved. Thus, if we choose the Gini index as the inequality metric, then both the expected Gini index and Gini of the expected income should come under consideration.

In this section for evaluating inequality under uncertainty, following Gajdos and Weymark (2005), we restrict attention to the framework considered by Ben-Porath, Gilboa, and Schmeidler (1997). This structure uses a multiple-priors (min-of-means) functional for the required purpose. A functional H defined on the set of distribution matrices M_2^n is referred to as a multiple-priors functional if there exists a compact and convex set C of probability measures over the product space $\{1, 2, \ldots, n\} \times Q$ such that for all $X \in M_2^n$, $H(X) = \min_{p \in C} \sum_{i,j} p_{ij} x_{ij}$, where $p = (p_{ij}) \in C$ is the $n \times d$ probability matrix whose (i, j)th entry p_{ij} assigns the probability on the (i, j)th entry x_{ij} of the distribution matrix X under consideration.[7] This type of functional, introduced by Gilboa and Schmeidler (1989), is referred to as min-of-means because for

---

[6] See also Myerson (1981).

[7] Compactness of the set C means that it should be bounded and closed. Since for each (i, j), p_{ij} is bounded from below by 0 and bounded above by 1, C is a bounded set. A set is closed if it contains its boundaries. Since 0 and 1 are respectively attainable lower and upper bounds of p_{ij}, C definitely contains its boundaries. Because for any $p, p' \in C$, $\lambda p + (1 - \lambda) p' \in C$, where $0 \leq \lambda \leq 1$ is arbitrary, and C is convex.

every X its value is the minimum over a set of values, each of which is a weighted average of entries of X, where weights are the appropriate probabilities.

Following Ben-Porath, Gilboa, and Schmeidler (1997), Gajdos and Weymark (2005) considered two min-of-means functionals J_1 and J_2 defined respectively on $\Re^n$ and $\Re^d$. For all $X \in M_2^n$, $J_1 * J_2$ is defined by first employing J_2 on each row of X and then employing J_1 on the emerging n dimensional vector. Likewise, $J_2 * J_1$ is defined by interchanging the roles of J_1 and J_2. In view of a proposition of Ben-Porath, Gilboa, and Schmeidler (1997, 202), we can claim that for any $\alpha \in [0,1]$, $J = \alpha(J_1 * J_2) + (1 - \alpha)(J_2 * J_1)$ becomes a min-of-means functional defined on M_2^n.

To illustrate the above general discussion, let us assume that J_1 is the relative Gini operator and J_2 is the expectation operator corresponding to the uniform probability distribution over the set of dimensions Q. Then J comes to be:

$$ J(X) = \alpha I_G(\mu(x_{1.}), \mu(x_{2.}), \dots, \mu(x_{n.})) + \frac{(1-\alpha)}{d} \sum_{j=1}^{d} I_G(x_{.j}), $$

(9.27)

where $X \in M_2^n$ is arbitrary, $I_G(x_{.j})$ is the relative generalized Gini index of the distribution of attainments in dimension $j \in Q$ across n persons, as defined in (9.7), and $\mu(x_{i.})$ is the mean of attainments of person i in different dimensions $1 \leq i \leq n$. Thus, J in (9.27) is a weighted average of the Gini index of expected values $I_G(\mu(x_{1.}), \mu(x_{2.}), \dots, \mu(x_{n.}))$, the ex post component, and the expected value of the Gini indices $\frac{1}{q} \sum_{j=1}^{q} I_G(x_{.j})$, the ex ante component.

Suppose that the distribution $Y \in M_2^n$ is obtained from the matrix $X \in M_2^n$ by a sequence of correlation increasing switches. Then $(\mu(x_{1.}), \mu(x_{2.}), \dots, \mu(x_{n.}))$ becomes Lorenz superior to $(\mu(y_{1.}), \mu(y_{2.}), \dots, \mu(y_{n.}))$. Given that the relative Gini index agrees with the Lorenz superiority relation, it follows that $I_{RG}(\mu(x_{1.}), \mu(x_{2.}), \dots, \mu(x_{n.})) < I_{RG}(\mu(y_{1.}), \mu(y_{2.}), \dots, \mu(y_{n.}))$. Note that the second term of $J(X)$ is insensitive to a correlation increasing switch. Thus, although in a situation characterized by certainty, the Gajos–Weymark index turns out to be insensitive to correlation increasing switches, its uncertain counterpart in

the Ben-Porath–Gilboa–Schmeidler framework is shown to possess
sensitivity with respect to such switches.

9.8 EXERCISES

(E-9.1) Consider the following 4×3 distribution matrix X whose
(i,j)th entry x_{ij} stands for person $i's$ achievement in
dimension j, where $i = 1, 2, 3, 4$ and $j = 1, 2, 3$.

$$X = \begin{bmatrix} 2,000 & 50 & 900 \\ 2,700 & 60 & 500 \\ 2,600 & 70 & 700 \\ 2,700 & 60 & 700 \end{bmatrix}.$$

Determine the values of the Kolm multidimensional
inequality index associated with the matrix X. Discuss its
ratio scale invariance property.

(E-9.2) Can a multidimensional inequality index deduced by
aggregating the dimension-wise inequality indices be
sensitive to a correlation increasing switch
unambiguously? If your answer is yes, prove it. If your
answer is no, give an example to justify your claim.

(E-9.3) Demonstrate rigorously that the Gajdos–Weymark
generalized Gini welfare functions satisfy the
Pigou–Dalton bundle transfer principle.

(E-9.4) Determine the values of the Tsui absolute inequality
index associated with the matrix X considered in Exercise
9.1, assuming the utilitarian form of the social welfare
function.

(E-9.5) In the 2×2 distribution matrix $Y = \begin{bmatrix} 2 & 1 \\ 1 & 2 \end{bmatrix}$, the (i,j)th
entry y_{ij} stands for person $i's$ achievement in dimension j,
where $i = 1, 2$ and $j = 1, 2$. Show that a switch of
achievements of the persons in dimension 2 increases the
correlation between the dimensional achievements.

(E-9.6) Consider the multidimensional inequality index $I_\theta(X) =$
$1 - \left[\frac{1}{n} \sum_{i=1}^{n} \frac{1}{q} \sum_{j=1}^{q} \left(\frac{x_{ij}}{\mu(x_{.j})} \right)^\theta \right]$, where each entry x_{ij} in the
$n \times q$ distribution matrix X is non-negative and $\mu(x_{.j})$
is the positive mean of the achievements in dimension j,
$1 \leq j \leq q$, and $0 < \theta < 1$ is a parameter.

(a) Rigorously analyze properties of the social evaluation
standard associated with this inequality metric.

(b) Can this inequality metric be used to measure
inequality under uncertainty in the Ben–Porath–
Gilboa–Schmeidler framework? Justify your claim
rigorously.

9.9   BIBLIOGRAPHICAL NOTES

Dominance criteria for multidimensional well-being distributions
have been analyzed, among others, by Kolm (1977), Trannoy (2006),
Savaglio (2006a), and Weymark (2006). The Atkinson–Kolm–Sen
multidimensional ethical inequality indices were characterized
by Tsui (1995). This structure evaluates individual achievements
with a utility function, thus obtaining a vector of distribution of
individual utilities, which are then aggregated in an unambiguous
way to arrive at an inequality standard. Bourgouignon's (1999)
two-dimensional extension of the single-dimensional Dalton (1920)
inequality index employed the symmetric utilitarian structure, as
followed by Tsui (1995). An innovative feature of this contribution
is that it can classify the dimension as complements or substitutes
using some parametric restrictions. Other inequality indicators that
fall within this category, referred to as the inclusive measure of
well-being approach, include the ones suggested by Maasoumi
(1986) and Bosmans, Decancq, and Ooghe (2015).[8]

The Gajdos–Weymark (2005) multidimensional generalized Gini
indices are examples of direct normative indicators of inequality. A

---

[8]   See also Savaglio (2006a) for a discussion.

generalized Gini family considered by Decancq and Lugo (2012) can also be accommodated within this grouping. The underlying social welfare functions are defined directly on the set of achievement matrices, and hence welfare evaluation does not rely on aggregation of utilities across individuals. Multidimensional extensions of the Gini inequality metric without any explicit normative foundations include, among others, those suggested by Koshevoy and Mosler (1996, 1997), List (1999), and Banerjee (2010). Hussain, Siersbæk, and Østerdal (2020) employed first-order dominance relation to compare multidimensional welfare.

As in the case of single-dimensional indices, descriptive non-Gini type inequality standards that do not make use of any social welfare function have been proposed in the multidimensional case as well. For example, Tsui (1999) characterized the family of multidimensional generalized entropy inequality metrics using a general notion of population subgroup decomposability. This family has been analyzed further by Lasso de la Vega, Urrutia, and Sarachu (2010). Weymark's (2006) survey article analyzes different approaches to multidimensional inequality in detail. More recent surveys of the literature are available in Chakravarty and Lugo (2016) and Chakravarty (2018).

REFERENCES

Acosta, L., J. Pineda, L. Galotto, P. Maharjan, and F. Sheng. 2019. *Assessment of Complementarities between GGGI's Green Growth Index and UNEP's Green Economy Progress Index*. GGGI Technical Report no. 10, Green Growth Performance Measurement (GGPM) Program, Global Green Growth Institute, Seoul.

Alkire, S., J. E. Foster, S. Seth, M. E. Santos, J. M. Roche and P. Ballon 2015. *Multidimensional Poverty Measurement and Analysis*. New York: Oxford University Press.

Atkinson, A. B. 1970. "On the Measurement of Inequality." *Journal of Economic Theory* 2 (3): 244–263.

Atkinson, A. B., and F. Bourguignon. 1982. "The Comparison of Multidimensioned Distributions of Economic Status." *Review of Economic Studies* 49 (2): 183–201.

Banerjee, A. K. 2010. "A Multidimensional Gini Index." *Mathematical Social Sciences* 60 (2): 87–93.

———. 2014. "A Multidimensional Lorenz Domination Relation." *Social Choice and Welfare* 42 (1): 171–191.

———. 2020. *Measuring Development: An Inequality Dominance Approach.* Singapore: Springer.

Bellani, L., and A. Fusco. 2018. "Social Exclusion: Theoretical Approaches." In *Handbook of Research on Economic and Social Well-Being*, edited by C. D'Ambrosio, 193–205. Cheltenham: Edward Elgar.

Ben-Porath, E., I Gilboa, and D. Schmeidler. 1997. "On the Measurement of Inequality under Uncertainty." *Journal of Economic Theory* 75 (1): 194–204.

Bosmans, K., K. Decancq, and E. Ooghe. 2015. "What Do Normative Indices of Multidimensional Inequality Really Measure?" *Journal of Public Economics* 130 (C): 94–104.

Bourguignon, F. 1999. "Comment on Multidimensioned Approaches to Welfare Analysis by E. Maasoumi." In *Handbook of Income Inequality Measurement*, edited by J. Silber, 477–84. London: Kluwer Academic.

Bourguignon, F., A. Bénassy-Quéré, S. Dercon, A. Estache, J. W. Gunning, R. Kanbur, S. Klasen, S. Maxwell, J.-P. Platteau, and A. Spadaro. 2008. "Millennium Development Goals at Midpoint: Where Do We Stand?" European Report on Development, Maastricht, The Netherlands.

———. 2010. "Millennium Development Goals: An Assessment." In *Equity and Growth in a Globalizing World*, edited by R. Kanbur and M. Spencer, chap. 2. Washington, DC: World Bank.

Bourguignon, F., and S. R. Chakravarty. 2003. "The Measurement of Multidimensional Poverty." *Journal of Economic Inequality* 1 (April): 25–49. Reprinted in *Measuring Poverty*, edited by S. Klasen, 594–617. Cheltenham: Edward Elgar, 2018. Also reprinted in *Poverty, Social Exclusion and Stochastic Dominance*, edited by S. R. Chakravarty, 83–107. Singapore: Springer, 2019.

Chakravarty, S. R. 2018. *Analyzing Multidimensional Well-Being: A Quantitative Approach.* New Jersey: John Wiley.

———. 2021. "An Axiomatic Analysis of Generalized Gini Air Quality Indices." In *Contemporary Research on Gini's Inequality Index and Beyond*, edited by N. Mukhopadhyay and P. P. Sengupta, 125–144. Florida: CRC Press.

Chakravarty, S. R., and N. Chattopadhyay. 2018. "Multidimensional Poverty and Material Deprivation: Theoretical Approaches." In *Handbook of Research on Economic and Social Well-Being*, edited by C. D'Ambrosio, 153–170. Cheltenham: Edward Elgar.

Chakravarty, S. R. and M. A. Lugo. 2016. "Multidimensional Indicators of Inequality and Poverty." In *Oxford Handbook of Well-Being and Public Policy*, edited by M. D. Adler and M. Fleurbaey, 246–285. New York: Oxford University Press.

Dalton, H. 1920. "The Measurement of the Inequality of Incomes." *Economic Journal* 30 (119): 348–361.

Dardanoni, V. 1996. "On Multidimensional Inequality Measurement." In *Research on Economic Inequality: Income Distribution, Social Welfare, Inequality and Poverty*, edited by C. Dagum and A. Lemmi, 6:201–205. Greenwich: JAI Press Inc.

Decancq, K., M. Fleurbaey, and E. Schokkaert. 2015. "Inequality, Income and Well-Being." In *Handbook of Income Distribution*, edited by A. B. Atkinson, and F. Bourguignon, 2A:67–140. Amsterdam: North Holland.

Decancq, K., and M. A. Lugo. 2012. "Inequality of Well-Being: A Multidimensional Approach." *Economica* 79 (316): 721–746.

Diez, H., C. L. de la Vega, and A. Urrutia. 2008. "Multidimensional Unit- and Subgroup-Consistent Inequality and Poverty Measures: Some Characterization Results." In *Inequality and Opportunity: Papers from the Second ECINEQ Society Meeting (Research on Economic Inequality, Vol. 16)*, edited by J. Bishop and B. Zheng, 189–211. Bingley: Emerald Group Publishing Limited. https://doi.org/10.1016/S1049-2585(08)16009-4.

Donaldson D., and J. A. Weymark. 1980. "A Single Parameter Generalization of the Gini Indices of Inequality." *Journal of Economic Theory* 22 (1): 67–86.

Duclos, J.-Y., and L. Tiberti. 2016. "Multidimensional Poverty Indices: A Critical Assessment." In *Oxford Handbook of Well-Being and Public Policy*, edited by M. D. Adler and M. Fleurbaey, 677–710. New York: Oxford University Press.

Durand, M. 2015. "The OECD Better Life Initiative: How's Life? and the Measurement of Well-Being." *Review of Income and Wealth* 61 (1): 4–17.

Dutta, I., P. K. Pattanaik, and Y. Xu. 2003. "On Measuring Deprivation and the Standard of Living in a Multidimensional Framework on the Basis of Aggregate Data." *Economica* 70 (278): 197–221.

Epstein, L. G., and S. M. Tanny. 1980. "Increasing Generalized Correlation: A Dentition and Some Economic Consequences." *Canadian Journal of Economics* 13 (1): 16–34.

Esty, D. C., C. Kim, T. Srebotnjak, M. A. Levy, A. de Sherbinin, and V. Mara. 2008. *Environmental Performance Index.* New Haven, CT: Yale Center for Environmental Law and Policy.

Ferreira, F. H. G., and V. Peragine. 2016. "Individual Responsibility and Equality of Opportunity." In *Oxford Handbook of Well-Being and Public Policy,* edited by M. D. Adler and M. Fleurbaey, 746–784. New York: Oxford University Press.

Fleurbaey, F. 2006. "Social Welfare, Priority to the Worst-Off and the Dimensions of Individual Well-Being." In *Inequality and Economic Integration,* edited by F. Farina and E. Savaglio, 222–263. London: Routledge.

Fleurbaey, M., and F. Maniquet. 2011. *A Theory of Fairness and Social Welfare.* New York: Cambridge University Press.

Fleurbaey, M., and A. Trannoy 2003. "The Impossibility of a Paretian Egalitarian." *Social Choice Welfare* 21 (2): 319–329.

Gajdos, T., and J. A. Weymark. 2005. "Multidimensional Generalized Gini Indices." *Economic Theory* 26 (2): 471–496.

Gilboa, I., and D. Schmeidler. 1989. "Maximin Expected Utility with Non-unique Prior." *Journal of Mathematical Economics* 18 (2): 141–153.

Guio, A.-C. 2018. "Multidimensional Poverty and Material Deprivation: Empirical Findings." In *Handbook of Research on Economic and Social Well-Being,* edited by C. D'Ambrosio, 171–192. Cheltenham: Edward Elgar.

Holmes, Kim R., Edwin J. Feulner, Mary Anastasia O'Grady, Anthony B. Kim, Daniella Markheim, and James M. Roberts. 2008. *2008 Index of Economic Freedom.* Washington, DC: The Heritage Foundation; New York, USA: Wall Street Journal.

Hoskins, B., J. Jesinghaus, M. Mascherini, G. Munda, M. Nardo, M. Saisana, D. Van Nijlen, D. Vidoni, and E. Villalba. 2006. "Measuring Active Citizenship in Europe." Eur Report no. 22530, Joint Research Center of the European Commission, Brussels, Belgium.

Hussain, M. A., N. Siersbæk, and L. P. Østerdal. 2020. "Multidimensional Welfare Comparisons of EU Member States before, during, and after the Financial Crisis: A Dominance Approach." *Social Choice and Welfare* 55 (4): 645–686.

Kolm, S. C. 1976. "Unequal Inequalities I." *Journal of Economic Theory* 12 (3): 416–442.

———. 1977. "Multidimensional Egalitarianism." *Quarterly Journal of Economics* 91 (1): 1–13.

Koshevoy, G., and K. Mosler. 1996. "The Lorenz Zonoid of a Multivariate Distribution." *Journal of the American Statistical Association* 91 (434): 873–882.

———. 1997. "Multivariate Gini Indices." *Journal of Multivariate Analysis* 60 (2): 252–276.

Lasso de la Vega, C., M. C. Urrutia, and A. Sarachu. 2010. "Characterizations of Multidimensional Inequality Measures Which Fulfil the Pigou–Dalton Bundle Principle." *Social Choice and Welfare* 35 (2): 319–329.

List, C. 1999. *Multidimensional Inequality Measurement*. Oxford: Nuffield College.

Lugo, M. A. 2005. "Comparing Multidimensional Indices of Inequality: Methods and Applications." Working Papers 14, ECINEQ, Society for the Study of Economic Inequality. Rome, Italy.

Maasoumi, E. 1986. "The Measurement and Decomposition of Multidimensional Inequality." *Econometrica* 54 (4): 991–997.

Marshall, A. W., I. Olkin, and B. Arnold. 2011. *Inequalities: Theory of Majorization and Its Applications*. 2nd edition. New York: Springer.

Mueller, G. 2015. *The Green Economy Progress Index*. Brussels: United Nations Environmental Program.

Muller, C., and A. Trannoy. 2012. "Multidimensional Inequality Comparisons: A Compensation Perspective." *Journal of Economic Theory* 147 (4): 1427–1449.

Myerson, R. 1981. "Utilitarianism, Egalitarianism, and the Timing Effect in Social Choice Problems." *Econometrica* 49 (4): 883–897.

Paes de Barros, R., F. H. G. Ferreira, J. R. Molinas Vega, and J. S. Chanduvi. 2009. *Measuring Inequality of Opportunities in Latin America and Caribbean*. Washington, DC: World Bank.

Pattanaik, P. K., S. Reddy, and Y. Xu. 2012. "On Measuring Deprivation and Living Standards of Societies of in a Multi-attribute Framework." *Oxford Economic Papers* 64 (1): 43–56.

Pattanaik, P. K., and Y. Xu. 2019. "Measuring Multidimensional Well-Being and Deprivation with Discrete Ordinal Data." In *Deprivation, Inequality and Polarization: Essays in Honor of S. R. Chakravarty*, edited by I. Dasgupta and M. Mitra, 3–14. New York: Springer.

Permanyer, I. 2013. "The Measurement of Success in Achieving the Millennium Development Goals." *Journal of Economic Inequality* 11 (3): 393–415.

Plaia, A. and M. Ruggieri. 2011. "Air Quality Indices: A Review." *Reviews in Environmental Science and Bio/Technology* 10 (2): 165–179.

Ravallion, M. 2011. "On Multidimensional Indices of Poverty." *Journal of Economic Inequality* 9 (2): 235–248.

Rawls, J. 1971. *A Theory of Justice*. Cambridge: Harvard University Press.

Roemer, J. E., and A. Trannoy. 2016. "Equality of Opportunity." In *Handbook of Income Distribution*, edited by A. B. Atkinson and F. Bourguignon, 2A:217–300. Amsterdam: North Holland.

Savaglio, E. 2002. "Multidimensional Inequality: A Survey." Working Paper No. 362, Dipartimento di Economia Politica, Università degli Studi di Siena.

———. 2006a. "Three Approaches to the Analysis of Multidimensional Inequality." In *Inequality and Economic Integration*, edited by F. Farina and E. Savaglio, 264–277. London: Routledge.

———. 2006b. "Multidimensional Inequality with Variable Population Size." *Economic Theory* 28 (1): 85–94.

Sen, A. K. 1985. *Commodities and Capabilities*. Amsterdam: North-Holland.

———. 1992. *Inequality Re-examined*. Cambridge, MA: Harvard University Press.

Seth, S., and A. Villar. 2018. "Human Development and Poverty: Theoretical Approaches." In *Handbook of Research on Economic and Social Well-Being*, edited by C. D'Ambrosio, 104–125. Cheltenham: Edward Elgar.

Shorrocks, A. F. 1980. "The Class of Additively Decomposable Inequality Measures." *Econometrica* 48 (3): 613–625.

———. 1982. "Inequality Decomposition by Factor Components." *Econometrica* 50 (1): 193–211.

Stiglitz, J. E., A. Sen, and J.-P. Fitoussi. 2009. *Report by the Commission on the Measurement of Economic Performance and Social Progress*. Report no. TD/TNC 102.763, CMEPSP, Paris, France, 291.

Streeten, P. 1981. *First Things First: Meeting Basic Human Needs in Developing Countries*. New York: Oxford University Press.

Tchen, A. 1980. "Inequalities for Distributions with Given Margins." *Annals of Probability* 8 (4): 814–27.

Trannoy, A. 2006. "Multidimensional Egalitarianism and the Dominance Approach: A Lost Paradise?" In *Inequality and Economic Integration*, edited by F. Farina and E. Savaglio, 284–302. London: Routledge.

Tsui, K. Y. 1995. "Multidimensional Generalizations of the Relative and Absolute Indices: The Atkinson–Kolm–Sen Approach." *Journal of Economic Theory* 67 (1): 251–265.

———. 1998. "Multidimensional Inequality and Multidimensional Generalized Entropy Measures: An Axiomatic Derivation." *Social Choice and Welfare* 16 (1): 145–157.

Townsend, P. 1979. *Poverty in the United Kingdom: A Survey of Household Resources and Standards of Living*. London: Peregrine Books.

UNDP. 1990. *Human Development Report* United Nations Development Program, New York: Oxford University Press.

———. 1997. *Human Development Report* United Nations Development Program, New York: Oxford University Press.

———. 2019. *Human Development Report* United Nations Development Program, New York: Oxford University Press.

US Environmental Protection Agency. 2013. *Technical Assistance Document for the Reporting of Daily Air Quality: The Air Quality Index*. North Carolina: US Environmental Protection Agency Research Triangle Park.

Weymark, J. A. 1981. "Generalized Gini Inequality Indices." *Mathematical Social Sciences* 1 (4): 409–430.

———. 2006. "The Normative Approach to the Measurement of Inequality." In *Inequality and Economic Integration*, edited by F. Farina and E. Savaglio, 303–328. London: Routledge.

SOCIAL CHOICE FUNCTIONS 10

10.1 **INTRODUCTION**

Social choices, by which we mean group or collective decisions, are made in two ways. In political voting, collective decision is typically used to make "political" decisions, and in the market mechanism, collective decision is typically used to make economic decisions. In this chapter, we concentrate exclusively on the former. Collective action (or social [group] choices) should be based on the preferences of individuals (or agents) in society. Therefore, an important aspect of social choice theory is a description and analysis of the way preferences of individual members of a group are aggregated into a decision of the group as a whole (see Arrow 1950; and Taylor 2005). We are interested in aggregating preferences of the agents into a social decision, which essentially means that we consider social choice functions that, for each possible individual preference profile, picks an alternative for society from the set of alternatives. This approach is different from social welfare function (discussed in Chapters 2–6) that for each possible individual preference profile picks an ordering for society (not just an alternative like the social choice function).

Social choice methods can be subject to strategic manipulation in the sense that an agent, by misrepresenting his preference, may secure an outcome he prefers to the outcome which would have been obtained if he had revealed his preference sincerely. This issue was first addressed by Gibbard (1973) and Satterthwaite (1975). They consider a situation where a collective decision has to be made by a group of individuals regarding the selection of an outcome. The choice of this outcome depends on the preferences that each agent has over the various feasible outcomes. However, these preferences are known only to the agents themselves, that is, each agent knows only his preference. The Gibbard–Satterthwaite theorem states that under very mild assumptions, the only procedures which will provide incentives for each individual to report his private information truthfully is one where the responsibility of choosing the outcome is left solely to a single individual (the dictator).

The chapter is organized as follows. In Section 10.2, we consider the framework and we also provide the statement of the Gibbard–Satterthwaite theorem. In Section 10.3, we provide two proofs of the theorem. The first proof is for the two-agent case that uses the notion of an "option set." Given a social choice function and given an agent $i \in N$, an option set of agent i is the set of alternatives that agent i can get as an outcome for society (by announcing different preferences), for any given preferences of all but agent i. If a social choice function is dictatorial, then the option set of the dictator is always the entire set of alternatives and the option of all other agents are always singletons. The second proof is a general one that uses Arrow's impossibility theorem to derive the result. We also introduce Maskin monotonicity (see Maskin 1999) and show its similarities with the strategyproofness requirement. Finally, in order to come out of the dictatorship conclusion, in Section 10.3 we impose single-peakedness restriction on the preferences of agents and provide two possibility results due to Moulin (1980).

10.2 THE FRAMEWORK AND THE GIBBARD–SATTERTHWAITE THEOREM

Let $N = \{1, \ldots, n\}, n \geq 2$, be the finite set of agents and A be the finite set of alternatives, where we assume that the cardinality of the set A is more than two (that is, $|A| \geq 3$). We assume that agents have strict preferences over the set of alternatives.[1] Let $\mathcal{P}$ be the set of all strict ordering on A. A typical *profile* is $\succ = (\succ_1, \ldots, \succ_n)$, where $\succ_i$ is agent i's strict preference. The set of all profiles is $\mathcal{P}^n$ while the set of *admissible profiles* is $D(\subseteq \mathcal{P}^n)$. A *social choice function* is a mapping from D to A, where $D \subseteq \mathcal{P}^n$, that is, $f : D \to A$. In other words, f associates an alternative to each profile $\succ = (\succ_1, \ldots, \succ_n) \in D$.

Definition 10.1 A social choice function $f : D \to A$ satisfies *unrestricted domain* if $D = \mathcal{P}^n$.

We define the notion of manipulable preference. A social choice function is *manipulable* at some profile by an agent if by misreporting the agent can induce an outcome that this agent prefers compared to what this agent would have got if he had reported truthfully. Formally, we have the following.

Definition 10.2 A social choice function $f : D \to A$ is *manipulable* at a profile $\succ$ by agent i via $\succ'_i$, if $f(\succ'_i, \succ_{-i}) \succ_i f(\succ)$, where $\succ_{-i} \in \mathcal{P}^{|N \setminus \{i\}|}$ represents a profile of all but agent i.

Clearly, if the preferences of the agents are private information, then having manipulable social choice function is not desirable. Hence, we have the next definition.

Definition 10.3 A social choice function $f : D \to A$ is *strategyproof* if it is not manipulable by any agent at any profile.

A social choice function is strategyproof if there is no agent who finds it beneficial to misreport under any profile. Therefore, if a social choice function is strategyproof, then truth telling is a dominant strategy for every agent under all profiles.

Before going to our next definition, we introduce some more relevant definitions. Let $\max(\succ_i; B)$ be the highest ranking element in $B(\subseteq A)$ according to $\succ_i$. For example, if $A = \{x, y, z\}$ and the preference of agent i is $z \succ_i x \succ_i y$, then $\max(\succ_i; \{x, y\}) = x$. For any $x \in A$, let $\mathcal{P}_x(\subset \mathcal{P})$ be such that for all strict preference $\succ_i \in \mathcal{P}_x$,

---

[1] At the end of this chapter we will relax this assumption of strict preferences.

we have $\max(\succ_i; A) = x$. Therefore, for any alternative $x \in A$, $\mathcal{P}_x$ is the set of all possible strict orders in $\mathcal{P}$ with x as the top element.

Definition 10.4 A social choice function $f : D \to A$ is *dictatorial* if there exists an agent $d \in N$ such that for all $\succ = (\succ_1, \ldots, \succ_n) \in D$, $f(\succ) = \max(\succ_d; A)$.

A dictatorial social choice function is clearly strategyproof. The dictator can only hurt himself by lying and other agents cannot change the outcome. Another uninteresting social choice function that satisfies strategyproof is the constant social choice function. A social choice function f is said to be a *constant* social choice function if there exists an alternative $x \in A$ such that for every profile $\succ = (\succ_1, \ldots, \succ_n) \in D$, we have $f(\succ) = x$. Clearly, a constant social choice function is strategyproof since no one can benefit by misreporting as the social choice remains unchanged under all preferences.

Definition 10.5 A social choice function $f : D \to A$ satisfies the *full-range* property if $range(f) = A$, that is, for each $x \in A$, there exists $\succ = (\succ_1, \ldots, \succ_n) \in D \subseteq \mathcal{P}^n$ such that $f(\succ) = x$.

A social choice function $f : D \to A$, satisfies the full-range property simply means that f is an onto function. Clearly, the constant social choice function fails to satisfy the full-range property since it is not onto.

Definition 10.6 A social choice function $f : D \to A$ satisfies *unanimity* if for any $x \in A$ and any $\succ = (\succ_1, \ldots, \succ_n) \in \mathcal{P}_x^n \cap D$, we have $f(\succ) = x$.

Unanimity requires that if all individuals select x as the top element, then society does so as well. If a social choice function satisfies unrestricted domain and unanimity, then it satisfies the full-range property. However, the converse is not true.

Definition 10.7 A social choice function $f : D \to A$ satisfies *weak Pareto* if for any $x, y \in A$ and any profile $\succ = (\succ_1, \ldots, \succ_n) \in D$ such that $x \succ_i y$ for all $i \in N$, we have $f(\succ) \neq y$.

Clearly, if a social choice function satisfies weak Pareto, then it satisfies unanimity, but the converse is not true. Therefore, if a social choice function satisfies unrestricted domain, then weak Pareto implies unanimity and unanimity implies full-range property.

The next theorem is known as the Gibbard–Satterthwaite theorem due to Gibbard (1973) and Satterthwaite (1975).

Theorem 10.1 Suppose the number of elements in the set of alternatives A is three or more and suppose that the social choice function $f : D \rightarrow A$ satisfies unrestricted domain and the full-range property. Then f is strategyproof if and only if it is dictatorial.

We know that if a social choice function is dictatorial, then it is strategyproof. To complete the proof of Theorem 10.1, we show that if a social choice function $f : D \rightarrow A$ satisfies unrestricted domain, the full-range property, and strategyproofness, then it is necessarily dictatorial.

10.3 TWO PROOFS OF THE GIBBARD–SATTERTHWAITE THEOREM

We provide two proofs of Theorem 10.1. The first one (due to Barberá and Peleg, 1990) is for the two-agent case and the second proof is a general one.

10.3.1 *Proof for the two-agent case using option sets*

The first proof of Theorem 10.1 uses the concept of an option set.

Definition 10.8 Fix any social choice function $f : D \rightarrow A$. The option set of any $i \in N$, given any preference profile $\succ_{-i} \in \mathcal{P}^{|N \setminus \{i\}|}$ of all but agent i, is

$$O_i(\succ_{-i}) = \{x \in A \mid \exists \; \succ_i \in \mathcal{P} \text{ such that } f(\succ_i, \succ_{-i}) = x\}.$$

Given any social choice function $f : D \rightarrow A$, and given any agent $i \in N$ and any profile $\succ_{-i}$ of all but agent i, the option set of agent i is the set of alternatives that agent i can induce for the society (under f) by selecting some announced profile $\succ_i \in \mathcal{P}$. Observe that $O_i(P_{-i}) \subseteq A$ and, more importantly, observe that if a social choice function $f : D \to A$ is strategyproof, then for any $i \in N$ and any profile $\succ = (\succ_i, \succ_{-i}) \in D \subseteq \mathcal{P}^n$,

$$f(\succ_i, \succ_{-i}) = \max(\succ_i; O_i(\succ_{-i})). \tag{10.1}$$

Condition (10.1) states that if a social choice function f is strategyproof, then for any agent $i \in N$ and any given profile $(\succ_i, \succ_{-i})$, the assigned alternative for the society $f(\succ_i, \succ_{-i})$ must be the best possible alternative from the option set $O_i(\succ_{-i})$ of agent i, given his true preference $\succ_i$. The reason being that if this is not the case, then $i \in N$ will manipulate by reporting a preference $\succ'_i$ ($\neq \succ_i$) that makes him strictly better off.

The proof of Theorem 10.1 uses four lemmas. The first lemma states that if f satisfies unanimity, that is, for any alternative $x \in A$ and any profile $\succ = (\succ_1, \succ_2)$, with both agents having x as the top element, the social choice function must also pick x as the chosen alternative for society.

Lemma 10.1 Suppose the number of elements in the set of alternatives A is three or more and consider any social choice function that satisfies unrestricted domain, the full-range property, and strategyproofness. For any $x \in A$, let $\succ = (\succ_1, \succ_2) \in \mathcal{P}_x^2$. Then we get $f(\succ) = x$.

Proof. Consider any $x \in A$. Since f satisfies the full-range property, there exists a profile $\succ' = (\succ'_1, \succ'_2) \in \mathcal{P}^2$ such that $f(\succ') = x$. Consider any preference $\succ_1$ of agent 1 with x as the top alternative, that is, consider $\succ_1 \in \mathcal{P}_x$. Assume that $f(\succ_1, \succ'_2) = z \neq x$. Since $x \in O_1(\succ'_2)$ (as $f(\succ') = f(\succ'_1, \succ'_2) = x$), and $x \succ_1 z$ (as $\succ_1 \in \mathcal{P}_x$), agent 1 manipulates at $(\succ_1, \succ'_2)$ via $\succ'_1$. Therefore, our assumption is incorrect and hence we must have $f(\succ_1, \succ'_2) = x$. Consider any preference $\succ_2$ of agent 2 with x as the top alternative, that is, let $\succ_2 \in \mathcal{P}_x$. Assume that $f(\succ_1, \succ_2) = y \neq x$. Since $x \in O_2(\succ_1)$ (as $f(\succ_1, \succ'_2) = x$), and $x \succ_2 y$ (as $\succ_2 \in \mathcal{P}_x$), agent 2 manipulates at $(\succ_1, \succ_2)$ via $\succ'_2$. Therefore, we must have $f(\succ_1, \succ_2) = x$. $\square$

The next lemma states that if we consider any two profiles of agent 1 with both preferences having a common alternative $x \in A$

as the top element, then under both these profiles the option set of agent 2 must remain unchanged.

Lemma 10.2 Suppose the number of elements in the set of alternatives A is three or more and consider any social choice function that satisfies unrestricted domain, the full-range property, and strategyproofness. Consider any alternative $x \in A$ and let $\succ_1, \succ_1' \in \mathcal{P}_x$. Then $O_2(\succ_1) = O_2(\succ_1')$.

Proof. Assume it is not, that is, assume that there exists an alternative $x \in A$ and a profile $\succ_1, \succ_1' \in \mathcal{P}_x$ such that $z \in O_2(\succ_1) \setminus O_2(\succ_1')$. From Lemma 10.1, it follows that $z \neq x$. Let $\succ_2$ be a preference for agent 2 such that $z \succ_2 x \succ_2 w$ for all $w \in A \setminus \{x, z\}$ (due to unrestricted domain, we can have such a preference for agent 2). Then, using condition (10.1), we get $f(\succ_1, \succ_2) = \max(\succ_2; O_2(\succ_1)) = z$. Moreover, $x \in O_2(\succ_1')$ since agent 2 can always report some $\succ_2^* \in \mathcal{P}_x$ and from Lemma 10.1, it then follows that $f(\succ_1', \succ_2^*) = x$. Therefore, given $x \in O_2(\succ_1')$ and $z \notin O_2(\succ_1')$, using condition (10.1), it follows that $f(\succ_1', \succ_2) = \max(\succ_2; O_2(\succ_1')) = x$. Under both $\succ_1$ and $\succ_1'$, agent 1's most preferred alternative is x. Therefore, agent 1 manipulates at $(\succ_1, \succ_2)$ via $\succ_1'$ and we have a contradiction to strategyproofness. $\square$

The next lemma states that for every preference of agent 1, either the option set of agent 2 is a singleton or the entire set A.

Lemma 10.3 Suppose the number of elements in the set of alternatives A is three or more and consider any social choice function that satisfies unrestricted domain, the full-range property, and strategyproofness. For every preference $\succ_1$ of agent 1, either $O_2(\succ_1) = A$ or $O_2(\succ_1)$ is a singleton.

Proof. Assume it is not, that is, there exists $\succ_1 \in \mathcal{P}$ such that $x, y \in O_2(\succ_1)$ and $z \notin O_2(\succ_1)$. An implication of Lemma 10.1 is that $\succ_1 \notin \mathcal{P}_z$. Let $\succ_1 \in \mathcal{P}_x$, where $x \neq z$. Applying Lemma 10.2, and using unrestricted domain, we can assume further that $x \succ_1 z \succ_1 y \succ_1 w$ for all $w \in A \setminus \{x, y, z\}$. Using unrestricted domain, suppose the preference $\succ_2$ of agent 2 is such that $z \succ_2 y \succ_2 v$ for all $v \in A \setminus \{y, z\}$. Therefore, using condition (10.1), we get $f(\succ_1, \succ_2) = \max\{\succ_2; O_2(\succ_1)\} = y$. However, at $(\succ_1, \succ_2)$, agent 1 can announce $\succ_1^* \in \mathcal{P}_z$ so that from Lemma 10.1, it follows that $f(\succ_1^*, \succ_2) = z \succ_1 f(\succ_1, \succ_2) = y$. Therefore, agent 1 manipulates at $(\succ_1, \succ_2)$ via $\succ_1^* \in \mathcal{P}_z$ and we have a contradiction to strategyproofness. $\square$

The next lemma states that either, for every preference of agent 1, the option set of agent 2 is a singleton throughout, or, for every preference of agent 1, the option set of agent 2 is the entire set A throughout.[2]

Lemma 10.4 Suppose the number of elements in the set of alternatives A is three or more and consider any social choice function that satisfies unrestricted domain, the full-range property, and strategyproofness. Either, $O_2(\succ_1) = A$ for all $\succ_1 \in \mathcal{P}$, or, $O_2(\succ_1)$ is a singleton for all $\succ_1 \in \mathcal{P}$.

Proof. Assume that there exist two preferences $\succ_1, \succ_1' \in \mathcal{P}$ for agent 1 such that $O_2(\succ_1) = A$ and $O_2(\succ_1') = \{x\}$ for some $x \in A$. Observe that $\succ_1 \notin \mathcal{P}_x$. The reason is the following. If $\succ_1 \in \mathcal{P}_x$, then, using unrestricted domain, assume $y \succ_2 z \succ_2 x$ and, by using Lemma 10.2, assume that $x \succ_1 y \succ_1 z$. Therefore, using condition (10.1), we get $f(\succ_1, \succ_2) = \max\{\succ_2; O_2(\succ_1)\} = \max\{\succ_2; A\} = y$ and $f(\succ_1', \succ_2) = \max\{\succ_2; O_2(\succ_1')\} = \max\{\succ_2; \{x\}\} = x$. Given $\succ_1$, agent 1 manipulates at $(\succ_1, \succ_2)$ via $\succ_1'$. Therefore, $\succ_1 \in \mathcal{P}_z$, where $z \neq x$. Using Lemma 10.2, we assume that $z \succ_1 x \succ_1 y$. Using unrestricted domain, let $\succ_2$ for agent 2 be such that $y \succ_2 w$ for all $w \in A \setminus \{y\}$. Then, applying condition (10.1), we get (I) $f(\succ_1, \succ_2) = \max\{\succ_2; O_2(\succ_1)\} = \max\{\succ_2; A\} = y$ and we also get (II) $f(\succ_1', \succ_2) = \max\{\succ_2; O_2(\succ_1')\} = \max\{\succ_2; \{x\}\} = x$. From (I) and (II), it follows that agent 1 manipulates at $(\succ_1, \succ_2)$ via $\succ_1'$. $\square$

Using the above four lemmas, we can now prove Theorem 10.1 for the two-agent case.

Proof of Theorem 10.1. Suppose that $O_2(\succ_1) = A$ for all $\succ_1 \in \mathcal{P}$. In that case, using condition (10.1), it follows that $f(\succ_1, \succ_2) = \max(\succ_2;$

---

[2] Note that the statement of Lemma 10.4 is different from that of Lemma 10.3. Lemma 10.3 allowed for the possibility that for some preferences of agent 1, the option set of agent 2 is a singleton and for some other preferences of agent 1, the option set of agent 2 is the entire set A. Lemma 10.4 eliminates these kinds of possibilities.

$O_2(\succ_1)) = \max(\succ_2; A)$ for all $\succ_1 \in \mathcal{P}$. Hence, agent 2 is the dictator. Suppose that $O_2(\succ_1)$ is a singleton for all $\succ_1 \in \mathcal{P}$. Consider any $x \in A$ and any $\succ_1 \in \mathcal{P}_x$. Since f satisfies unanimity (Lemma 10.1), $f(\succ_1, \succ_2) = x$ if $\succ_2 \in \mathcal{P}_x$. Since, by Lemma 10.4, $O_2(\succ_1)$ is a singleton, $f(\succ_1, \succ_2) = x$ for all $\succ_2 \in \mathcal{P}$, given $\succ_1 \in \mathcal{P}_x$. Therefore, $f(\succ_1, \succ_2) = \max(\succ_1; A) = x$, given any $\succ_1 \in \mathcal{P}_x$. Since for any $x \in A$ this must be true, agent 1 must be the dictator. $\qquad\square$

10.3.2 *The proof using the Arrow impossibility theorem*

There are a number of proofs of Theorem 10.1. A natural line of reasoning is to exploit the connection with the Arrow's impossibility theorem. The main idea here is to construct a social welfare function from a social choice function and then demonstrate that if the latter satisfies the property of unrestricted domain, unanimity, and strategyproofness, then the former satisfies weak Pareto, independence of irrelevant alternative axioms, and rationality of social preferences.

The proof presented here is due to Schmeidler and Sonnenschein (1978). For brevity, we will use the following notations: $\succ = (\succ_1 \ldots, \succ_n) \in \mathcal{P}^n$, $\succ|\succ'_i = (\succ'_i, \succ_{-i})$, $\succ'|\succ_1, \ldots, \succ_m = (\succ_1, \ldots, \succ_m, \succ'_{m+1}, \ldots, \succ'_n)$ and $\succ'|\succ_m, \ldots, \succ_n = (\succ'_1, \ldots, \succ'_{m-1}, \succ_m, \ldots, \succ_n)$. For any non-empty subset $B \subset A$, let $\succ^B = (\succ_1^B, \ldots, \succ_n^B)$ be the profile obtained from $\succ$ by moving the elements in B to the top of $\succ$ in such a way that the relative order between elements in B is preserved and the relative order between elements in $A \setminus B$ is also preserved. That is, (a) for all $x, y \in B$, and any $i \in N$, $x \succ_i^B y \Leftrightarrow x \succ_i y$, (b) for all $a, b \in A \setminus B$, and any $i \in N$, $a \succ_i^B b \Leftrightarrow a \succ_i b$, and (c) for all $v \in B$, all $w \in A \setminus B$, and all $i \in N, v \succ_i^B w$.

Proof of Theorem 10.1. We prove the result in four steps. The first step is to show that the social choice function f satisfies unanimity.

Step 1: f must satisfy unanimity.

Proof of Step 1. The proof is omitted as it is an obvious extension of Lemma 10.1. $\qquad\square$

The next step is related to weak Pareto. Step 2 requires that if for any profile we have any two alternatives $x, y \in A$ such that x

is strictly preferred to y by all agents, then y cannot be a chosen outcome for the society.

Step 2: f must satisfy weak Pareto, that is, for all $\succ \in \mathcal{P}^n$ and $x, y \in A$, if $x \succ_i y$ for all $i \in N$, then $f(\succ) \neq y$.

Proof of Step 2. Assume that the statement in Step 2 is not true. Then there exists a profile $\succ = (\succ_1, \ldots, \succ_n) \in \mathcal{P}^n$ and a pair of alternatives $x, y \in A$ such that $x \succ_i y$ for all $i \in N$ and yet we have $f(\succ) = y$. Let $\succ^x = (\succ_1^x, \ldots, \succ_n^x)$ be the profile obtained from $\succ = (\succ_1, \ldots, \succ_n)$ by moving x to the top. By unanimity (that is, by Step 1), $f(\succ^x) = x$. Therefore, there exists an $i \in N \setminus \{1\}$ such that $f(\succ|\succ_1^x, \ldots, \succ_{i-1}^x) = y$ and $f(\succ|\succ_1^x, \ldots, \succ_i^x) = z \neq y$. If $z \neq x$, then either $z \succ_i y$ or $y \succ_i z$. If $z \succ_i y$, then i manipulates at $\succ|\succ_1^x, \ldots, \succ_{i-1}^x$ via $\succ_i^x$. If $y \succ_i z$, then, it is also true that $y \succ_i^x z$, and hence, i manipulates at $\succ|\succ_1^x, \ldots, \succ_i^x$ via $\succ_i$. The remaining possibility is $f(\succ|\succ_1^x, \ldots, \succ_i^x) = x$. By assumption, $x \succ_i y$ for all $i \in N$ and therefore, i manipulates at $\succ|\succ_1^x, \ldots, \succ_{i-1}^x$ via $\succ_i^x$. □

Before going to the next step, we introduce one more concept. For any $B \subset A$ and $\succ \in \mathcal{P}^n$, let $F(B; \succ) = f(\succ^B)$. Note that from Step 2 we have $F(B; \succ) \in B$. The next step is about independence of irrelevant alternatives. Step 3 requires that if, while moving from one profile $\succ$ to another profile $\succ'$, the relative ranking between any two alternatives $x, y \in A$ remains the same across agents, then, for the two new profiles, obtained from $\succ$ and $\succ'$ by moving x and, y to the top (by keeping all other relative rankings intact), the social choice function prescribes the same outcome for these two new profiles.

Step 3: Consider any $x, y \in A$. If $\succ, \succ' \in \mathcal{P}^n$ are such that $\succ_i|_{\{x,y\}} = \succ_i'|_{\{x,y\}}$ for all $i \in N$, then $F(\{x, y\}; \succ) = F(\{x, y\}; \succ')$.

Proof of Step 3. Assume it is not. Then there exists a pair of alternatives $x, y \in A$ and a pair of profiles $\succ, \succ' \in \mathcal{P}^n$ such that the relative ranking between x and y across agents are identical in the two profiles (that is, $\succ_i|_{\{x,y\}} = \succ_i'|_{\{x,y\}}$ for all $i \in N$) and yet we have $F(\{x, y\}; \succ) = f(\succ^{\{x,y\}}) = x$ and $F(\{x, y\}; \succ') = f((\succ')^{\{x,y\}}) = y$. Define two new profiles obtained from $\succ$ and $\succ'$ by moving x and y to the top and keeping everything else unchanged, that is, define $\succ^{\{x,y\}} := \succ^* = (\succ_1^*, \ldots, \succ_n^*)$ and define $(\succ')^{\{x,y\}} := \succ^{**} = (\succ_1^{**}, \ldots, \succ_n^{**})$. Therefore, $f(\succ^{**}) = x$, $f(\succ^{**}) = y$

and there exists an $i \in N$ such that $f(\succ^*|\succ_1^{**}, \ldots, \succ_{i-1}^{**}) = x$ and $f(\succ^*|\succ_1^{**}, \ldots, \succ_i^{**}) = y$. From rationality of strict preferences, either $y \succ_i^* x$ or $x \succ_i^* y$. If $y \succ_i^* x$, then i manipulates at $\succ^*|\succ_1^{**}, \ldots, \succ_{i-1}^{**}$ via $\succ_i^{**}$. If $x \succ_i^* y$ then, by assumption, $x \succ_i^{**} y$ and i manipulates at $\succ^*|\succ_1^{**}, \ldots, \succ_i^{**}$ via $\succ_i^*$. □

Observe that for any profile $\succ = (\succ_1, \ldots, \succ_n) \in \mathcal{P}^n$, if we consider $F(\{x, y\}; \succ)$ for all $x, y \in A$, then we get a complete social preference, say $\overline{F}^*(\succ)$. Thus, for each $\succ = (\succ_1, \ldots, \succ_n) \in \mathcal{P}^n$, we have a social preference rule $\overline{F}^*(\succ)$. Step 2 implies $\overline{F}^*(.)$ satisfies weak Pareto and Step 3 implies that the social preference rule $\overline{F}^*(.)$ satisfies independence of irrelevant alternatives. In Step 4, we prove that this social preference rule is a social welfare function by proving that it satisfies transitivity.

Step 4: The social preference rule $\overline{F}^*(.)$ is an ordering, that is, it satisfies transitivity.

Proof of Step 4. Assume it is not. Then there exists a triplet $x, y, z \in A$ and a profile $\succ = (\succ_1, \ldots, \succ_n) \in \mathcal{P}^n$ such that, when we put x and y to the top of the preference $\succ$ by keeping all other relative orderings unchanged, we get $F(\{x, y\}; \succ) = y$; when we do the same thing for the preference $\succ$ with x and z, we get $F(\{x, z\}; \succ) = x$; and when we do the same thing for the preference $\succ$ with y and z, we get $F(\{y, z\}; \succ) = z$. This means that $\overline{F}^*(\succ)$ gives $y \succ x \succ z \succ y$ implying a violation of acyclicity and hence also a violation of transitivity. Let $\succ^* := \succ^{\{x, y, z\}}$ be the profile obtained from $\succ$ by moving x, y, z to the top (by keeping all other relative orderings unchanged). Assume, without loss of generality, that $F(\{x, y, z\}; \succ) = f(\succ^*) = x$. Let $\succ^{**} = (\succ^*)^{\{x, y\}}$, that is, $\succ^{**}$ is the profile constructed from $\succ^*$ by moving alternative z just below x and y. By assumption $F(\{x, y, z\}; \succ) = f(\succ^*) = x$, and, by Step 3, $F(\{x, y\}; \succ^*) = F(\{x, y\}; \succ) = f(\succ^{**}) = y$. Therefore, there exists an $i \in N$ such that $f(\succ^*|\succ_1^{**}, \ldots, \succ_{i-1}^{**}) = x$ and $f(\succ^*|\succ_1^{**}, \ldots, \succ_i^{**}) = w \neq x$. By Step 2, $w \in \{y, z\}$. If $w = z$, then, given $x \succ_i^{**} z$, i manipulates at $\succ^*|\succ_1^{**}, \ldots, \succ_i^{**}$ via $\succ_i^*$. If $w = y$, then, using rationality of strict preferences of the agents, we get either $y \succ_i^* x$ or $x \succ_i^* y$. If $y \succ_i^* x$, then i manipulates at $\succ^*|\succ_1^{**}, \ldots, \succ_{i-1}^{**}$ via $\succ_i^{**}$. If $x \succ_i^* y$, then, by assumption $x \succ_i^{**} y$ and i manipulates at $\succ^*|\succ_1^{**}, \ldots, \succ_i^{**}$ via $\succ_i^*$. □

From Steps 2–4, it follows that F generates a social ordering $\overline{F}^*(.)$, which is a social welfare function $\overline{F}^* : \mathcal{P}^n \to \mathcal{P}$ that also satisfies weak Pareto and independence of irrelevant alternatives. Moreover, by assumption we have unrestricted domain (since $D = \mathcal{P}^n$). Therefore, by Arrow's impossibility theorem, the social welfare function $\overline{F}^*(.)$ is dictatorial, that is, there exists an agent $d \in N$ such that for each preference $\succ = (\succ_1, \ldots, \succ_n) \in \mathcal{P}^n$, we have $\overline{F}^*(\succ) = \succ_d$ implying $f(\succ) = \max(\succ_d; A)$.   □

10.3.2.1 *Generalizing the result*

Consider a more general social choice function $f : \mathcal{Q}^n \to A$ that also allows for all orderings. We can extend the Gibbard–Satterthwaite theorem (that is, Theorem 10.1) to this enlarged domain as well. We argue that the dictator over $\mathcal{P}^n$ is also the dictator over the enlarged domain $\mathcal{Q}^n$. Specifically, a social choice function $f : \mathcal{Q}^n \to A$ is *dictatorial on this enlarged domain* if there exists an agent $d \in N$ (referred to as the dictator) such that for all $\succsim = (\succsim_1, \ldots, \succsim) \in \mathcal{Q}^n$, $f(\succsim) \in M(A; \succsim_d)$, where $M(A; \succsim_d)$ is the set of maximal elements of $\succsim_d$. Assume, without loss of generality, that agent 1 is the dictator over $\mathcal{P}^n$. Suppose that there exists a profile $\succsim = (\succsim_1, \ldots, \succsim_n)$ such that $f(\succsim) \notin M(A; \succsim_1)$. Let us consider a profile of strict preferences $\succ = (\succ_1, \ldots, \succ_n) \in \mathcal{P}^n$ such that for all $y \in M(A; \succsim_1)$ and all $z \in A \setminus M(A; \succsim_1)$, $y \succ_1 z$ and $z \succ_j y$ for all $j \in N \setminus \{1\}$. Clearly, by construction of $\succ$ from $\succsim$, it follows that $f(\succ) \in M(A; \succsim_1)$. Therefore, there exists $i \in \{1, \ldots, n\}$ such that $f(\succsim|\succ_i, \ldots, \succ_n) \in M(A; \succsim_1)$ and $f(\succsim|\succ_{i+1}, \ldots, \succ_n) \notin M(A; \succsim_1)$. If $i = 1$, then agent 1 will manipulate at $(\succsim_1, \succ_{-1}) := \succsim|\succ_2, \ldots, \succ_n$ via $\succ_1$. If $i > 1$, then i manipulates at $\succ|\succ_i, \ldots, \succ_n$ via $\succsim_i$.

10.3.3 *Monotonicity and the Gibbard–Satterthwaite theorem*

Consider any social choice function $f : D \to A$, where the number of alternatives in A is at least three and there are two or more agents. Let $m(x, \succ_i)$ be the set of alternatives below x in preference ordering $\succ_i$ for any agent $i \in N$. Formally, $m(x, \succ_i) := \{y \in A : x \succ_i y\}$.

Definition 10.9   A social choice function $f : D \to A$ (with $D \subseteq \mathcal{P}^n$) is *Maskin monotone* if for any pair of preferences $\succ, \succ' \in D$ with $m(f(\succ); \succ_i) \subseteq m(f(\succ); \succ'_i)$ for all $i \in N$, we have $f(\succ) = f(\succ')$.

The next result is due to Muller and Satterthwaite (1977) that links Maskin monotonicity with strategyproofness.

Proposition 10.1 If a social choice function $f : D \rightarrow A$ is strategyproof, then it is Maskin monotonic. Moreover, every Maskin monotone social choice function $f : D \rightarrow A$ defined on unrestricted domain (that is, with $D = \mathcal{P}^n$) is strategyproof.

Proof. Suppose $f : D \rightarrow A$ is a strategyproof social choice function. Consider two profiles $\succ = (\succ_1, \ldots, \succ_n), \succ' = (\succ'_1, \ldots, \succ'_n)$ $\in D$ and consider an alternative $x \in A$ such that $f(\succ) = x$ and $m(f(\succ); \succ_i) \subseteq m(f(\succ); \succ'_i)$ for all $i \in N$. Assume that $f(\succ'_1, \succ_{-1}) = z \neq x$. Since $\succ_1$ is a strict ordering, either $z \succ_1 x$ or $x \succ_1 z$. If $z \succ_1 x$ holds, then agent 1 manipulates at $\succ$ via $\succ'_1$. If $x \succ_1 z$ holds, then by the hypothesis we also have $x \succ'_1 z$ and agent 1 manipulates at the profile $(\succ'_1, \succ_{-1})$ via $\succ_1$. Hence, we must have $f(\succ'_1, \succ_{-1}) = x$. Now progressively switch the preferences of agents 2 through n from $\succ_2 \ldots \succ_n$ to $\succ'_2 \ldots \succ'_n$. At each stage, an argument similar to the one given for agent 1 can be applied to show that the outcome remains fixed at x. Hence, $f(\succ') = x$ and f satisfies Maskin monotonicity.

Suppose that the social choice function $f : \mathcal{P}^n \rightarrow A$ satisfies Maskin monotonicity but is not strategy proof. Then, there exists $i \in N$, a preference profile $\succ = (\succ_1, \ldots, \succ_n) \in \mathcal{P}^n$ and a preference $\succ'_i \in \mathcal{P}$ for agent i such that $f(\succ'_i, \succ_{-i}) \succ_i f(\succ)$. Let $f(\succ) = x$ and $f(\succ'_i, \succ_{-i}) = y$. Let $\succ''_i$ be a preference for agent i such that y is the top-ranked alternative and x is the second-ranked alternative. Such a preference $\succ''_i$ is always possible due to the assumption of unrestricted domain. Observe that $y \succ'_i z$ implies $y \succ''_i z$ since $m(f(\succ'_i, \succ_{-i}); \succ'_i) \subseteq m(f(\succ_i, \succ_{-i}); \succ''_i)$ by construction. Since $f(\succ'_i, \succ_{-i}) = y$ and f satisfies Maskin monotonicity we must have (I) $f(\succ''_i, \succ_{-i}) = y$. Also observe that $x \succ_i z$ implies $x \succ''_i z$, since the only alternative ranked above x under $\succ''_i$ is y and y is also ranked above x under $\succ_i$. Therefore, given $f(\succ) = x$, we have $m(f(\succ); \succ_i) \subseteq m(f(\succ); \succ''_i)$ and, using Maskin monotonicity, we get (II) $f(\succ''_i, \succ_i) = x$. However, from (I) and (II) we get $y = f(\succ''_i, \succ_i) = x$, which is not possible since $x \neq y$. Hence, we have the required contradiction. $\square$

Corollary 10.1 Consider any social choice function $f : D \to A$, where the number of alternatives in A is at least three. If the social choice function $f :\to A$ satisfies unrestricted domain, the full-range property, and Maskin monotonicity, then it must be dictatorial.

The proof of Corollary 10.1 follows quite easily from Proposition 10.1 and Theorem 10.1.

In this section, we have proved that we have dictatorship whenever one wants the social choice function to satisfy unrestricted domain, the full-range property, and either strategy proofness or Maskin monotonicity. Again, like in the case of Arrow's impossibility theorem, if we want to come out of the dictatorship conclusion, then the key assumption to relax is unrestricted domain. In the next section, we try and analyze what happens if we impose the assumption of single-peakedness of individual preferences.

10.4 SINGLE-PEAKED PREFERENCES

Recall that $\mathcal{Q}_{\geq}$ represents the set of all single-peaked preferences with respect to the linear order $\geq$ (see Chapter 5). In this section, we assume further that the linear order is the real line $\mathbb{R}$. Therefore, we shall denote the peak of any individual preference $\succsim_i \in \mathcal{Q}_{\geq}$ of any agent $i \in N$ as $\tau(\succsim_i) \in \mathbb{R}$ and we assume that the peak $\tau(\succsim_i)$ is finite. Throughout this section, we assume that agents are mutually aware that their preferences are single-peaked and we also assume that each agent reports his peak. In particular, a vector $x = (x_1, \ldots, x_n) \in \mathbb{R}^n$ summarizes a single-peaked preference profile $\succsim = (\succsim_1, \ldots, \succsim_n) \in \mathcal{Q}_{\geq}^n$ if and only if $x_i = \tau(\succsim_i)$ for all $i \in N$. Accordingly, we can define the social choice function as a mapping from $\mathbb{R}^n$ to $\mathbb{R}$, that is, a social choice function is now given as $f : \mathbb{R}^n \to \mathbb{R}$. We start with two uncontroversial requirements of the social choice function.

Definition 10.10 A social choice function $f : \mathbb{R}^n \to \mathbb{R}$ is *anonymous* if for any onto function $\pi : N \to N$, $f(x) = f(x_\pi)$, where $x_\pi = (x_{\pi(1)}, \ldots, x_{\pi(n)})$ with π being any reordering of $\{1, 2, \ldots, n\}$.

Definition 10.11 A social choice function $f : \mathbb{R}^n \to \mathbb{R}$ is *efficient* if for any profile $x \in \mathbb{R}^n$ with $x_i = \tau(\succsim_i)$ for all $i \in N$, there does not exist $a \in \mathbb{R}$ such that $a \succ_i f(x)$ for all $i \in N$.

That is, in any efficient social choice function, for any profile x, we cannot find an alternative $a \in A$ that is strictly preferred by all agents in comparison to the alternative $f(x)$ chosen for the society.

Proposition 10.2 The following statements are equivalent:

(a) A social choice function $f : \mathbb{R}^n \to \mathbb{R}$ is efficient.

(b) For any $x \in \mathbb{R}^n$, $f(x) \in [\inf\{x_1, \ldots, x_n\}, \sup\{x_1, \ldots, x_n\}]$.

According to Proposition 10.2, a social choice function, as a function of single-peaked preferences of individuals, is efficient if and only if it is bounded between the infimum and the supremum of single-peaked individual preferences.

Proof of Proposition 10.2. We first prove (a) implies (b). Consider any given vector of peaks $x = (x_1, \ldots, x_n) \in \mathbb{R}^n$ and any $b_1 < \inf\{x_1, \ldots, x_n\}$. Observe that any $a \in (b_1, \inf\{x_1, \ldots, x_n\})$ is such that $a \succ_i b_1$ for all $i \in N$ since, for every individual $i \in N$, any such a is closer to his peak x_i in comparison to b_1. Hence, any such b_1 cannot be efficient. Therefore, if a social choice function is efficient, then (I) $f(x) \geq \inf\{x_1, \ldots, x_n\}$. Similarly, consider any $b_2 > \sup\{x_1, \ldots, x_n\}$ and note that any $a' \in (\sup\{x_1, \ldots, x_n\}, b_2)$ is such that $a' \succ_i b_2$ for all $i \in N$ since, for every individual $i \in N$, any such a' is closer to the peak x_i in comparison to b_2. Therefore, if a social choice function is efficient, then (II) $f(x) \leq \sup\{x_1, \ldots, x_n\}$. From (I) and (II), the necessity of $f(x) \in [\inf\{x_1, \ldots, x_n\}, \sup\{x_1, \ldots, x_n\}]$ for any $x \in \mathbb{R}^n$ follows.

Next, we prove (b) implies (a). Suppose that (b) holds but f is not efficient. Then there exists $x = (x_1, \ldots, x_n) \in \mathbb{R}^n$ and $a \in \mathbb{R}$ such that $f(x) \in [\inf\{x_1, \ldots, x_n\}, \sup\{x_1, \ldots, x_n\}]$ and $a \succ_i f(x)$ for all $i \in N$. Let $i(1) \in N$ be such that $x_{i(1)} = \inf\{x_1, \ldots, x_n\}$, and $i(2) \in N$ be such that $x_{i(2)} = \sup\{x_1, \ldots, x_n\}$. If $a < \inf\{x_1, \ldots, x_n\}$, then for agent $i(1)$ we have $f(x) \succ_{i(1)} a$ implying that we cannot have $a \succ_i f(x)$ for all $i \in N$. Similarly, if $a > \sup\{x_1, \ldots, x_n\}$, then for agent $i(2)$ we have $f(x) \succ_{i(2)} a$, and hence we cannot have $a \succ_i f(x)$ for all $i \in N$. Finally, if $a \in [\inf\{x_1, \ldots, x_n\}, \sup\{x_1, \ldots, x_n\}]$, then due to single-peakedness, $f(x) \succ_{i(1)} a$ if $a > f(x)$ and $f(x) \succ_{i(2)} a$ if $a < f(x)$. Hence, in both these cases, we cannot have $a \succ_i f(x)$ for all $i \in N$. □

Definition 10.12 A social choice function $f : \mathbb{R}^n \to \mathbb{R}$ is *strategyproof* if for any profile $x = (x_1, \ldots, x_n) \in \mathbb{R}^n$, any $i \in N$ such that $x_i = \tau(\succsim_i)$ and any x_i', $f(x) \succsim_i f(x_i', x_{-i})$.

For any odd positive integer K, let $y = (y_1, \ldots, y_K)$ be a K element vector, where $y_j \in \mathbb{R} \cup \{-\infty, +\infty\}$ for each $j = 1, \ldots, K$. Let $m(y) = a$ be the median ranked number from the elements in y, that is, $m(y) = a$ is such that $|\{j \mid a \geq y_j\}| \geq (K+1)/2$ and $|\{j \mid a \leq y_j\}| \geq (K+1)/2$. The following theorem is due to Moulin (1980).

Theorem 10.2 The following two statements are equivalent:

(M1) A social choice function $f : \mathbb{R}^n \to \mathbb{R}$ is anonymous, efficient, and strategyproof.

(M2) There
exists $(n-1)$ real numbers $\alpha_1, \ldots, \alpha_{n-1} \in \mathbb{R} \cup \{-\infty, +\infty\}$ such that for any vector of peaks $x = (x_1, \ldots, x_n) \in \mathbb{R}^n$, we have $f(x) = m(x_1, \ldots, x_n, \alpha_1, \ldots, \alpha_{n-1})$.

By assuming that the social choice function is a voting procedure and calling each agent a voter, one can interpret Theorem 10.2 in the following way. *Every strategyproof, efficient, and anonymous voting scheme is obtained by adding $(n-1)$ fixed ballots to the n voters' ballot and then choosing the median of this large set of ballots.*
Let k be an integer such that $1 \leq k \leq n$. If the real numbers $x_1, \ldots, x_n$ are reordered by increasing value, we denote by $r_k(x_1, \ldots, x_n)$ the number ranked k-th. Observe that $r_1(x_1, \ldots, x_n) = \sup\{x_1, \ldots, x_n\}$ and also observe that $f_n(x_1, \ldots, x_n) = \inf\{x_1, \ldots, x_n\}$. Using this definition, we try to understand condition (M2) of Theorem 10.2.

(1) If *none* of the numbers $\alpha_1, \ldots, \alpha_{n-1}$ is finite, then the voting scheme f is one of the F_k described above, or, more precisely:

- $f(x) = m(x_1, \ldots, x_n, -\infty, \ldots, -\infty) = \inf\{x_1, \ldots, x_n\} = F_1(x_1, \ldots, x_n)$,

- $f(x) = m(x_1, \ldots, x_n, +\infty, -\infty, \ldots, -\infty) = F_2(x_1, \ldots, x_n),$

$$\vdots \qquad\qquad \vdots \qquad\qquad \vdots \qquad\qquad \vdots$$

- $f(x) \quad = \quad m(x_1, \ldots, x_n, +\infty, \ldots, +\infty, -\infty) \quad =$
  $F_{n-1}(x_1, \ldots, x_n)$ and

- $f(x) = m(x_1, \ldots, x_n, +\infty, \ldots, +\infty) = \sup\{x_1, \ldots, x_n\} = F_n(x_1, \ldots, x_n).$

(2) If *all* of the numbers $\alpha_1, \ldots, \alpha_{n-1}$ are finite, then this amounts to saying that "society" has $(n-1)$ votes whereas each individual has one single vote; therefore unanimous agents can enforce any arbitrary alternative, but as soon as the agent's preferences differ, then the "social votes" $\alpha_1, \ldots, \alpha_{n-1}$ matters. For instance, if every x_i is greater than (less than) than $\sup \alpha_j$ ($\inf \alpha_j$), then the selected alternative is $\inf x_i$ ($\sup x_i$).

(3) The voting schemes in condition (M2) of Theorem 10.2 also contain the schemes where "society" has only $(n-3)$ votes (take $\alpha_1 = +\infty, \alpha_2 = -\infty$, and all other α_js are finite), or $(n-5)$ votes (take $\alpha_1 = \alpha_2 = +\infty, \alpha_3 = \alpha_4 = -\infty$, and all other α_js are finite), and so on.

Proof of Theorem 10.2. We only prove that (M2) implies anonymity, efficiency, and strategyproofness. Consider any $x = (x_1, \ldots, x_n) \in \mathbb{R}^n$ and any onto function $\pi : N \to N$. Observe that by definition we have $f(x) = m(x_1, \ldots, x_n, \alpha_1, \ldots, \alpha_{n-1}) = m(x_{\pi(1)}, \ldots, x_{\pi(n)}, \alpha_1, \ldots, \alpha_{n-1}) = f(x_\pi)$ implying anonymity. Next, we show efficiency of the social choice function. In the one extreme, if (a) $\alpha_1 = \ldots = \alpha_{n-1} = -\infty$, then, for any vector of peaks $x = (x_1, \ldots, x_n) \in \mathbb{R}^n$, we get $f(x) = m(x_1, \ldots, x_n, \alpha_1, \ldots, \alpha_{n-1}) = r_1(x_1, \ldots, x_n) = \inf\{x_1, \ldots, x_n\}$. Similarly, in the other extreme, if (b) $\alpha_1 = \ldots = \alpha_{n-1} = +\infty$, then for any vector of peaks $x = (x_1, \ldots, x_n) \in \mathbb{R}^n$, $f(x) = m(x_1, \ldots, x_n, \alpha_1, \ldots, \alpha_{n-1}) = r_n(x_1, \ldots, x_n) = \sup\{x_1, \ldots, x_n\}$. Hence, given these two extreme cases (a) and (b), for any given $\alpha_1, \ldots, \alpha_{n-1} \in \mathbb{R} \cup \{-\infty, +\infty\}$, we have $f(x) \in [\inf\{x_1, \ldots, x_n\}, \sup\{x_1, \ldots, x_n\}]$, and hence we get efficiency. Finally, to show strategyproofness, consider any profile of peaks $x = (x_1, \ldots, x_n)$ such that $f(x) = a$. Consider any agent

$i \in N$. Agent i has no incentive to manipulate if $a = x_i$. Suppose $x_i < a$. In this case, the only way agent i can change the outcome is by changing the median, which he can only do by changing his peak to the right of a. But that will shift the median to the right of a, which for agent i is inferior to getting a. Therefore, agent i cannot benefit from such a deviation. Similarly, suppose $x_i > a$. In this case, the only way agent i can change the outcome is by changing the median, which he can only do by changing his peak to the left of a. But that will shift the median to the left of a, which for agent i is inferior to getting a. Therefore, agent i cannot benefit from such a deviation either. Hence, (M2) implies startegyproofness. For the other part of the result, that is, for a proof of (M1) implies (M2), see Moulin (1980).   □

Another important result proved by Moulin (1980) in this context considers the possibility of dropping efficiency. It states the following.

Proposition 10.3 The social choice function $f : \mathbb{R}^n \rightarrow \mathbb{R}$ is anonymous and strategyproof if and only if there exists $(n + 1)$ real numbers $\alpha_1, \ldots, \alpha_{n+1} \in \mathbb{R} \cup \{-\infty, +\infty\}$ such that for any $x = (x_1, \ldots, x_n) \in \mathbb{R}^n$, we have $f(x) = m(x, \alpha_1, \ldots, \alpha_{n+1})$.

For a proof of this result, see Moulin (1980).

10.5 EXERCISES

For explanations or definitions of the notation, see the main text of Chapter 10.

(E-10.1) Consider any social choice function $f : D \rightarrow A$, where the number of alternatives in the set A is at least three, there are two or more agents and the social choice function satisfies unrestricted domain so that $D = \mathcal{P}^n$.

(a) Show that if $f : \mathcal{P}^n \rightarrow A$ satisfies unanimity, then it satisfies the full-range property.

(b) Show that if $f : \mathcal{P}^n \to A$ satisfies weak Pareto, then it satisfies unanimity. Do we need unrestricted domain to derive this result?

(c) Show that if $f : \mathcal{P}^n \to A$ satisfies the full-range property and strategyproofness, then it satisfies unanimity.

(E-10.2) Consider the domain of single-peaked preferences as defined in Section 10.4. Answer the following questions:

(a) Show that the social choice function $f_M : \mathbb{R}^n \to \mathbb{R}$ with the property that for all $x = (x_1, \ldots, x_n) \in \mathbb{R}^n$, $f_M(x) = \max\{x_1, \ldots, x_n\}$, is strategyproof.

(b) Consider the social choice function $f^* : \mathbb{R}^n \to \mathbb{R}$ with the property that for each $x = (x_1, \ldots, x_n) \in \mathbb{R}^n$,

$$f^*(x) = \frac{\min\{x_1, \ldots, x_n\} + \max\{x_1, \ldots, x_n\}}{2}.$$

Is the social choice function f^* strategyproof? Justify your answer.

10.6 BIBLIOGRAPHICAL NOTES

- There are papers that prove the Gibbard–Satterthwaite theorem using its link with the Arrow impossibility theorem. Instances of this approach are Gibbard's original proof (Gibbard 1973) and the first proof in Schmeidler and Sonnenschein (1978). Reny (2001) further strengthens the connection between Arrow's impossibility theorem and the Gibbard–Satterthwaite theorem by providing a single proof that yields both the results.

- The notion of Maskin monotonicity (Maskin 1999), introduced in Definition 10.9 of this chapter, is the most crucial requirement for social choice functions to be Nash implementable.

A social choice function is Nash implementable whenever one can design a mechanism such that for every preference profile and Nash equilibrium of the game induced by the mechanism, the Nash equilibrium outcome coincides with the alternative chosen by the social choice function, given the profile of preferences. A mechanism means a communication system through which individuals can exchange their messages with each other and messages that jointly govern the settlement of the outcome. Under Nash equilibrium, holding the strategies of other players unchanged, no player can derive a higher payoff by selecting a different strategy.

- There is now a substantial literature dealing with strategy proof social choice with single-peaked preferences and multidimensional generalizations of single-peakedness. See, for example, papers by Barberá et al. (1993), Sprumont (1995), and Weymark (2011).

REFERENCES

Arrow, K. J. 1950. "A Difficulty in the Concept of Social Welfare." *Journal of Political Economy* 58 (4): 328–346.

Barberá, S., and B. Peleg. 1990. "Strategy-Proof Voting Schemes with Continuous Preferences." *Social Choice and Welfare* 7 (March): 31–38.

Barberá, S., F. Gul, and E. Stachetti. 1993. "Generalized Median Voters Schemes and Committees." *Journal of Economic Theory* 61 (2): 262–289.

Gibbard, A. 1973. "Manipulation of Voting Schemes: A General Result." *Econometrica* 41 (4): 587–601.

Maskin, E. 1999. "Nash Equilibrium and Welfare Optimality." *Review of Economic Studies* 66 (1): 23–38.

Moulin, H. 1980. "On Strategyproofness and Single Peakedness." *Public Choice* 35 (1): 437–455.

Muller, E., and M. Satterthwaite. 1977. "The Equivalence of Strong Positive Association and Strategy-Proofness." *Journal of Economic Theory* 14 (2): 412–418.

Reny, P. J. 2001. "Arrow's Theorem and the Gibbard–Satterthwaite Theorem: A Unified Approach." *Economics Letters* 70 (1): 99–105.

Satterthwaite, M. 1975. "Strategyproofness and Arrow's Conditions: Existence and Correspondence Theorems for Voting Procedures and Social Welfare Functions." *Journal of Economic Theory* 10 (2): 187–217.

Schmeidler, D., and H. Sonnenschein. 1978. "Two Proofs of the Gibbard–Satterthwaite Theorem on the Possibility of a Strategy-Proof Social Choice Function." In *Decision Theory and Social Ethics*, edited by H. W. Gottinger and W. Leinfellner, 227–234. Dordrecht, The Netherlands: D. Reidel.

Sprumont, Y. 1995. "Strategyproof Collective Choice in Economic and Political Environments." *Canadian Journal of Economics* 48 (1): 68–107.

Taylor, A. D. 2005. *Social Choice and the Mathematics of Manipulation*. New York: Cambridge University Press.

Weymark, J. A. 2011. "A Unified Approach to Strategy-Proofness for Single-Peaked Preferences." *SERIEs* 2 (December): 529–550.

STRATEGYPROOFNESS ON QUASI-LINEAR DOMAINS

11.1   **INTRODUCTION**

Following the Gibbard–Satterthwaite theorem, several relaxations of the unrestricted domain assumption have been investigated. We have already discussed single-peaked preferences in the previous chapter, which is a relaxation of the unrestricted domain assumption. A second relaxation of the unrestricted domain assumption amounts to assuming that side-payments are allowed among agents (implying the cardinality of their utility functions). Specifically, in this second kind of relaxation, it is assumed that agents have quasi-linear preferences that are represented with quasi-linear utility functions. This assumption of quasi-linearity creates several strategyproof mechanisms. The economic implications of these strategyproof mechanisms are numerous and have been systematically investigated in the vast literature about Vickrey–Clarke–Groves (or VCG) mechanisms (see Vickrey 1961; Clarke 1971; and Groves 1973). The VCG mechanisms, in its most general form, was specified by Groves (1973), though its special cases were identified earlier—first by Vickrey (1961), who specified the second price auction in the context of auction theory, and then by Clarke (1971), who provided the pivotal mechanism for the non-excludible pure public goods problem. There is another class of mechanisms, known as Roberts' mechanisms for affine maximizers, that generalizes the VCG mechanisms (Roberts 1980). In this chapter, we discuss these strategyproof mechanisms for quasi-linear domains. The problem of designing strategyproof mechanisms is also referred to as dominant strategy mechanism design problem under incomplete information.

In Section 11.2, we introduce a non-excludible pure public goods problem and introduce the VCG mechanisms and show that this is the unique class of mechanisms that satisfies outcome efficiency (that maximizes the sum of utilities of all the agents from the public decision) and strategyproofness (also called dominant strategy incentive compatibility). We then argue that for the pure public goods problems, the VCG mechanisms fail to satisfy Pareto optimality. We then discuss some nice properties of the pivotal mechanism, which is a specific mechanism in the class of VCG mechanisms that was first identified by Clarke (1971). In Section 11.3, we introduce a single indivisible private good allocation problem and show that the pivotal mechanism of Clarke (1971) is identical to the second price Vickrey auction (Vickrey 1961). Finally, in Section 11.4, we discuss what happens when we relax the requirement of outcome efficiency and look for dominant strategy incentive compatible mechanisms. We discuss Roberts' theorem on affine maximizers in this context.

11.2 THE PURE PUBLIC GOODS PROBLEM

We consider a social planner's (or a team's) problem of whether to build or not to build a non-excludible public good (for example, a bridge or a park) for a set of agents $N = \{1, \dots, n\}$. The public good is produced at a fixed cost $C = 0$.[1] The planner's (or team's) decision problem is denoted by $d \in \{0, 1\}$, where $d = 0$ means that the public good is not produced and $d = 1$ means that the public good is produced. Utility of any agent $i \in N$ is quasi-linear and

---

[1] This assumption is for simplicity and can easily be relaxed to allow for non-zero fixed cost C.

is given by $U_i(d, t_i; \theta_i) = d\theta_i + t_i$, where $\theta_i \in \mathbb{R}$ is the valuation of the public good to agent i and t_i is the monetary transfer to agent i. The valuation of the public good to any agent i is private information. This means that the valuation θ_i of any agent $i \in N$ is not known either to the planner or to any other agent $j \in N \setminus \{i\}$ and it is common knowledge that θ_i is some number from the real line $\mathbb{R}$. A vector $\theta = (\theta_1, \ldots, \theta_n) \in \mathbb{R}^n$ represents a state of the world or simply a profile. We will use the notation (θ_i', θ_{-i}) to represent $(\theta_1, \ldots, \theta_{i-1}, \theta_i', \theta_{i+1} \ldots, \theta_n)$. The planner's (team's) objective is to ensure outcome efficiency, that is, to maximize the sum of agents' utilities from the public decision.

Definition 11.1 A decision d^* is said to be *outcome efficient* if for each $\theta \in \mathbb{R}^n$, $d^*(\theta) \in \arg\max_{d \in \{0,1\}} \sum_{j \in N} d\theta_j$.

Outcome efficiency implies that (*a*) the public good is produced whenever the sum of all valuations is positive, and (*b*) the public good is not produced whenever this sum is negative. Observe that when the sum of all valuations is zero, the planner is indifferent between producing and not producing the public good and hence whether we select $d^*(\theta) = 1$ or $d^*(\theta) = 0$, we get the same aggregate utility from the public decision. To make the selection of outcome efficient decision single-valued, we assume that if the sum of all valuations is non-negative, then the public good is produced. Thus,

$$d^*(\theta) = \begin{cases} 1 \text{ if } \sum_{j \in N} \theta_j \geq 0 \\ 0 \text{ if } \sum_{j \in N} \theta_j < 0. \end{cases}$$

11.2.1 *Incomplete information*

We have assumed that the valuations are private information and that the agents are utility maximizers. The planner's objective is to ensure outcome efficiency. There is a possibility that if adequate incentives are not given, then agents will be strategic in the sense that they can manipulate their announcement to maximize private benefit. What class of mechanisms can induce agents to be truthful?

Definition 11.2 A mechanism $M = (d(.); t_1(.), t_2(.), \ldots, t_n(.))$ is a state-contingent selection of a decision and a vector of transfers for the set of agents.

The mechanism works in the following sequence: The planner asks the agents to (simultaneously) report their type (or valuation). Based on the announcements of the agents, we have an announced state (or profile) $x = (x_1, \ldots, x_n) \in \mathbb{R}^n$. Based on this announcement, the mechanism $M = (d(.); t_1(.), t_2(.), \ldots, t_n(.))$ specifies a decision $d(x)$ and a transfer vector $(t_1(x), \ldots, t_n(x))$. These mechanisms are referred to as the direct revelation mechanisms in the literature. Given $M = (d(.); t_1(.), t_2(.), \ldots, t_n(.))$, the utility of an agent i, with true valuation θ_i, in some announced state x is given by $U_i(d(x), t_i(x); \theta_i) = d(x)\theta_i + t_i(x)$. Therefore, a mechanism $M = (d(.); t_1(.), \ldots, t_n(.))$ is a game designed by the planner. In this game, the strategy space of each agent is $\mathbb{R}$ because each agent $i \in N$ announces a type (or some valuation) $x_i \in \mathbb{R}$. Based on the announcement of all agents, we have an announced state $x = (x_1, \ldots, x_n)$. The outcome of this game is given by the decision $d(x)$ and a transfer $t_i(x)$ for each $i \in N$. The payoff of agent i, with true valuation θ_i, for the announced state $x = (x_1, \ldots, x_i, \ldots, x_n)$, is the utility $U_i(d(x), t_i(x); \theta_i) = d(x)\theta_i + t_i(x)$. Our first objective is to identify mechanisms that satisfy the following properties:

(a) Outcome efficiency

(b) Dominant strategy incentive compatibility (or non-manipulability or strategyproofness or cheat-proofness or implementability)

Definition 11.3 A mechanism $M = (d(.); t_1(.), t_2(.), \ldots, t_n(.))$ satisfies *dominant strategy incentive compatibility* if for each $i \in N$, each (true type) $\theta_i \in \mathbb{R}$, all $x_i \in \mathbb{R}$ (announcements by agent i) and all $x_{-i} \in \mathbb{R}^{n-1}$ (announcements of all $j \in N \setminus \{i\}$),

$$U_i(d(\theta_i, x_{-i}), t_i(\theta_i, x_{-i}); \theta_i) \geq U_i(d(x_i, x_{-i}), t_i(x_i, x_{-i}); \theta_i).$$

Dominant strategy incentive compatibility means that no matter what others are reporting, truth-telling is a dominant strategy for each individual. To understand the incentive issue, consider the following mechanism. The planner tells each agent to announce his or her valuation and, based on the announcement of all agents, the planner takes the following decision: If the announced state is

$x = (x_1, \ldots, x_n) \in \mathbb{R}^n$, then the decision is

$$d^*(x) = \begin{cases} 1 \text{ if } \sum_{j \in N} x_j \geq 0 \\ 0 \text{ if } \sum_{j \in N} x_j < 0 \end{cases}$$

and the transfer is $t_i(x) = 0$ for all $i \in N$ and for all $x \in \mathbb{R}^n$. The mechanism suggested above is $M^0 = (d^*(.); t_1(.), \ldots, t_n(.))$, where for each announced state $x = (x_1, \ldots, x_n) \in \mathbb{R}^n$, the mechanism specifies a decision $d^*(x)$, which is outcome efficient in terms of the announced state x and a vector of transfers $(t_1(x) = 0, \ldots, t_n(x) = 0)$ for the set of agents. Is the mechanism M^0 dominant strategy incentive compatible? The answer is no. Suppose that the true state is $\theta = (\theta_1 = 10, \theta_2 = -5, \theta_3 = -4)$ and assume that agents 1 and 2 are truthful (that is, $x_1 = \theta_1$ and $x_2 = \theta_2$). Consider two possible reports of agent 3. First, if agent 3 is truthful, that is, if $x_3 = \theta_3$, then the announced state is $x = (x_1 = \theta_1, x_2 = \theta_2, x_3 = \theta_3)$ (which is also the actual state). The mechanism M^0 specifies that $d^*(x = \theta) = 1$ and the vector of transfers is $(t_1(\theta) = 0, t_2(\theta) = 0, t_3(\theta) = 0)$. The utility (or payoff) of agent 3 is $U_3(d^*(\theta), t_3(\theta); \theta_3) = d^*(\theta)\theta_3 + t_3(\theta) = 1.(-4) + 0 = -4$. If, instead, agent 3 misreports the valuation as $x_3' = -6$, then the announced state is $x_3', x_{-3} = x_3', \theta_{-3} = (x_1 = \theta_1, x_2 = \theta_2, x_3' = -6)$. Now the outcome efficient decision is $d^*(x_3', \theta_{-3}) = 0$ (since $10 - 5 - 6 = -1 < 0$), $t_1(x_3', \theta_{-3}) = t_2(x_3', \theta_{-3}) = t_3(x_3', \theta_{-3}) = 0$. The utility of agent 3 is $U_3(d^*(x_3', \theta_{-3}), t_3(x_3', \theta_{-3}); \theta_3) = d^*(x_3', \theta_{-3})\theta_3 + t_3(x_3', \theta_{-3}) = 0.(-4) + 0 = 0$. The benefit of agent 3 from misreporting is $U_3(d^*(x_3', \theta_{-3}), t_3(x_3', \theta_{-3}); \theta_3) - U_3(d^*(\theta), t_3(\theta); \theta_3) = 0 - (-4) = +4 > 0$. Therefore, given the reports of agents $\{1, 2\}$, agent 3 has an incentive to report his or her valuation to be $\tilde{x}_3' < -5$ so that the public good is not produced. Thus, the mechanism M^0 cannot induce agents to be truthful. The reason is the following: Given M^0, the planner's objective is to select a decision $d \in \{0, 1\}$ that maximizes social benefit (that is, $\sum_{j \in N} d\theta_j$) while each agent i is announcing a valuation x_i to maximize personal benefit $d\theta_i$. Due to this conflict of interest, the mechanism M^0 fails to induce truthful revelation of private information. What is the class of mechanisms that satisfy outcome efficiency and dominant strategy incentive compatibility?

Theorem 11.1 An outcome efficient mechanism $M^* = (d^*(.);$ $t_1(.), \ldots, t_n(.))$ satisfies dominant strategy incentive compatibility if and only if for all $\theta = (\theta_1, \ldots, \theta_n) \in \mathbb{R}^n$,

$$t_i(\theta) = \sum_{j \neq i} d^*(\theta)\theta_j + h_i(\theta_{-i}), \tag{11.1}$$

where for each $i \in N$, $h_i : \mathbb{R}^{|N \setminus \{i\}|} \to \mathbb{R}$ is any function that depends on the profile of all but agent i.

Using outcome efficiency, one can rewrite the transfer given by (11.1) as

$$t_i(\theta) = \begin{cases} \sum\limits_{j \neq i} \theta_j + h_i(\theta_{-i}) & \text{if } \sum_{j \in N} \theta_j \geq 0 \\ h_i(\theta_{-i}) & \text{if } \sum_{j \in N} \theta_j < 0. \end{cases}$$

Note that in (11.1), for any $i \in N$, we can select any h_i function and for each such selection $h = (h_1, \ldots, h_n)$ we get a mechanism M^* which satisfies dominant strategy incentive compatability. Hence, in Theorem 11.1, we have specified a class of mechanisms. This class of mechanisms with transfer given by (11.1) is called VCG mechanism (see Groves 1973).

The main features of VCG mechanism are the following:

(a) In a VCG mechanism, given the announcements θ_{-i} of agents $j \neq i$, agent i's transfer depends on her announced type (θ_i say) only through her announcement's effect on the public decision $d^*(\theta)$.

(b) The change in agent i's transfer that results when her announcement changes the decision d is exactly equal to the effect of this change in d on agents $j \neq i$. In other words, the change in i's transfer reflects exactly the externality that she imposes on other agents.

(c) In a VCG mechanism, agent i internalizes this externality and announces truthfully, which leads to a level of d that maximizes the joint payoff of the agents from the public decision, that is, $\sum_{j \in N} d\theta_j$.

Proof of Theorem 11.1. We first prove that if, for an outcome efficient mechanism M, the transfer is given by (11.1), then it satisfies dominant strategy incentive compatability. Assume it is not. Then there exists an agent i, a true type θ_i, and an announced state θ'_i, θ_{-i} with $\theta'_i \neq \theta_i$ such that $U_i(d^*(\theta'_i, \theta_{-i}), t_i(\theta'_i, \theta_{-i}); \theta_i) > U_i(d^*(\theta_i, \theta_{-i}), t_i(\theta_i, \theta_{-i}); \theta_i)$. This means that

$$d^*(\theta'_i, \theta_{-i})\theta_i + t_i(\theta'_i, \theta_{-i}) > d^*(\theta_i, \theta_{-i})\theta_i + t_i(\theta_i, \theta_{-i}). \tag{11.2}$$

Using (11.1) in (11.2), and then simplifying it (by canceling out $h_i(\theta_{-i})$ from both sides), we get

$$\sum_{j \in N} d^*(\theta'_i, \theta_{-i})\theta_j > \sum_{j \in N} d^*(\theta_i, \theta_{-i})\theta_j. \tag{11.3}$$

Condition (11.3) is a violation of outcome efficiency of decision for the state $\theta = (\theta_i, \theta_{-i})$. Hence, we have a contradiction.

To prove the other part, consider the mechanism $M^* = (d^*(.); t_1(.), \ldots, t_n(.))$ with transfer of the following general form:

$$t_i(\theta) = \sum_{j \neq i} d^*(\theta)\theta_j + H_i(\theta), \tag{11.4}$$

for all $i \in N$ and for all $\theta \in \mathbb{R}^n$. To prove the result, we show that $H_i(\theta) = h_i(\theta_{-i})$ for all i, that is, the function $H_i(\theta)$ is independent of θ_i. From the definition of dominant strategy incentive compatibility, it follows that for all pairs $(\theta_i, \theta'_i) \in \mathbb{R}^2$ and for all $\theta_{-i} \in \mathbb{R}^{n-1}$,

(1) $U_i(d^*(\theta), t_i(\theta); \theta_i) \geq U_i(d^*(\theta'_i, \theta_{-i}), t_i(\theta'_i, \theta_{-i}); \theta_i)$,

(2) $U_i(d^*(\theta'_i, \theta_{-i}), t_i(\theta'_i, \theta_{-i}); \theta'_i) \geq U_i(d^*(\theta), t_i(\theta); \theta'_i)$.

Simplifying (1) and (2) by using the general transfer (11.4), we get

$$\Delta(\theta'_i, \theta_i; \theta_{-i}) \left(\sum_{j \in N} \theta_j \right) \geq H_i(\theta'_i, \theta_{-i}) - H_i(\theta)$$

$$\geq \Delta(\theta'_i, \theta_i; \theta_{-i}) \left(\sum_{j \neq i} \theta_j + \theta'_i \right), \tag{11.5}$$

where $\Delta(\theta'_i, \theta_i; \theta_{-i}) = d^*(\theta) - d^*(\theta'_i, \theta_{-i})$. We can have two possibilities, that is, either $d^*(\theta) = d^*(\theta'_i, \theta_{-i})$ or $d^*(\theta) \neq d^*(\theta'_i, \theta_{-i})$.

If $d^*(\theta) = d^*(\theta'_i, \theta_{-i})$, then from (11.5) it follows that

$$H_i(\theta) = H_i(\theta'_i, \theta_{-i}). \tag{11.6}$$

Therefore, using the conclusion of (11.6), define $H_i(x_i, \theta_{-i}) = h_i^0(\theta_{-i})$ for all $x_i \in \mathbb{R}^n$ such that $d^*(x_i, \theta_{-i}) = 0$ and define $H_i(y_i, \theta_{-i}) = h_i^1(\theta_{-i})$ for all $y_i \in \mathbb{R}^n$ such that $d^*(y_i, \theta_{-i}) = 1$. Suppose that $d^*(\theta) \neq d^*(\theta'_i, \theta_{-i})$ and, without loss of generality, let $d^*(\theta) = 1 > d^*(\theta'_i, \theta_{-i}) = 0$. From (11.5) we get

$$\sum_{j \in N} \theta_j \geq h_i^0(\theta_{-i}) - h_i^1(\theta_{-i}) \geq \sum_{j \neq i} \theta_j + \theta'_i. \tag{11.7}$$

Condition (11.7) must be true for all θ_i such that $d^*(\theta)(= d^*(\theta_i, \theta_{-i})) = 1$ and for all θ'_i such that $d^*(\theta'_i, \theta_{-i}) = 0$. Let $\sum_{j \neq i} \theta_j + \hat{\theta}_i = 0$. From the definition of outcome efficiency, it follows that $d^*(\hat{\theta}_i, \theta_{-i}) = 1$. From (11.6), it follows that $H_i(\theta) = H_i(\hat{\theta}_i, \theta_{-i}) = h_i^1(\theta_{-i})$ for all $\theta_i > \hat{\theta}_i$. Moreover, from (11.6), it also follows that $H_i(\theta'_i, \theta_{-i}) = h_i^0(\theta_{-i})$ for all θ'_i such that $d^*(\theta'_i, \theta_{-i}) = 0$. Since condition (11.7) must hold for all θ_i such that $d^*(\theta) = 1$, we can rewrite (11.7) after substituting $\theta_i = \hat{\theta}_i$ and $\sum_{j \neq i} \theta_j = -\hat{\theta}_i$. This gives:

$$0 \geq h_i^0(\theta_{-i}) - h_i^1(\hat{\theta}_i, \theta_{-i}) \geq (\theta'_i - \hat{\theta}_i). \tag{11.8}$$

for all θ'_i such that $d^*(\theta'_i, \theta_{-i}) = 0$ (that is, for all $\theta'_i < \hat{\theta}_i$). Let $\theta'_i = \hat{\theta}_i - \epsilon$, where $\epsilon > 0$.

$$0 \geq h_i^0(\theta_{-i}) - h_i^1(\theta_{-i}) \geq -\epsilon \tag{11.9}$$

for all $\epsilon > 0$. Condition (11.9) implies that $h_i^0(\theta_{-i}) = h_i^1(\theta_{-i}) := h_i(\theta_{-i})$ and the result follows. $\qquad \square$

11.2.2 *Budget-balanced VCG mechanisms*

The planner would prefer to solve the incentive problem using a VCG mechanism that satisfies budget balance.

Definition 11.4 A mechanism $M = (d(.); t_1(.), \ldots, t_n(.))$ is said to be *budget balanced* if for all $\theta = (\theta_1, \ldots, \theta_n) \in \mathbb{R}^n$, $\sum_{j \in N} t_j(\theta) = 0$.

If we can find a budget-balanced VCG mechanism for the public goods model, then that VCG mechanism is first best implementable or fully efficiency or Pareto optimal. Why? The reason is very simple: Suppose that the agents, valuation for the public good is common knowledge. The planner can always ensure outcome efficiency without making any transfer to the agents (that is, with zero tranfers to all agents). This also implies that an outcome efficient decision can be implemented in a way such that the sum of transfers is equal to zero (budget balance). With private information, if we find a budget-balanced VCG mechanism, then information extraction is costless for the planner (and hence for society) as the transfer in each state is confined to exchanges within the agents with the property that some agents pay while other agents get in a way such that sum of transfers is zero. Thus, we get outcome efficiency of the decision along with budget balance, which is neither Pareto inferior nor Pareto superior to what we can achieve when agents, valuation is common knowledge. Hence, obtaining a budget-balanced VCG mechanism implies achieving first best or Pareto optimality. However, we will see that it is impossible to get a budget-balanced VCG mechanism for the public goods problem.

An implication of a budget-balanced mechanism was provided by Walker (1980), better known as the cubical array lemma, which is stated below. Before stating the cubical array lemma, we introduce some more notation. For any profile $\theta \in \mathbb{R}^n$, let $V(\theta) = \sum_{i \in N} d^*(\theta)\theta_i$. For any pair of states $\theta = (\theta_1, \theta_2, \ldots, \theta_n)$ and $\theta' = (\theta'_1, \theta'_2, \ldots, \theta'_n)$ and any $S \subseteq N$, let $\theta(S) = (\theta_1(S), \theta_2(S) \ldots, \theta_n(S)) \in \mathbb{R}^n$ be a profile such that $\theta_j(S) = \theta_j$ if $j \notin S$ and $\theta_j(S) = \theta'_j$ if $j \in S$. Observe that $\theta(S = \emptyset) = \theta$, $\theta(S = \{i\}) = (\theta'_i, \theta_{-i})$, $\theta(S = \{i,j\}) = (\theta'_i, \theta'_j, \theta_{-i-j})$, and so on, $\theta(S = N \setminus \{i\}) = (\theta_i, \theta'_{-i})$, and $\theta(S = N) = \theta'$.

Lemma 11.1 A VCG mechanism is budget balanced only if for all distinct profile pairs θ, θ', $\sum_{S \subseteq N} (-1)^{|S|} V(\theta(S)) = 0$.

For $N = \{1, 2\}$, budget balancedness implies that for all profiles $\theta \in \mathbb{R}^2$, $V(\theta_1, \theta_2) = g_1(\theta_2) + g_2(\theta_1)$. Thus, $\sum_{S \subseteq N} (-1)^{|S|} V(\theta_1(S), \theta_2(S)) = V(\theta_1, \theta_2) - V(\theta'_1, \theta_2) - V(\theta_1, \theta'_2) + V(\theta'_1, \theta'_2) = g_1(\theta_2) + g_2(\theta_1) - g_1(\theta_2) - g_2(\theta'_1) - g_1(\theta'_2) - g_2(\theta_1) + g_1(\theta'_2) +$

$g_2(\theta_1') = 0$ for all $\theta, \theta' \in \mathbb{R}^2$. Lemma 11.1 is a generalization of this idea.

Theorem 11.2 There is no balanced VCG mechanism for the pure public goods problem.

Proof. Let $\theta = (-1, \ldots, -1)$ and $\theta' = (\frac{1}{2}, 0, \ldots, 0)$. Observe that $d^*(\theta(S = N)) = d^*(\theta') = 1$ and $d^*(\theta(S)) = 0$ for all $S \subset N$. Therefore, $\sum_{S \subseteq N}(-1)^{|S|}V(\theta(S)) = (-1)^{|N|}\frac{1}{2} \neq 0$ and we have a violation of Lemma 11.1, which is a necessary condition for the existence of a balanced VCG mechanism. $\qquad\square$

11.2.3 *Feasibility and the pivotal mechanism*

We have argued that the class of mechanisms that solves the incentive problem is the VCG mechanisms. Since budget-balanced VCG mechanisms cannot be obtained, the planner would prefer to solve the incentive problem using a VCG mechanism that satisfies feasibility.

Definition 11.5 A mechanism $M = (d(.); t_1(.), \ldots, t_n(.))$ is said to be *feasible* if for all $\theta = (\theta_1, \ldots, \theta_n) \in \mathbb{R}^n$, $\sum_{j \in N} t_j(\theta) \leq 0$.

Clearly there are VCG mechanisms that are not feasible. For example, consider the VCG mechanism $M^1 = \langle d^*(.); t_1(.), \ldots, t_n(.) \rangle$, where for all $i \in N$, $h_i(\theta_{-i}) = 0$ for all $\theta_{-i} \in \mathbb{R}^{n-1}$. For M^1, $\sum_{j \in N} t_j(\theta) = (n-1)\sum_{j \in N} d^*(\theta)\theta_j$. Consider a state $\theta = (\theta_1, \ldots, \theta_n)$ such that $\sum_{j \in N} \theta_j > 0$. Clearly, for the state θ, $d^*(\theta) = 1$, and hence $\sum_{j \in N} t_j(\theta) = (n-1)\sum_{j \in N} \theta_j > 0$. Hence, the VCG mechanism M^1 is not feasible. Can we find a VCG mechanism that satisfies feasibility? A special case of VCG mechanism was discovered independently by Clarke (1971) and is known as the pivotal mechanism. One can prove that the pivotal mechanism is feasible.

Definition 11.6 A mechanism $M = (d^*(.); t_1(.), \ldots, t_n(.))$ is said to be a *pivotal mechanism* if for all announcements $\theta = (\theta_1, \ldots,$

$\theta_n) \in \mathbb{R}^n,$

$$t_i(\theta) = \sum_{j \neq i} d^*(\theta)\theta_j - \sum_{j \neq i} d^*(\theta_{-i})\theta_j, \qquad (11.10)$$

where for any given $i \in N$, $d^*(\theta_{-i}) \in \arg\max_{d \in \{0,1\}} \sum_{j \neq i} d\theta_j$ for all $\theta_{-i} \in \mathbb{R}^{n-1}$.

Under the pivotal mechanism, for any given profile θ, the transfer of any agent i reflects the difference in benefit of all other agents $N \setminus \{i\}$ of the society caused by the presence and absence of agent i. Specifically, the term $\sum_{j \neq i} d^*(\theta)\theta_j$ reflects the benefit of all other agents in the presence of agent i and the term $\sum_{j \neq i} d^*(\theta_{-i})\theta_j$ reflects the benefit of all other agents in the absence of agent i. Observe that the pivotal mechanism is a VCG mechanism with $h_i(\theta_{-i}) = -\sum_{j \neq i} d^*(\theta_{-i})\theta_j$ for all i and all $\theta_{-i} \in \mathbb{R}^{n-1}$. Therefore, from Theorem 11.1, it follows that the pivotal mechanism satisfies dominant strategy incentive compatibility.

Proposition 11.1 The pivotal mechanism is feasible.

Proof. To show feasibility, it is sufficient to show that for all agent $i \in N$, $t_i(\theta) \leq 0$ for all $\theta \in \mathbb{R}^n$. This would imply that no matter what state we are in, the sum of transfers is non-negative.

Case 1: $d^*(\theta) = d^*(\theta_{-i})$. From condition (11.10), it follows that $t_i(\theta) = 0$.

Case 2: $d^*(\theta) = 1 > d^*(\theta_{-i}) = 0$. This means that $\sum_{j \in N} \theta_j \geq 0$ and $\sum_{j \neq i} \theta_j < 0$. From (11.10), it follows that $t_i(\theta) = \sum_{j \neq i} \theta_j < 0$.

Case 3: $d^*(\theta) = 0 < d^*(\theta_{-i}) = 1$. This means that $\sum_{j \in N} \theta_j < 0$ and $\sum_{j \neq i} \theta_j \geq 0$. From transfer (11.10), it follows that $t_i(\theta) = -\sum_{j \neq i} \theta_j \leq 0$.

From cases 1–3, it follows that the transfer of any agent i, under the pivotal mechanism M^p, for any state θ is non-positive, that is, $t_i(\theta) \leq 0$ for all $\theta \in \mathbb{R}^n$. Hence, $\sum_{j \in N} t_j(\theta) \leq 0$ for all $\theta \in \mathbb{R}^n$. $\qquad \square$

For the pivotal mechanism $M^p = (d^*(.); t_1(.), \ldots, t_n(.))$, one can rewrite the transfer of an agent $i \in N$, for any (announced) state

$\theta = (\theta_1, \ldots, \theta_n) \in \mathbb{R}^n$, in the following way:

$$t_i(\theta) = \begin{cases} -\left| \sum_{j \neq i} \theta_j \right| & \text{if } d^*(\theta) \neq d^*(\theta_{-i}), \\ 0 & \text{if } d^*(\theta) = d^*(\theta_{-i}). \end{cases}$$

The main features of the pivotal mechanism are the following:

(a) Under the pivotal mechanism, an agent i's transfer is zero if the agent's announcement does not change the public decision relative to what would be outcome efficient for the agents $j \neq i$ (that is, if $d^*(\theta) = d^*(\theta_{-i})$).

(b) Agent i's transfer is non-positive if the agent is "pivotal," that is, if the agent's announcement changes the public decision relative to what would be outcome efficient for the agents $j \neq i$ ($d^*(\theta) \neq d^*(\theta_{-i})$).

(c) The pivotal mechanism satisfies outcome efficiency, dominant strategy incentive compatibility, and feasibility.

11.2.4 *Domains for which VCG mechanisms are unique*

The VCG mechanisms induce agents to reveal true information about preferences for public decisions under the assumption that preferences are additively separable and linear in money. Subsequently, Green and Laffont (1977) proved that VCG mechanisms are unique in this respect when a universal domain of preference profiles (or a domain containing all continuous profiles) is allowed. Holmström (1979) proved that VCG mechanisms are unique on any domain which is "smoothly connected." A domain is smoothly connected if for any two preference profiles in the domain, there exists a differentiable deformation of one profile into the other within the domain (that is, the domain is a differentiably homotopic class). An important class of domains that are smoothly connected is the class of convex domains. Thus, one may a priori take preferences to be convex, differentiable, polynomial, and so on, without altering the uniqueness result.

11.3 ALLOCATION OF A SINGLE INDIVISIBLE OBJECT

Let $N = \{1, \ldots, n\}$ be the set of agents. One indivisible object needs to be allocated to any one of these agents.[2] Each agent's valuation for this object is private information. The valuation $\theta_i \in \mathbb{R}_+$. Utility of agent i is $U_i(d_i, t_i; \theta_i) = d_i\theta_i + t_i$, where $d_i \in \{0, 1\}$. Here, $d_i = 0$ means that the good is not allocated to agent i and $d_i = 1$ means that the good is allocated to agent i. Observe that the decision problem is to allocate one indivisible object. Let D be the set of possible decisions. A vector $d = (d_1, \ldots, d_n) \in D$ if and only if $d_i \in \{0, 1\}$ for all $i \in N$ and $\sum_{j \in N} d_j = 1$. A state of the world is $\theta = (\theta_1, \ldots, \theta_n) \in \mathbb{R}_+^n$.

Outcome efficiency for the single indivisible object allocation problem is to select $d^*(\theta) = (d_1^*(\theta), \ldots, d_n^*(\theta)) \in \arg\max_{d \in D} \sum_{j \in N} d_j\theta_j$ for all $\theta \in \mathbb{R}_+^n$. Outcome efficiency means that for any state $\theta = (\theta_1, \ldots, \theta_n) \in \mathbb{R}_+^n$, the object goes to the agent with the highest valuation.[3] Since the valuation is private information, we are interested in designing a mechanism that achieves outcome efficiency and dominant strategy incentive compatibility. A mechanism for the indivisible object allocation problem is $M = (d(.) = (d_1(.), \ldots, d_n(.); t_1(.), \ldots, t_n(.))$. A mechanism M specifies a state-contingent allocation $d(.) \in D$ and a vector of transfers $(t_1(.), \ldots, t_n(.)) \in \mathbb{R}^n$ for the set of agents. Consider the pivotal mechanism for this problem. The mechanism $M^{piv} = (d^*(.) = (d_1^*(.), \ldots, d_n^*(.); t_1(.), \ldots, t_n(.))$ is the pivotal mechanism for the single indivisible object allocation problem if for all announced states $\theta \in \mathbb{R}_+^n$ and all $i \in N$,

$$t_i(\theta) = \sum_{j \neq i} d_j^*(\theta)\theta_j - \sum_{j \neq i} d_j^*(\theta_{-i})\theta_j, \tag{11.11}$$

---

[2] Note that the allocating authority may be an auctioneer or a planner (government) or a team.
[3] If there is a tie, then the person with the lowest index gets the object, that is, if, for a profile θ, agents i and j have the highest valuations and $i < j$, then agent i gets the good.

where the decision for the profile θ_{-i} of all but agent i, that is, $d^*(\theta_{-i}) = (d_1^*(\theta_{-i}), \ldots, d_{i-1}^*(\theta_{-i}), d_{i+1}^*(\theta_{-i}), \ldots, d_n^*(\theta_{-i}))$, is outcome efficient for the agents in $N \setminus \{i\}$.

Consider a state $\theta = (\theta_1, \ldots, \theta_n) \in \mathbb{R}_+^n$ such that agent $h \in N$ has the highest valuation and agent $s \in N \setminus \{h\}$ has the second-highest valuation. Under the pivotal mechanism, the transfer of the agent with the highest valuation is $t_h(\theta) = 0 - \theta_s = -\theta_s$. The transfer of the agent with the second-highest valuation is $t_s(\theta) = \theta_h - \theta_h = 0$. Finally, the transfer of any agent $i \in N \setminus \{h, s\}$ is $t_i(\theta) = \theta_h - \theta_h = 0$. Therefore, for the single indivisible object allocation problem, the pivotal mechanism specifies that in any state θ, the person with the highest announced valuation (or bid) pays the second-highest valuation (or bid) and the object goes to the highest bidder. For all bidders, other than the highest bidder, the transfer is zero and they do not get the object. Thus, the single indivisible object outcome efficient allocation problem with the pivotal mechanism is equivalent to the Vickrey (or second price) auction. The Vickrey auction was developed by Vickrey (1961).

Proposition 11.2 The Vickrey auction (or outcome efficient allocation of one indivisible object with the pivotal mechanism) is dominant strategy incentive compatible.

The proof of Proposition 11.2 is quite easy and is hence omitted.

11.4 RELAXING OUTCOME EFFICIENCY: AFFINE MAXIMIZERS

What more can we achieve if we relax outcome efficiency and simply require dominant strategy incentive compatibility from allocation problems under quasi-linear utility specifications? Roberts (1979) proved that under certain conditions the only dominant strategy incentive compatible mechanisms with unrestricted domain are the affine maximizers. Here we briefly present his framework and state his result.

Let $N = \{1, \ldots, n\}$ be the finite set of agents and $A = \{x, y, z, \ldots\}$ be the finite set of alternatives. Each agent's valuation is given by the vector $v_i = (v_i(x), v_i(y), v_i(z), \ldots) \in V_i \subseteq \mathbb{R}^{|A|}$. A profile $v =$

$(v_1, \ldots, v_n) \in V := \prod_{j \in N} V_j$, that is, the profile v is an element of the Cartesian product of the sets V_j, $j = 1, \ldots, n$. For any given $i \in N$, denote v_{-i} as a vector in $V_{-i} := \prod_{j \in N \setminus \{i\}} V_j$ so that for any v and for any $i \in N$, we can write $v = (v_i, v_{-i})$ and hence, given v, for any given $i \in N$, (v_i', v_{-i}) is a profile obtained from v by replacing v_i with v_i'. Utility of any agent $i \in N$ from an alternative $x \in A$ when his valuation is $v_i \in V_i$ and when his payment is $p_i \in \mathbb{R}$ is given by $U_i(x, p_i; v_i) = v_i(x) - p_i$. The domain of preference V is *unrestricted* if $V_i = \mathbb{R}^{|A|}$ for all $i \in N$. An allocation rule or simply a *rule* is $f : V \to A$. Given any rule f, the *payment function* for any agent $i \in N$ is $p_i : V \to \mathbb{R}$. A rule f is said to be *dominant strategy incentive compatible* if for each $i \in N$, there exists a payment function $p_i : V \to \mathbb{R}$ such that for all $v_{-i} \in V_{-i}$ and for all $v_i, v_i' \in V_i$, $U_i(f(v), p_i(v); v_i) \geq U_i(f(v_i', v_{-i}), p_i(v_i', v_{-i}); v_i)$, that is, $v_i(f(v)) - p_i(v) \geq v_i(f(v_i', v_{-i})) - p_i(v_i', v_{-i})$.[4]

Definition 11.7 A rule f satisfies *weak monotonicity* if for any $i \in N$, any $v_{-i} \in V_{-i}$ and any $v_i, v_i' \in V_i$ such that $f(v) = x$ and $f(v_i', v_{-i}) = y$, we have $v_i'(y) - v_i(y) \geq v_i'(x) - v_i(x)$.

Weak monotonicity requires that if the allocation rule $f(.)$ is such that for the profile v it selects $f(v) = x$ and for any other profile (v_i', v_{-i}) (that differs in valuation of agent i only), the allocation rule selects $f(v_i', v_{-i}) = y$, then the incremental benefit of getting y across valuations v_i' and v_i for agent i is no less than the incremental benefit of getting x across the same valuations v_i' and v_i for agent i. The next lemma is due to Bikhchandani et al. (2006) that establishes the necessity of weak monotonicity for achieving dominant strategy incentive compatibility.

Lemma 11.2 Every dominant strategy incentive compatible rule f satisfies weak monotonicity.

Proof. Consider any implementable rule f. If for any $i \in N$, any $v_{-i} \in V_{-i}$, and any $v_i, v_i' \in V_i$ we have $f(v) = x$ and

---

[4] A mechanism $M(.) = (f(.), p_1(.), \ldots, p_n(.))$ in this context is a state-contingent specification of an allocation and a vector of payments. That is, for every $v \in V$, a mechanism specifies $M(v) = (f(v), p_1(v), \ldots, p_n(v))$ that consists of an allocation $f(v)$ and a payment $p_i(v)$ for each $i \in N$.

$f(v'_i, v_{-i}) = y$, then from the definition of implementability we must have the following: (i) $v_i(x) - p_i(v) \geq v_i(y) - p_i(v'_i, v_{-i})$ and (ii) $v'_i(y) - p_i(v'_i, v_{-i}) \geq v'_i(x) - p_i(v)$. From (i) and (ii) we get $v'_i(y) - v'_i(x) \geq p_i(v'_i, v_{-i}) - p_i(v) \geq v_i(y) - v_i(x)$, which implies $v'_i(y) - v_i(y) \geq v'_i(x) - v_i(x)$ and we have weak monotonicity. □

Definition 11.8 A rule f satisfies *positive association of differences* if for any $v, v' \in V$ such that $f(v) = x$ and $v'_i(x) - v_i(x) > v'_i(y) - v_i(y)$ for all $y \in A \setminus \{x\}$ and all $i \in N$, we have $f(v') = x$.

Positive association of differences requires that for any two valuation vectors $v, v' \in V$ such that (i) the allocation rule picks x for the valuation vector v (that is, $f(v) = x$), and we also know that (ii) for any alternative y different from x (that is, any $y \in N \setminus \{x\}$) and every agent $i \in N$, the incremental benefit of getting x across valuations v'_i and v_i for agent i is more than the incremental benefit of getting y across the same valuations v'_i and v_i for agent i, then for the profile v' also we must pick x, that is, we must have $f(v') = x$. The next lemma, due to Roberts (1979), establishes the necessity of positive association of differences in order to obtain dominant strategy incentive compatible rule on unrestricted domain.

Lemma 11.3 Every dominant strategy incentive compatible rule f on an unrestricted domain satisfies positive association of differences.

Proof. Consider any implementable rule f. By Lemma 11.2, it satisfies weak monotonicity. Fix some $v, v' \in V$ such that $f(v) = x$ and $v'_i(x) - v_i(x) > v'_i(y) - v_i(y)$ for all $y \in A \setminus \{x\}$ and all $i \in N$. For positive association of differences, we need to prove $f(v') = x$. Let $v^0 = v$, $v^n = v'$ and for any $i = 1, \ldots, n-1$, define $v^i = (v'_1, \ldots, v'_i, v_{i+1}, \ldots, v_n)$. To prove the result, we show that for any $i = 1, \ldots, n$, if $f(v^{i-1}) = x$, then $f(v^i) = x$. Suppose not, that is, for some i assume that $f(v^{i-1}) = x$ and $f(v^i) = y$, where $y \in A \setminus \{x\}$. Then by weak monotonicity, $v'_i(y) - v_i(y) \geq v'_i(x) - v_i(x)$, which, for agent i, contradicts the strict inequality $v'_i(x) - v_i(x) > v'_i(y) - v_i(y)$ with alternative $y \neq x$. Hence, if $f(v^{i-1}) = x$, then $f(v^i) = x$. Since for any $i \in N$ this is true, the result follows. □

Roberts' theorem (Roberts 1979), stated below, specifies that the only dominant strategy incentive compatible rules that are onto, defined over the full domain, and are defined for domains having at least three alternatives are the weighted variants of the outcome efficiency condition called affine maximizers.

Definition 11.9 An allocation rule f is *outcome efficient* if for every valuation vectors $v \in V$,

$$f(v) \in \arg\max_{x \in A} \left\{ \sum_{j \in N} v_j(x) \right\}.$$

Definition 11.10 An allocation rule f is an *affine maximizer* if there exists non-negative weights $k_1, \ldots, k_n$ not all zero and constants $\{c_x\}_{x \in A}$ such that for all $v \in V$,

$$f(v) \in \arg\max_{x \in A} \left\{ \sum_{j \in N} k_j v_j(x) + c_x \right\}.$$

Theorem 11.3 Suppose the set of alternatives A has at least three elements and suppose that V is unrestricted. Then every dominant strategy incentive compatible rule f is an affine maximizer.

For a proof of Theorem 11.3, see Roberts (1979). Observe that the outcome efficient rule is a special case of Roberts' affine maximizer rules with $k_i = 1$ for all $i \in N$ and $c_x = 0$ for all $x \in A$. Given any affine maximizer rule, the payment functions that help achieve dominant strategy incentive compatibility is of the following form: For each $v \in V$ and each $i \in N$,

$$p_i(v) = \begin{cases} -\frac{1}{k_i} \left[\sum_{j \neq i} k_j v_j(f(v)) + c_{f(v)} \right] + \mathcal{H}_i(v_{-i}) & \text{if } k_i > 0 \text{ and} \\ \mathcal{H}_i(v_{-i}) & \text{if } k_i = 0, \end{cases}$$

where for each $i \in N$, $\mathcal{H}_i : V_{-i} \to \mathbb{R}$ is any function that depends on the profile of all but agent i. This family of payment functions is also referred to as the generalized VCG transfers for obvious reasons.

11.5 EXERCISES

For explanations or definitions of the notation, see the main text of Chapter 10.

(E-11.1)   For the pure public goods problem developed in Section 11.2, try to derive all the results by assuming that the pure public good is produced with a positive fixed cost $C > 0$.

(E-11.2)   Prove Proposition 11.2.

(E-11.3)   Like the single indivisible good allocation problem developed in Section 10.3, try to develop a double identical indivisible goods allocation problem where each agent has need for only one good.[5] To make the allocation problem non-trivial, assume that there are at least three agents. Try to identify the pivotal mechanism in this context. Is the pivotal mechanism in this double identical indivisible goods allocation problem like the *third price auction* where agents having the highest and the second-highest valuation gets one good each and both of them pay as price the third highest-valuation? Justify your answer.

11.6   BIBLIOGRAPHICAL NOTES

- The proof technique used in the proof of the necessity of the VCG mechanisms (see Theorem 11.1) is due to Makowski and Mezzetti (1994).

- The cubical array Lemma 11.1 (due to Walker [1980]) was also applied by Hurwicz and Walker (1990) to establish a generic impossibility result on balanced VCG mechanisms.

- The pivotal mechanism (due to Clarke [1971]) was characterized by Moulin (1986).

- The paper by Lucking-Reiley (2000) presents the history of the Vickrey auction.

- One of the problems about Roberts' theorem (that is, Theorem 11.3) is that its proof is extremely involved. Researchers have

---

[5]   This means that the marginal value of getting the second good to an agent who already has one good is zero.

tried to simplify Roberts' original proof (Roberts 1979). Two alternative proofs were provided by Lavi, Mu'alem and Nisan (2009). By adding the neutrality axiom, a proof of Roberts' theorem was also provided by Mishra and Sen (2012).

REFERENCES

Bikhchandani, S., S. Chatterjee, R. Lavi, A. Mu'alem, N. Nisan, and A. Sen. 2006. "Weak Monotonicity Characterizes Deterministic Dominant Strategy Implementation." *Econometrica* 74 (4): 1109–1132.

Clarke, E. H. 1971. "Multi-part Pricing of Public Goods." *Public Choice* 11 (September): 17–33.

Green, J., and J-J. Laffont. 1977. "Characterization of Satisfactory Mechanisms for the Revelation of Preferences for Public Goods." *Econometrica* 45 (2): 727–738.

Groves, T. 1973. "Incentives in Teams." *Econometrica* 41 (4): 617–631.

Holmström, B. 1979. "Groves' Schemes on Restricted Domains." *Econometrica* 47 (5): 1137–1144.

Hurwicz, L., and M. Walker. 1990. "On the Generic Non-optimality of Dominant Strategy Allocation Mechanisms: A General Theorem That Includes Pure Exchange Economies." *Econometrica* 58 (3): 683–704.

Lavi, R., A. Mu'alem, and N. Nisan. 2009. "Two Simplified Proofs for Roberts' Theorem." *Social Choice and Welfare* 32 (3): 407–423.

Lucking-Reiley, D. 2000. "Vickrey Auctions in Practice: From Nineteenth-Century Philately to Twenty-First-Century E-commerce." *Journal of Economic Perspectives* 14 (3): 183–192.

Makowski, L., and C. Mezzetti. 1994. "Bayesian and Weakly Robust First Best Mechanisms: Characterizations." *Journal of Economic Theory* 64 (2): 500–519.

Mishra, D., and A. Sen. 2012. "Roberts' Theorem with Neutrality: A Social Welfare Ordering Approach." *Games and Economic Behavior* 75 (1): 283–298.

Moulin, H. 1986. "Characterizations of the Pivotal Mechanism." *Journal of Public Economics* 31 (1): 53–78.

Roberts, K. W. S. 1979. "The Characterization of Implementable Social Choice Rules." In *Aggregation and Revelation of Preferences*, edited by

J-J. Laffont, 321–349. Amsterdam, The Netherlands: North-Holland Publications.

———. 1980. "Price Independent Welfare Prescriptions." *Journal of Public Economics* 13 (3): 277–297.

Vickrey, W. S. 1961. "Counterspeculation, Auctions and Competitive Sealed Tenders." *Journal of Finance* 16 (1): 8–37.

Walker, M. 1980. "On the Non-existence of Dominant Strategy Mechanisms for Making Optimal Public Decisions." *Econometrica* 48 (6): 1521–1540.

INDEX